The Crisis of the Self in the Age of Information

D1196430

What is happening to the self in post-industrial society?

Computers, like automobiles before them, are not merely useful instruments, they are also culturally and psychologically influential icons. But the meanings associated with these two technologies are not the same. Whereas mechanical technologies support masculine fantasies of individuality and autonomy, information technologies interact with us in ways that merge private and public, mind and environment. Hence this irony: although information-handling systems and networks augment human powers of organization and integration, they also subvert the traditional Western concept of the separate and independent subject.

In *The Crisis of the Self in the Age of Information* Raymond Barglow shows how contemporary technological environments furnish the unconscious with internal objects that hark back to a time in our lives prior to personal boundary formation and identity. The consequence is that our technological involvements help to disrupt and dismantle the ideal of the unified and sovereign self that in the past technology fostered.

Throughout the book Raymond Barglow interweaves critical theory and psychoanalysis with an examination of artistic representations, media imagery and dreams to explore the conflictual dynamics of contemporary self-formation and self-representation.

Raymond Barglow holds doctorates in both clinical psychology and philosophy. In this book he draws upon his experience as a teacher, clinician, systems analyst and consultant. He has taught at Trinity College, Connecticut, and is currently on the faculty of the Saybrook Institute in San Francisco.

Critical Psychology
Series editors

John Broughton
Columbia University, New York

David Ingleby
Rijksuniversiteit, Utrecht

Valerie Walkerdine
Goldsmiths' College, London

Since the 1960s there has been widespread disaffection with traditional approaches in psychology, and talk of a 'crisis' has been endemic. At the same time, psychology has encountered influential contemporary movements such as feminism, neo-marxism, post-structuralism and postmodernism. In this climate, various forms of 'critical psychology' have developed vigorously.

Unfortunately, such work – drawing as it does on unfamiliar intellectual traditions – is often difficult to assimilate. The aim of the Critical Psychology series is to make this exciting new body of work readily accessible to students and teachers of psychology, as well as presenting the more psychological aspects of this work to a wider social scientific audience. Specially commissioned works from leading critical writers will demonstrate the relevance of their new approaches to a wide range of current social issues.

Titles in the series include:

The crisis in modern social psychology
And how to end it
Ian Parker

The mastery of reason
Cognitive development and the production of rationality
Valerie Walkerdine

The psychology of the female body
Jane M. Ussher

Child-care and the psychology of development
Elly Singer

Significant differences
Feminism in psychology
Corinne Squire

Rewriting the self
History, memory, narrative
Mark Freeman

Lev Vygotsky
Revolutionary scientist
Fred Newman and Lois Holzman

Deconstructing developmental psychology
Erica Burman

The Crisis of the Self in the Age of Information

Computers, dolphins, and dreams

Raymond Barglow

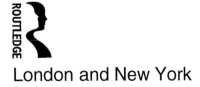

London and New York

First published 1994
by Routledge
11 New Fetter Lane, London EC4P 4EE

Simultaneously published in the USA and Canada
by Routledge
29 West 35th Street, New York, NY 10001

©1994 Raymond Barglow

Typeset in Times by Michael Mepham, Frome, Somerset

Printed and bound in Great Britain by
Biddles Ltd, Guildford and King's Lynn

British Library Cataloguing in Publication Data
A catalogue record for this book is available from the British Library

Library of Congress Cataloging in Publication Data
A catalog record for this book is available from the Library of Congress

ISBN 0–415–10142–5 (hbk)
ISBN 0–415–10143–3 (pbk)

The separation of subject and object is both real and illusory. True, because in the cognitive realm it serves to express the real separation, the dichotomy of the human condition, a coercive development. False because the resulting separation must not be ... magically transformed into an invariant ... If speculation on the state of reconciliation were permitted, neither the undistinguished unity of subject and object nor their antithetical hostility would be conceivable in it; rather the communication of what was distinguished.

Theodor Adorno, "Subject and Object"

Contents

Preface and acknowledgements

When I began this study, my intuition was that recently developed technological objects – computers, in particular – double as psychoanalytic "internal objects" that organize and mobilize unconscious fantasies and fears in new ways. But how could one investigate that? Because people may not be aware of nor able to put into words the character of their involvements with technological systems, certain standard research methods would not be sufficient. This investigation began without any well-formed methodology. I fastened instead on any fragment I could find to begin building a picture – a few sentences from a dream here, an advertising image there, an observation made by an acquaintance, a bit of my own experience. I didn't know at the outset, a decade ago, what the picture would eventually look like.

Now that the book has been completed, I see that the collage I've created has a certain order. Can it be said that the truth has been found and is contained in the following pages? Can it be said at least that I have expressed *my* view on this subject? The trouble is, I find certain paradoxes more puzzling here at the end than they seemed at the beginning. I set out to describe that dialectic whereby we see ourselves reflected in environments we ourselves have created. But we "see through a glass darkly," scarcely recognizing the one who peers back at us from behind the mirror. In particular, I found the "self," on which this study is focussed, to be an enigmatic notion that was not easy to write about coherently.

Notwithstanding such problems, I certainly received every encouragement from my dear friends for pursuing this intriguing project. I appreciate that they condoned, even abetted my obsession. John Broughton discussed each draft with me and was immensely helpful every step of the way. Margret Schaefer's careful reading and rereading helped to shape both form and content.

Nina Wax, Bob Griffin, David Ingleby, Mike Pincus, and Dave Lomba read the manuscript and pointed out problems that needed to be addressed. Discussions with Charles Webel and Richard Lichtman also helped move the project forward toward publication. Vivien Ward, my editor at Routledge, deftly handled matters of final editing, cover design, and production.

I am thankful as well to the people who were willing to talk to me about their experiences with information technologies, their observations, and even their dreams. What I say in this book reflects what I have learned – or mislearned, as the case may be – from them.

Finally, I would like to acknowledge permission to use the following illustrations: Figure 7.1 and Figure 8.2 by permission of the Biblioteque Royal, Brussels, Belgium; Figure 12.3 from Georgius Agricola, *De Re Metallica*, edited by Herbert Hoover and Lou Hoover (New York: Dover, 1950); Figure 13.1, by Peter Breugel, from H. Arthur Klein, *Graphic Worlds of Peter Breugel* (New York: Dover, 1963); Figure 13.2 by permission of Apple Computer, Inc.

Introduction

Sandy's dream: *I was a dolphin sailing through the waves, pure thought cutting through the water like a knife, silent and invisible.*

Associations: When someone is using a [computer] program I've written, all they see of me are some symbols splashed on their screen. Hope I amount to more than that.

I noticed yesterday that I had lost some weight. Well, if here I am looking down at the scale, I thought to myself, then I must certainly still exist!

FROM AUTOMOBILES TO COMPUTERS

Ours is an "Information Age," an age of databases and electronic spreadsheets, desk-top publishing and automated tellers, computer-assisted instruction, virtual realities, and "artificial intelligence." Intelligence once was the privileged domain of human beings. Now it appears that we have to share that honor with the new devices brought to us by IBM and Apple. The information-processing carried out by millions of circuits etched into a silicon chip is astonishingly swift, far outracing the human brain.

When I was growing up in the 1940s and 1950s, on the other hand, technology was still mainly mechanical, consisting of physical parts that push and pull one another. Although the electronics industry was getting underway, automotive technology remained symbolically as well as economically supreme. The American four-wheeled sedan exemplified nothing less than the good life: affluence, mobility, comfort, elegance – the freedom of the individual to go wherever he or she might desire. The automobile served as an emblem not only of material prosperity but also of our liberty, pride of accomplishment, and even self-esteem.

Today, in the final decade of the twentieth century, we are still taken with our cars, to be sure, but their glamour has been eclipsed, in the media and the marketplace, by a higher technology. As cars represent the values of industrial culture, so computers represent those of post-industrialism, defined as a social order in which the leading economic sector is the production, distribution, and processing of information. In each case, the artifact itself, automobile or computer, is an ideological apparatus, a carrier of a mythology that articulates but also conceals how the world we inhabit is put together.

Not all technological artifacts are created equal in their cultural impact, however. The automobile is a familiar metaphor, and has been one of the cornerstones of modernity, a universally acknowledged symbol of industrial society. The computer, however, is relatively new, and its symbolic implications remain unclear. What we can say with some confidence though, even at this early stage of our involvement with information technologies, is that they too will influence our ways of perceiving nature, the social world, and human subjectivity. Science and technology do not dispense with imagination and fantasy; on the contrary, they provide rich material for the elaboration of images, dreams, and ideals in new forms. I intend in this book to look into the ways in which various technologies express different models not only of social organization and conflict, but also of personal integration and fragmentation. Computers, like automobiles before them, echo back to us metaphorical representations of our own experience and agency. Human identity itself is entwined with technological circumstance: information technology, like previous forms of mastery of nature, serves to fashion not only objects outside ourselves but also human subjects.

That we are shaped in relation to the devices we create and manipulate is a truth as ancient as our earliest inventions: spears and shields make warriors; plows, farmers; hammers and nails, carpenters; printing presses, publishers and readers. What changes from one cultural or historical context to another is not the existence of reciprocal relationships between instruments and their users, but the forms that these relationships assume. Even within a single context, this dialectic of subject and object does not unfold in the same way for everyone. Personal identity formation is an individual matter, as are the varieties of empowerment and disempowerment that we experience in relation to the machines that serve us and that sometimes we serve.

Yet there are discernible historical patterns and continuities. Consider, for example, the autonomy and mastery that mental activity promises. Exaltation of the life of the mind is nothing new. Plato, Aristotle, St Augustine, and Descartes have been among its most famous exponents. The scientific discoveries and technological innovations centered in Europe and North America during the eighteenth and nineteenth centuries seemed to provide further evidence that the mind is godlike in its powers and scope of understanding. The recent displacement of mechanical in favor of information technologies has also contributed to the idea that what is mental is distinct from and elevated above what is physical, that work of the mind is superior to manual labor. But this historical dialectic is today taking a curious turn. For work of the mind has become something that machines can now imitate, if not duplicate. It becomes questionable, then, whether mental capacities are as ennobling as we had previously believed, or whether they can even serve to distinguish persons from inanimate objects, to define what it is to be human. In Sandy's dream of a dolphin, quoted at the beginning of this Introduction, her awareness of herself as a thinking being seems to affirm her existence. Yet she remains "silent and invisible," and her associations to the dream indicate that she is not entirely reassured by this affirmation. In my conversations with Sandy, the Cartesian question arose again and again: I think, but do I exist?

One of the contemporary hallmarks of the successful individual is mental alacrity and competence. From birth, the cognitive development of the individual assumes a critical importance, as the acute anxieties of parents, especially in middle-class homes, regarding the intelligence of their children attest. But is cognitive functioning, no matter how adept, sufficient to establish a human identity? In Sandy's dream, it is not. She identifies with a dolphin, an animal whose resemblance to human beings is uncertain.

DOLPHIN AS METAPHOR FOR ENDANGERED SUBJECTIVITY

Researchers have been observing dolphins for some time, without being able to arrive at a consensus on the issue of whether they really are "intelligent" creatures. Can they communicate not only with one another, but perhaps even with us? Does there exist, "behind their behavior," so to speak, an experiencing creature anything like the creatures we take ourselves to be?

Although observed by humans, dolphins remain to some extent enigmatic and invisible to them. Sandy experiences a similar predicament; notwithstanding her apparently intelligent performances, in composing a computer program, for example, she remains invisible to others: "all they see of me are some symbols splashed on their screen." This predicament is a common one in contemporary social settings; hidden behind, or perhaps feeling reduced to, the roles we play, involved in institutions that depersonalize our interactions, we are concealed from others, perhaps even from ourselves. When we witness dolphins splashing about in the sea, we know little about what is "going on" in them internally. We may find ourselves equally inscrutable, unable to say what it is that makes us distinctively human, that differentiates us from dolphins or from the "thinking machines" that imitate us.

Traditionally in the West, we have regarded the possession of a "soul" or "self" as essential to our humanity. Yet this subjective center or core, which seems most intimately connected and essential to the person one is, eludes our conceptual grasp. The "self" is presumably something internal, so we look inside to find it. But when we ask, "Who am I? What is it that makes up my identity, my uniqueness, my self?", the answer may not come to us simply through this act of introspection. We are apt to discover instead a certain emptiness, or encounter this particular perception, or that particular thought, but where are we to locate the perceiver, the thinker, the one who *has* these experiences?

Perhaps the quest for the self requires a more circuitous pathway. When any two people regard one another, it is in a sense themselves that they see. The eyes, it is said, are the gateway to the soul: the soul of the other, but also my own which I see reflected in the other person. Yet our knowledge of others, however extensive, cannot unlock the key to our own identity, since we understand their fundamental nature no better than we understand our own. In this sense, others are too similar to ourselves to unlock the key to our own nature. Without denying that we are social beings whose identities are formed through our affiliations with others, we can still ask whether there is something basic about us that cannot be fully defined in terms of this inter-human network.

We are drawn, then, to casting our net wider, looking beyond ourselves – beyond, in any event, the conscious mind that seeks self-understanding – to find a source of knowledge about who we are. I chose the title for this book shortly after hearing Sandy's dream. Its imagery, while expressing her unique life experience, may help to illuminate our own. Computers, dolphins, and dreams, which at first glance seem to be utterly dissimilar notions, have this in common: they represent mirrors of a kind in which we might hope to recognize ourselves. Freud's interpretations of his patients' dreams, the cognitive scientist's efforts to build "artificial intelligence," Jane Goodall's "conversations" with primates, and John Lilly's experiments in communicating with dolphins can be seen as projects that carry on this pursuit of a reflection or echo that will unravel the mystery of our own being.

The dolphin metaphor, however, functions quite differently from the analogy between human beings and computers. Computers are best at simulating conscious, procedural intelligence; they can be regarded as models for the reasoning apparatuses, operating within the psyche or externally organized as institutional protocols, that order our lives. The dolphin, on the other hand, reflects back to us something more intuitive and spontaneous about ourselves, something that relates human beings to a natural world existing prior to the systematizing, regulating discourses of everyday life. Another difference between these two metaphorical vehicles is that, whereas computers represent one of the triumphs of a technologically advanced social order, dolphins may be regarded as among its victims. When people protest the fishing industry's slaughter of dolphins and whales, or the use of animals for experimentation, or for that matter the clear-cutting of the redwoods, they also affirm something precious about themselves, reflected in the cherished object that they wish to save.

In the case of the dolphins, in particular, this "something precious" involves qualities of inwardness, subjectivity, and perhaps forms of communication and cooperation that the lens of Western science has in the past been too narrow to recognize.[1] This same lens, when focused upon human beings, may overlook our essential nature as well. The image of the dolphin, suffering under captivity or destroyed by modern fishing practices, carries the message that something vitally significant about ourselves gets lost in a world that dissects and manipulates nature without understanding it. This sense of loss – the feeling of lack or emptiness when we peer into the mirror to discern who we are – is by no means dispelled by the wealth of factual information made available to us through access to the new technologies. On the contrary, there are many links between technological abundance, on the one hand, and subjective deprivation on the other.

AN OUTLINE OF OUR INQUIRY

This deprivation takes many forms and is difficult to characterize in a general way, although we use clichéd expressions like "crisis of the self" to begin to talk about it. Exploration of this "crisis" is the aim of this book, which I have organized as follows:

I Crisis of the self

The closely linked notions of "self," "individual," and "subject," long central to the Western canon, no longer provide a satisfactory foundation for human identity. The Western ideal of the "autonomous individual," understood as a self-initiating and self-determining human agent, remains important in a post-industrial order. But the ideology of that order is at odds with itself, since it emphasizes adaptation as well as independence, connectedness as well as separation. These values are somewhat inconsistent, and a life that tries to fulfill them all somewhat incoherent. Viewed by ourselves or others as detached individuals, we are expected to assume by and for ourselves the responsibility for our own self-formation, instead of having our identity handed to us by any external agency. No longer compelling is the idea that traditional roles, assigned to us by our gender, family, or community ties, should define who we are. On the contrary, we learn that what we are supposed to do is literally to construct ourselves. Although this ideal is often attributed to members of the upper and middle social classes, and to men more than to women, contemporary culture communicates the values of self-determination and self-realization to everyone in the society, through such channels as the mass media and educational institutions: "Be all you can be."

But how many of us can live up to this standard? What can "self-formation" or "autonomy" mean, given the many ways that human lives are institutionally coordinated and regimented? Given also our realization that modeling personal identity after the allegedly free-standing, separate individual will not necessarily strengthen or fulfill us, but might even reinforce patterns of isolation and inner impoverishment. The traditional image of the self-determining individual – "master of himself and of the universe," as the seventeenth-century dramatist Corneille put it – which has for centuries been the cornerstone of Western thought, is no longer adequate. But if we give up this image of personhood and individuality, what will replace it?

II Technological objects and divided subjects

Information technologies contribute to this predicament. On the one hand, the enormous power and versatility of our machines seem to assure our mastery over the world we inhabit. On the other hand, ours is becoming a *programmed society* in which rationalization (planning, organization, and automation) leaves little room for independent action or spontaneity on the part of specialized actors. While it may appear that information technologies help to affirm and empower centered subjects or "selves," communicating across secure boundaries, the opposite often turns out to be the case. The more powerful and "intelligent" the machines that serve us, and the more capable they become of replacing the mental as well as the physical capacities of human beings, the less confident we become that there remains an irreplaceable human subject to be served.

The irony is that although information technologies are tools of organization and integration, they also serve, in their dual role as material instruments and as culturally influential icons, to render problematic the traditional Western ideal of the unified subject. Mechanical instruments such as automobiles support fantasies of individuality and autonomy: submission of the "external world" to a masterful subject. Computers, on the other hand, tend to function in the unconscious as internal objects harking back to a time in children's lives prior to personal differentiation and identity. Connection rather than separation becomes the predominant technological idiom of our lives; the historical shift from mechanical to information technologies helps to subvert the notions of sovereignty and self-sufficiency that have provided an ideological anchoring for "individual identity" since Greek philosophers elaborated the concept more than two millenniums ago. In short, technology is helping to dismantle the very vision of the world that in the past it fostered.

III Internal colonization and response

Technology accomplishes nothing by itself, however. It is influential only within the social context of its invention and employment. We in the West take pride in our capacity to think about and take charge of the world around us. Scientific and technological innovations make possible the modernization of industry, transportation, communications, and education, testifying to the power of human reason to reconstruct social and natural environments.

But not everyone participates equally in exercising this power. Nor does its exercise necessarily enhance the well-being or freedom of those under its jurisdiction. The German social theorist Jürgen Habermas speaks of an "internal colonization of the lifeworld:"[2] the structures of modernity have a destructive impact on kinship, communal, religious, and ethnic affiliations. Like a colonial regime that administers the lives of those subject to its rule, institutional systems rationalize and reorganize the "lifeworld" (the domain of everyday taken-for-granted human experiences and relationships) in keeping with technocratic priorities and procedures. This administration gives rise to a host of irrationalities and dilemmas ranging from discordant gender roles to problems of structural unemployment, homelessness, pollution of the environment, and so on. These contradictions divide the social world against itself at many levels, contributing to such polarized relationships as public versus private, bureaucrat versus client, ego versus other, elites versus masses, mind versus body. The crisis of the self emerges from this historically constituted constellation of opposites.

Does a scientifically and technologically sophisticated culture require these divisions? Is it naive to believe that there could be a relationship between subject and object that would amount neither to an absolute and unnegotiable separation nor, in Theodor Adorno's words, to an *"erpresste Versöhnung"* (forced reconciliation)? In recent years, new social movements have taken up these questions in a way that challenges the models of subjectivity, rationality and progress that prevail in advanced industrial societies.[3] The feminist, peace, ecology, and New Age movements in the West, along with similar movements in Eastern Europe and Third World countries, propose new ways of understanding our relationships to one another and to nature, as well as our status as individual human subjects. But do they offer a viable alternative to the currently prevailing forms of rationalization? What part will technology play in the more humane world these movements hope to build? Consideration of what is technologically possible is relevant both to the utopian prospects that motivate, and to the practical constraints that limit, the creation of new forms of community and personal identity.

LOOKING FOR ANSWERS: A PERSONAL NOTE

Looking back over what I have written above, I notice a tension in my argument. Inasmuch as that argument aims to represent accurately the emerging structures of post-industrial society, it has to be distanced from my own particular experiences. On the other hand, those experiences will of course enter into the social analysis I build. In my own life, the meanings of technology have been many and contradictory.

Even as a child I took an interest in technological aspects of my surroundings. I found such toys as model trains and erector sets especially attractive. Later on, I was a bespectacled kid eager to learn everything about engineering and science. I found dealing with things less problematic than dealing with people. In my school work, math and science were the most exciting subjects. Socially, I felt backward, although I became friends with a boy who shared with me an interest in technical matters.

But the isolation and inferiority that I experienced in relation to most of my peers turned out, to my surprise, not to be set in stone. I was a senior in high school when the launching of the Soviet satellite Sputnik occurred. I remember an evening in the autumn of 1957, when teachers and students gathered on the campus to view the Soviet miracle as it passed overhead. A tiny speck in the sky, and yet the object of the attention and respect of everyone on earth, I imagined. Of interest to me was the use of cybernetic communication and control to manage satellite trajectories; information technology was already becoming essential to the conquest of space.

It did not have to be explained to me that, however inept I might seem in the social world, there might be a satisfactory place for me in the realm of scientific and technical exploration. When Sputnik took off, my fortune also went into orbit. After all, it would be my responsibility, would it not, to help our nation catch up with the Russians! I applied to attend college at the California Institute of Technology in Pasadena, California, and was accepted. My career was launched.

I mention this history because it reflects not just my own coming of age but also a larger historical transition. Almost overnight, it seemed, science and technology became very much respected, virtually godlike. And I was invited to join the ranks of the exalted priesthood. Whatever the petty, everyday difficulties I experienced elsewhere in my life, I would be supported and sustained by my relationship to scientific inquiry and knowledge.

Indeed I remained a devoted believer until, a few years later, something went wrong with my religion. In the 1960s, science and technology lost their aura of sanctity. Along with many other young men and women of my generation, I became aware of the horribly destructive purposes that technical understanding could serve. In university classrooms and laboratories, I had been learning about the marvelously intricate physical structure of nature. But was it not knowledge of this kind that, a few thousand miles away, was being put to use in Indo-China? Napalm, cluster bombs, Agent Orange, and the electronic battlefield were among our "finest" technological achievements. Under these circumstances, could one continue to believe in the nobility of scientific ideals and the value of technological innovation? On a more personal level, could I remain committed to my technical studies? Disillusioned, I dreamt of seeing myself attending my own wedding ceremony; the bride wears white, but her wedding dress scarcely conceals the monstrous fact that, underneath, she is a machine.

A decade later, when the war was over, I revived my technical interest by taking up with computers. I still find it amazing that we can get a silicon chip to act a little bit as if it thinks. But for reasons that will become evident in this book, I have lost some of my respect for information technologies too. The path I have taken – enchanted early on with the prospect of a mathematical and scientific understanding of the world, then disenchanted, impressed subsequently with "thinking machines," then disillusioned with them also, currently re-evaluating my earlier evaluations – leads to this writing. I cannot say that along the way I have arrived at the truth. But perhaps when the final page has been completed ...

Part I

Crisis of the self

Chapter 1

The technological mirror

THE CONTEMPORARY SEARCH FOR THE SELF

What a strange object to be trying to find: oneself. Surely the self is very near to us, the basis of our being. Yet somehow it escapes us. Something vital or central about ourselves remains absent or hidden, and we seek to remedy this ignorance and uncertainty.

Concern for the self is historically nothing new. Recall the Socratic maxim "Know thyself," the "care for the self" prescribed in Plato's *Alcibiades*, Augustine's intensely personal quest for salvation in *The Confessions*, and Rousseau's *amour de soi*.[1] In these instances, however, concern for oneself was a patiently pursued, lifelong project. Today, there is a more obsessive, even desperate, quality about the search for the self. Christopher Lasch has argued that a "culture of narcissism," preoccupied with securing and satisfying the self, has become a defining feature of industrially advanced societies.[2] Caring for the self certainly provides many professionals with their work: psychologists attempt to heal the self; entrepreneurs develop commercial products that cater to its needs. In leadership training seminars, corporate managers learn that they must look after the "self-esteem requirements" of their subordinates. Advertisements for the military announce that young people can truly discover and realize themselves in the armed forces.

But who is this "self" that longs for validation, nurturing, and realization, and why is it that at this particular juncture in the history of Western societies the very identity of the self becomes problematic? The common keywords used to characterize psychological health – "centredness," "grounding," "wholeness," and the like – point to a new vulnerability, an insecurity about the very coherence of the personal identities we construct for ourselves.

Information technologies, while appearing to empower us, may contribute to this insecurity by challenging the status of our own subjectivity. Indeed, as technological devices become more sophisticated and do more for us, there seems to be less for us to do, perhaps less for us to *be* – less that establishes us as uniquely human. The seventeenth-century philosopher René Descartes, observing the analogy between the most advanced mechanical devices of his time and the mechanistic functioning of the body, hypothesized that the body is essentially a machine. But this conjecture did not imply, for Descartes, that human beings are nothing more than material objects. Inhabiting the human body is a mind, interacting with the biological "vessel" of our being. Descartes' idea was to cede the human body to physical science, while celebrating the mind as the domain of freedom and autonomy. The body might be understood as just another material entity in the world, no less objective and public than any other. The mind, however, as the essence of the human subject, would remain something divine. In agreement with Plato, Aristotle, and the scholastics of the Middle Ages, Descartes held that what distinguishes human subjects from other species and from the inanimate world is their reasoning capacity.

In Descartes' time there was not even the prospect of a machine that could simulate thinking, the activity that he regarded as the hallmark of a uniquely human identity. Today, on the other hand, that machine has been invented; arguably, what it does is something like thinking. Harvard psychologist George Miller articulates a perspective now accepted by many within his profession: "Psychologists have come to take it for granted in recent years that men and computers are merely two different species of a more abstract genus called 'information-processing systems'."[3] Until recently, machines could enhance or supplant only our physical powers, giving rise to the analogy: machine = body. But the new, information-processing machines imitate or supplant our mental capacities, thereby making available a new metaphor: machine = mind.

One may object that the mind is significantly more sophisticated and subtle than a machine of any kind. Even the most advanced computer cannot simulate realistically human experiences or relationships. I agree with this critique, but, there is an underlying issue that it does not address, regarding the diminishing role allowed to subjectivity in a world that is technologically organized and scientifically understood. While there may be human attributes that no machine, however "intelligent," could possibly replicate – such as creativity, insight, intuition – it is far from clear that these attributes attest to the existence of a "self" or "subject" in any traditional sense.[4] Although the idea of the mind as software is oversimplified, it points in the direction of an analysis of subjectivity – in social, psychological and biological, if not cognitivist, terms – that is at odds with our fundamental notions of who we are. For if the mind is a "structure" or "system" that can be brought within the framework of scientific explanation, what becomes of the distinctively human and free subject or "self" we take ourselves to be? This is the profoundly unsettling question that scientific and technological advance raises.

Information systems, by providing not only evidence of the efficacy of scientific knowledge, but also new ways of perceiving and organizing the world, contribute to this uneasiness. Older, industrial technologies could be understood in traditional Cartesian terms as belonging to an "external" physical reality that human beings confront and master. Even when the human body itself is drawn within the scope of scientific inquiry, this still leaves the subject at least potentially in control; as free and autonomous agents, we own and make use of our bodies, as we do of our automobiles. The newer, computer-based analogy, on the other hand, which seeks to explain human experiences of agency and decision-making in information-processing terms, appears to dispense with the human subject altogether.

One obvious argument against this conjecture is that it exaggerates the cultural influence of technological objects; after all, aren't computers merely machines, for most people, with little significance beyond that of their everyday usefulness? The computer serves as a tool, like any other, and its typical user does not know or care much about the technical details of its operations. So it is unlikely, on this view, that the ways in which these new machines operate internally will have much meaning for those whose involvement is at a non-technical level. Nor should we anticipate that most people will be inclined to compare their own cognitive powers to those of machines. "Artificial intelligence" interests a few academics and engineers, but is otherwise irrelevant to the concerns of everyday life.

But consider again the cultural impact of such mechanical technologies as clocks or automobiles. Our industrial environment is populated by machines, and even people who live in rural areas see around them such things as trucks, tractors, and harvesters. Someone who grows up in such surroundings can hardly avoid forming at least a vague impression of how mechanical things work. One does not have to be a technician, an auto mechanic or watch-maker for example, to form the idea that the physical world, including our own bodies, functions in a mechanical way. I do not know very much about what goes on under the hood of an automobile, for instance, although I have nevertheless an elementary image of how the pistons, gears, and axles push and pull or turn one another so that, ultimately, the wheels are set into motion.

Similarly, with regard to my own physical structure, I know very little about how it works – I have a vague idea about the pumping of the heart, but am entirely in the dark about how the kidneys or the liver function. But here again, inasmuch as I accept the traditional medical model, I imagine that there are physical processes going on inside me, and when something goes wrong, I hand myself over to experts who presumably understand the "mechanics" of the body: namely, doctors. The point is that we need not be knowledgeable about technical matters in order for mechanism to influence our lives. For that influence is as much a matter of imagination and fantasy as of technical familiarity and know-how. Paradoxically, the less well informed we are about how mechanical objects work, the more powerful and influential may be the metaphors based on our perceptions of these objects. Many everyday expressions rely on an unsophisticated, shared experience of technological objects. Even people who dislike and avoid automobiles are apt to be familiar with phrases that link what goes on in human beings to what goes on in these machines: "revved up," "in the driver's seat," "running on empty," "putting on the brakes," "only going along for the ride."

Technological metaphor, then, can work quite effectively even for people who remain relatively ignorant about technical matters. This is as evident with computers as with any previous technology; as they become ubiquitous in our environment, they too will influence our basic assumptions about how the world is put together. Computers process information; they function not by the mechanical movements of their parts, but by carrying out invisible procedures called "programs." This minimal conception is enough to set into motion a transformation of the ways in which people conceive of themselves and their surroundings. We not only attribute human qualities of intelligence, friendliness, memory to the new machines, but are also inclined to attribute their features to ourselves. The image of human beings as "information-processors," whether vaguely articulated in pop psychology workshops or more precisely in cognitive science laboratories, has certainly come into its own during the past several years. Other terms with originally technological meanings, such as "input," "feedback," and "interface," have been incorporated into our everyday conversations about human interactions.

TECHNOLOGY AND THE CONSTRUCTION OF THE SELF

Computer metaphor, however, differs qualitatively from the metaphorical talk that has been built up around previous technologies. Whereas mechanical technology provides us with a vocabulary that supports the conception of autonomously acting and interacting individuals, information technology does not. Our employment of the older technologies (driving a car, using a handtool) presupposed human agency. A car goes nowhere without a driver; a tool without a tool-wielder is lifeless. Information-processing, on the other hand, may turn out to be an activity that is essentially subjectless. Our language indicates as much: terms like "feedback" and "interface" describe relationships among people as if they were relationships among cybernetic processes or objects. As our lives get more involved with information technologies, and information-processing concepts become culturally as well as technically more influential, we may find that these involvements call into question the notions of centered, coherent subjectivity and personal freedom that have traditionally propped up our ideals of selfhood and individuality.

The difference between our interactions with mechanical and with information technologies can be viewed psychoanalytically. The automobile is an exemplary Oedipal object, especially for men. It fulfills the classical male fantasy of penetration without entrapment: one hurtles through space to one's destination, but one can stop and exit any time one wants. Conversely, the rage experienced when one's trajectory is impeded expresses a kind of castration. The computer, on the other hand, tends to operate in the unconscious at a more fundamental level, as a pre-Oedipal object related to its user as a mother is bonded to her child before its own boundaries and personal identity have been consolidated.[5] This may partly explain why personal (non-networked) computers, unlike automobiles, are rarely given nicknames by their owners. Possibly, their existence is not sufficiently independent of our own to qualify as a nameable something. On the contrary, the "intelligence" of an information-processing system may be experienced as joined to that of its users. The language of information technologies indicates the closeness of this link: a "word-processor" designates at once the person, the software, and the device on which it runs. Similarly an "information system" is simultaneously subjective and objective, uniting human beings and machines.

TECHNOLOGY AS A SOCIAL LINK

It is important to remember that these connections between the technical and the experiential are always socially mediated. Technologies help to define user *communities*, including their traditions and ways of life. Hence, one of the ways of distinguishing various cultures from each other is in terms of the technology used.[6] Hunters do not employ the same implements as gatherers, nor gatherers the same implements as shepherds. The earliest civilizations were defined to some extent by the technical instruments that entered into the economic reproduction of everyday life.

More recently, technology has played an essential role in defining modern societies. The material wealth of the United States, Japan, and European nations has been built upon a base of machine-driven industrial manufacture that distinguishes their political economies from those of the Third World. Ours has been a world of machines, beginning with the mechanical toys that entertained European royalty 500 years ago, proceeding through the enormous expansion of the factory system in the eighteenth and nineteenth centuries, and culminating in the mass production of automobiles, computers, and other electronic devices in the twentieth century. This economic history is also a cultural history, a history not only of the ways in which we understand and handle things, but also of the views we take of one another and of ourselves.

The cultural consequences of technological innovation are often described, however, as if they were generated automatically – as if laws of nature govern not only the internal functioning of machines, but also the social context that surrounds them. A language of technological determinism articulates our understanding of the Information Age: qualitatively new forces of production are becoming dominant in industrial societies. Detroit declines and rusts, replaced in the media and the imagination by the greening of Silicon Valley. The older "sunset" industry is buried, and "sunrise" industry is born. Popular imagery of this kind not only celebrates contemporary change, but simultaneously informs us of its apparent inevitability. Apparently as natural as life and death, as the end of one day and beginning of another, is the replacement of one generation of technological instruments by another. Technology itself seems to propel this evolution, leaving to us the task of adapting to a technical world whose basic contours are formed beyond our own powers of knowledge or control.

This determinist view typically assumes that "autonomous technology" is overwhelmingly beneficial. The fundamental well-being of the global economy is thought to rest upon the unimpeded advance of technical innovation, upon "high technology" in particular. But in the United States, where unemployment, poverty, and corporate/financial bankruptcy have become symptoms of an economy chronically in recession, and where capitalist enterprise looks abroad to locate inexpensive labor resources and new markets, we have little reason to believe that technological advance will succeed either in restoring the material affluence of previous decades or in sustaining the set of values that have been associated with liberal capitalism and the welfare state. What kind of world, then, will the new technologies administer? What changes will our entry into a post-industrial era, organized around the global production and circulation of information, inaugurate in human social relations and self-understanding? Can traditional values of community and family, of work and leisure, of economic and psychological security survive? If not, what will replace them? Does technological innovation contribute to the "crisis of the self" that afflicts Western societies?

These are among the questions to be explored in this book. I assume that the answers are *not* predetermined by technology itself, independent of human interest and will. Advanced industrial societies are undergoing transformations involving not only economic and political restructuring but also changes in the ways we identify and understand ourselves. My intention here is not to sort out "good" technological applications and influences from "bad" ones, but to begin to reflect more generally upon the cultural and psychological foundations of the world that we reproduce daily and that reproduces us.

THEORETICAL FRAMEWORK

In the past decade, I have studied computer literacy in high school and college settings. As I learned more about the ways in which young people interact with information technologies, it occurred to me that these interactions might be associated with significant changes in students' self-image and self-esteem. I also conjectured that what I was observing in classrooms might reflect a society-wide transformation, and I set out to write this book about the subjective dimensions of that transformation. I interviewed or talked informally with about fifty persons regarding their involvements with computer technologies. Among them were computer programmers, systems analysts, and office workers. They were not "experimental subjects" in the scientific sense. Some were people I came to know through my work as a consultant. Some I saw in psychotherapy. Others, hearing of my interest in this subject, approached me to share their experiences of information-processing instruments and situations.

It was not only their conscious perceptions that I found illuminating, however. Technology, like everything else in our environment, is meaningful in ways of which we are unaware; technological objects are objects also of the unconscious. One of the ways of learning about this dimension of our experience is via the "royal road" (Freud) afforded by our dreams. I began to collect dreams – my own and others' – with a special interest in those that involved information technology in some way. My idea is that as our world becomes populated with new technological devices, they are apt to show up in our dreams in ways that may reveal their significance for us.

The interviews I have conducted and dreams I have gathered provide "observational evidence" that is relevant to the conjectures in this book. But empirical data can never be understood in the absence of an interpretive framework. Even in the most rigorous science, the facts never "speak for themselves." They are inevitably culled, interpreted, marshaled, even fabricated.[7] This is especially apparent with regard to the "evidence" that dreams offer. Does there exist such a thing as the "raw dream" itself, aside from any reading that may be given of it? Even at its first report, a dream is already being interpreted by its teller, as it is brought into words. The dreams and dream associations that were told to me surely took the dreamer's understanding of my expectations, as interviewer, into account. By asking certain questions and not others of the interviewees, I encouraged exploration of their dreams along certain lines and not others. So I cannot say that there is anything empirically pure about the dreams or any of the experiences reported to me during these interviews.

In short, observations, however empirically close they may pretend to be to their subject matter, are never meaningful in themselves, but are given meaning only by human perceivers who inevitably approach them with their own preconceptions. In writing this book, I have found several theoretical traditions helpful. The first is Critical Theory, also known as the "Frankfurt School."[8] Those who inaugurated this tradition in Germany in the 1920s, including Horkheimer, Adorno, and Marcuse, were influenced by Marxism, but were much more skeptical than Marx about the progressive cultural implications of technological innovation. Of specific relevance to the issues discussed in this book is their conjecture that technology advances organization and domination not only of the external physical world but also of internal nature, of subjectivity. This negative dialectic, whereby human beings become vulnerable to the social and technical structures that supposedly serve them, is one of Critical Theory's central themes. The best-known contemporary representative of this school is Jürgen Habermas. His account of the colonizing character of contemporary social institutions – of the ways in which they submit everyday experience to administrative rationalization – provides a context for examining the subjective consequences of involvements with information technologies.[9]

Also relevant are object relations theory and self-psychology. These psychoanalytic traditions, including the work of such figures as Klein, Winnicott, Kohut, and Jessica Benjamin, illuminate aspects of human relationships and experience – the constitution and vulnerability of the self, in particular – that are relevant to this study. Drawing upon this psychoanalytic thinking, we may distinguish between the different ways that mechanical technologies and information technologies function as internal objects.[10]

I have been influenced as well by post-structuralist and feminist critiques of psychoanalytic theory, and by the work of Jacques Lacan.[11] Some of these critiques argue that the "self" is an artifact, if not an illusion. Human subjectivity is culturally formed within diverse contexts of gender, social class, ethnic, and technological relationships.

UNDERSTANDING THE "POST-INDUSTRIAL REVOLUTION"

Theory works best when the domain it investigates is circumscribed and relatively stable. But the technological circumstances of our lives are evolving so rapidly and with such diverse and far-flung consequences that we are scarcely in any position to account for them definitively. It may be the case, as futurologists like Daniel Bell and Alvin Toffler have argued, that contemporary Western societies are undergoing a seachange as fundamental as the Industrial Revolution. But let us recall that the best theoretical explanations for *that* revolution, including the accounts given by Marx, Durkheim, and Weber, had to wait until it had been under way for several centuries before they were constructed. The German philosopher Hegel summarizes this lesson beautifully: "The owl of Minerva (goddess of wisdom) takes wing only at dusk." Understanding of the truly "big events" in our cultural history (perhaps this is true of our personal histories as well) becomes possible only *post facto*.

If so, then we cannot expect to construct an adequate picture of the times we are living through. Our historical situation may be comparable to that of the inhabitants of the late medieval cities in Western Europe. These townspeople were involved in a revolution of a kind: the transition from feudalism to capitalism, with new forms of production and mechanisms of commodity exchange, but they could make only limited sense of their own experience. Not everyone thrived under these changing economic and cultural circumstances. Most of the people living in European cities during the Renaissance suffered oppressive conditions of labor, material impoverishment, or epidemic diseases. But in the writings of those who flourished – the merchants, humanists, and educated artisans of fifteenth-century Florence, for instance – there is an unmistakable excitement and exuberance about the technological and cultural innovations of the time. Most compelling about their accounts, however, is not their theoretical explanations, but rather the personal observations and descriptions they offer of their transformed lives.

Similarly, modern industrial societies are undergoing changes that our traditional categories of political economy and culture can no longer grasp. In part, this transformation is technological; ours is becoming a world of "artificial intelligence" in which the automatic generation, management, and communication of information play a more important role in our daily lives than ever before. Computers have become ubiquitous: at home, at school and at work, there they sit staring at us, their video-monitors bursting with screenfuls of information. How are we to understand ourselves as making sense of and fitting into this strange new environment of our own creation?

Chapter 2

Narcissism, mastery, and identity

> Life is nothing. To be means to build oneself.
> Luigi Pirandello[1]

Crisis signifies that something is endangered: liable to come apart or collapse, perhaps to vanish altogether. Can we speak in this sense of a contemporary "crisis of the self"? Before we begin our examination of this phenomenon, we might ask whether it actually exists. Could it be that the proclaimed "crisis of the self" has been contrived by a handful of disaffected popular authors, abetted by another handful of academics? Although talking of "crisis" here may amount to an exaggeration, it does seem that a sense of isolation and anonymity, of uncertainty about one's place and purpose in life, is indeed characteristic of contemporary experience. Our surroundings are constantly being transformed: technology develops at breakneck speed; banks, corporations, families, and friendships form and dissolve. These changes continue a dynamic of modernization that, as Max Weber argued early in this century, mercilessly uproots tradition and "disenchants" the world.[2] The human bonding that we nostalgically associate with small communities, durable kinship relations, and older economic and political institutions is commonly perceived as disrupted or dissolved, contributing to feelings of loss and failure.

Under these conditions, one's very sense of oneself as a coherent center of comprehension and agency, as an internally unified subject capable of integrating subjective experiences, relations to others, and personal history, may become unstable. Called into question is the security, possibly even the very identity, of the person or alleged "self" one is assumed to be. Such anxiety has been a favorite subject not only of social theory but also of art, as in the existentialist writings of Sartre and Camus; the literature of women like Woolf, Sarraute, and Dumas; the avant-garde theater of Ionesco and Beckett. This is a theme, then, that is not exclusive to the late twentieth century. Yet it is noteworthy that the subject of the "self" has today become so commonplace, of interest no longer only to a few intellectuals and artists but to a much larger public, as a host of self-improvement and self-esteem bestsellers attest.

Paradoxically, the more uncertain the status of the self becomes, the more we want to secure it. We remain attached to the notion as if our own survival as distinctively human individuals depends on *its* survival. However elusive the self may seem, many of us remain committed to its existence, to the belief that there is or should be a personal core or center of a kind that uniquely identifies each of us – if not a *soul*, then at least a *self*. As has been said of God, if the self did not exist, we would have had to have invented it. For even if we go along with a postmodern account of the self as a construction to which nothing in objective "reality" actually corresponds, this still leaves us with a constellation of issues – having to do with self-esteem, self-deception, self-determination, and the like – that lend themselves to formulation and discussion in terms of a "self."[3]

At the same time, the notion of the self is a battlefield that has been crosscut so often by various warring disciplines and discourses that there is no consensus whatever on what it means. Since the self is the subject of this book, though, some preliminary remarks are in order. Let me begin with what I take to be an inadequate definition. "Self" does not refer simply to the reasoning agency or "ego" that cognitive psychology postulates and that artificial intelligence simulates with information-processing models. This view of the self overlooks the emotive, social, and embodied aspects of human subjectivity and agency.[4] These aspects are better captured in the object relations accounts of the self that have been given by people like Winnicott, Jacobson, and Jessica Benjamin. Kohut's self-psychology also belongs to this tradition. Complementing these psychoanalytic theories are con- tributions to our understanding of the social construction of the self that have been made by Durkheim, Mead, Dewey, and others in the social-interactionist tradition.

By citing these "authorities" I do not mean to lay to rest qualms about the ontological status of the self. Possibly the "self" is far more fragmentary and dispersed than the psychoanalytic and sociological views mentioned above admit. I will return later to the question of whether, and in what sense, the self can even be said to exist. Bracketing that question for the time being, however, it seems that in any event, the "self" does play a role in the lives of those who believe in it.

SELF-FORMATION AND PRESENTATION

The role of the self is public as well as private: the self is something "within" us that we may present and represent to others. As the target of self-improvement programs, of recriminations should these fail, of transformation in therapy, the self receives our constant attention and painstaking cultivation.

Robert Coles, in his study of children from affluent families, observes that they learn early on to experience themselves "from outside," as it were. They learn not only to master their surroundings, but also to shape themselves:

> With none of the other American children I have worked with have I heard such a continuous and strong emphasis put on the "self." In fact, other children rarely if ever think about themselves in the way children of well-to-do and rich parents do – with insistence, regularity, and, not least, out of a learned sense of obligation.[5]

This "obligation" is not only to traditional virtues such as honesty, helpfulness, and obedience, but above all to the very construction of the person one will be. The children interviewed by Coles understand this clearly. A boy remarks:

> It's this way: first you build *yourself* up. You learn all you can. Later, you can *give of yourself.* That's what Dad says: you can't help others until you've learned to help *yourself.* It's not that you're being selfish.[6]

This child is internalizing strategies for adult "success," which will eventually be applied toward a career in, say, medicine, law, or business administration. The most important requirement here is not the acquisition of specific skills, but the capacity for consciously directed development and presentation of oneself.

The self that gets constructed in this way is a symbolic product formed, Michel Foucault argues, out of discourses of knowledge and power. The manner of this formation changes historically. Foucault writes that in the West, a transition in the conception of the self has occurred. Definition of the self in terms of its social affiliations have been eclipsed by first-person language about the self, in which one legitimates oneself in front of others.[7]

Whereas in the past it may have been in a religious context or in the privacy of one's personal relations that talk about the self predominated, today this language has invaded the marketplace, where the exchange value of the self is handled like that of any commodity – gold, silver, or pork bellies. Professionals market not only their skills but, most importantly, themselves. One of young girls' favorite role models, the Barbie Doll, which began as a fashion model in the 1950s, later became an "American Airlines Flight Attendant" or "Registered Nurse," complete with the accoutrements of her profession. A stewardess or female nurse is someone who has built a career for herself, and has developed a certain persona or self in keeping with that career. Vocations designated as appropriate for women, like those for men, call for the rationalized and linguistically mediated presentation of oneself to others.

Shaping oneself in a way that first parents and later teachers and other authority figures find acceptable does not come easily for everyone, however. Even for the relatively privileged children in Coles' study, mentioned above, the possibility that they may "fall behind" is often a source of chronic anxiety; although educated to succeed, they will not necessarily fulfill either their parents' expectations or their own. Coles notes that approval from oneself as from others depends upon one's performance, upon "constant exertion, lest he [the child] fail to 'measure up' ... One measures up because one *must.* No allowance is made for any possible lack of ability or endowment."[8] In school, students are expected, in the words of one educator, to become "managers of their own cognitive resources."[9] If one does not "measure up," does not succeed in "making something" of oneself, then one's very identity may be endangered.

In this way, the project of self-formation is apt to become problematic, first for children and subsequently for the adults they become. Given the enormous enterprise devoted to the self's establishment, cultivation, and fulfillment, it seems right to describe the times we live in as the "Age of the Self." But the intensity of the narcissistic pursuit of the self is matched only by the precarious status of its object. Christopher Lasch points out that "Narcissism signifies a loss of selfhood, not self-assertion. It refers to a self threatened with disintegration and by a sense of inner emptiness."[10]

Lasch's analysis fails to differentiate, however, the ways in which selfhood is experienced by people belonging to various social classes. True, ideals of self-construction and self-presentation are widely influential in modern societies. Yet, the paths that are accessible to one person for forming a self may not be accessible to another. Technology is one of the relevant variables here, since relationships to machines correlate with social power and status, and even with self-conception. Hence, we cannot speak simply of "the influence of information technologies upon *our* lives." The pronoun "our" here conceals important differences differences of gender and social status, among others. Mechanical technologies, for example, have long been gender-typed: washing machines, stoves, and garbage disposals pertain to "women's work," while machine tools and automobile technology belong to "a man's world." Information technologies, too, contribute to gender differentiation: most data-entry clerks are female, most database administrators male.

MILITARY SELF-FORMATION: COMPUTERS VERSUS TANKS

The domain of military vocations illustrates this cultural functioning of technological objects. We learn not only about the military from recruitment advertisements (Figures 2.1 and 2.2), for instance, but also about the market at which they are aimed: teenage America. Each addresses this audience in a different way. The Army version, featuring a head-on photograph of a tank, makes a traditional appeal to teenagers' interest in things mechanical, and is reminiscent of the 1950s. At that time, automobiles were the rage. If you owned one, or could at least drive mom and dad's, you were someone. If you didn't, you were a nobody. Many of us spent a lot of time working on our automobiles, and auto mechanics was of greater interest than anything we learned in school. Cars were nothing less than the key to the good life: power, social status, sex. The bigger the better. More "sophisticated" information-processing technologies had not yet arrived to serve as symbols of power and prestige. This was before "Small is beautiful," before compact cars and microcomputers became popular. Something (or someone) had to be big and physically intimidating to be impressive.

The old-fashioned Army advertisement taps this admiration for machines. "52 Tons of Steel"! No car could ever compare. You too can get behind that gun barrel and drive a vehicle larger than any you ever imagined. Although the tank is represented as a formidable machine, the technology remains subordinate to human direction: "We'll help put you in the driver's seat with technical training, pay and other benefits." Human beings remain in charge. The machine has not yet acquired a mind and a will of its own.

While the Army advertisement speaks most effectively to adolescents from

Figure 2.1 US Army recruitment advertisement

traditional working-class backgrounds, the Air Force advertisement targets profession-bound middle class youth. "There's no telling where technology is going in the future. But with Air Force training, you've always got a future to look forward to." Technology is represented here as a pseudo-autonomous force, with a

Figure 2.2 US Air Force recruitment advertisement

direction and purpose of its own, promising the good life to those who connect with it. The video-screen reveals all, teaches all. And those who are willing to learn shall be saved. This secular religion proclaims a new gospel: computer technology "lets you program your own destiny." One learns to program not merely the computer, but, simultaneously, oneself. Technology, rather than God, parents, or teachers determines human fate.

The notion of destiny here is not without Christian precedent. But the Calvinist notion of a *calling*, to which an individual is *pre*destined, has been replaced here by another, that of *self*-destination: one is fully responsible for establishing one's own identity. A calling establishes personal and moral relationships between an individual and other members of a community; the contemporary emphasis upon self-construction, on the other hand, downplays the ethical and social implications of vocational choice. In the Army advertisement lipservice is still given to patriotism; its bottom line is "Americans At Their Best." Even this brief mention of service to one's country has been elided in the Air Force advertisement. One joins the military and takes up a technological vocation to benefit oneself, not to serve the nation or God or any ideal beyond the self.

The Air Force advertisement redefines power. Decades ago, when Detroit was the automobile capital of the world and the American economy was based on industries involved in manufacturing these vehicles, driving one of them certified a person's individuality, attractiveness, and status. Today, on the other hand, it is abstract motion – motion of the mind in the process of thought – not that of huge machines that is likely to impress. Some high school kids still soup up their jalopies. But they aren't the ones who are really going somewhere. The brainy kid who takes up computers has a far brighter future, we are told, since this is the Information Age. The male teenager who masters the computer will probably still be perceived by his peers as less "sexy" than the car jock. But with today's redefinitions of gender identities and sexual fantasies, even this ordering might be overturned.[11] Moreover, automotive technology is increasingly computerized, so that one needs to know about information technology even to work on cars. "Electronics and computer equipment can be state-of-the-art today. And ready for the garbage can tomorrow," the advertisement informs us. There is an implication here that a young man, too, can end up in the garbage if he does not take care to program his future. Like the children in Coles' study, adolescents learn that they need to attend to the selves they hope to become. We associate this lesson especially with middle-class high school students who intend to go on to college. But it also influences those who consider a military career as a plausible alternative.

MILITARY RATIONALIZATION

The recruitment ads we have looked at represent military service as an exciting and rewarding relationship with technology, without reference to an adversary or "enemy" of any kind. Good and evil have been replaced by another pair of opposites: competence and ignorance. Military service becomes, then, a profession like any other, harnessing the detached intelligence of the professional to the performance of technical obligations. The human "targets" of the technical system exist only at its remote periphery, invisible to those who direct the system from the center.

Information-processing systems accentuate this distancing of actors from the consequences of their actions. Such systems differ from mechanical devices in the way that they interpose themselves between subject and object. Returning to the advertisements discussed above, the drivers of a tank are sheltered by the machine's armor from the dangerous terrain they traverse; nevertheless it is on that terrain that war is fought. For the Air Force recruit seated at the computer console, on the other hand, the battlefield is rendered more abstract. He processes data, images on a screen, remote from the physical realities of warfare. (Today's tank driver, too, may observe a screen, which to some extent distances him from the "outside world.") Representation of the enemy carries as little real-world significance as that of an electronic adversary in a video-arcade game. In the film *Top Gun*, an Air Force pilot's target is reduced to a blip on a video display. Missiles are directed at the object and it explodes, denying the reality of the Soviet pilot who loses his life.

The Persian Gulf War in 1991 illustrates the way in which forms of abstraction made available by "high technology" may serve ideological ends, including denial of the realities of war. It was thrilling to see on television "our" missiles encountering and vanquishing those of the "enemy." Rarely were Iraqi targets represented in the mass media as actual human beings. The war seemed to be less a physical than a mental enterprise, fought by smart bombs from a distant aerial perspective that prevented detailed observation of the havoc wreaked below. Wounded and dead bodies were excluded from consciousness, although they might be mentioned for certain strategic purposes, as in the fabricated "incubator incident" in which Iraqi soldiers were alleged to have removed babies from their incubators in a Kuwaiti hospital.

Although the separation of image from reality, of technological means from human consequences, is dramatically exemplified in contemporary military campaigns, it is to some extent built into technological applications in any domain. For this reason, the conventional wisdom that "technology is neutral and can serve either good or bad ends" is misleading. Granted, the dehumanizing consequences of a technological system depend in most cases on the social context and the aims of its deployment. The construction of a personnel database, for example, does not *entail* the manipulation or exploitation of the human beings who are entered into it as records. Yet the very process of abstraction whereby the individual becomes a statistic, a data packet that the computer can process, lends itself to these purposes.

In a variety of settings, corporate and non-corporate, it has been observed that there is a tendency on the part of the designers and producers of information systems, notwithstanding their good intentions, to lose sight of the particular needs and perspectives of those allegedly served by their work. The challenging complexity of the project itself tends to obscure any reality beyond that of the technical system. Once the technological spectacles have been put on, and one becomes accustomed to seeing the world through them, they can hardly be removed. Those who work closely with abstract systems may come to view themselves abstractly as well. For the process of mapping the world into a matrix of binary representations, even if its intention is to target only objects outside oneself, is apt to turn inward and objectify the subject. The subject belongs, after all, to the processed world and therefore falls within the scope of its own processing. The systems analyst or programmer who designs the system – an automated bank-teller, for instance – is also, in his or her role as client, the processed object of that system.

THE LANGUAGE OF FRAGMENTATION

Rationalization and professionalization emphasize measurable aspects of military performance; subjective factors, including such traditional reasons for service in the armed forces as love of country or solidarity with one's peers, are played down.[12] Van Creveld suggests that motivational problems in the armed forces stem in part from military planners' use of information technology:

> Since numbers are all that computers can work with, there is a tendency of computer-based quantitative analysis to disregard every factor that cannot be quantified ... factors such as morale, resolution, fighting spirit, and endurance, which could not be easily quantified, tended to be overlooked by the systems analysts.[13]

Drawing on Max Weber's theory of modernity, sociologists have pointed out that processes of rationalization, whether they take place in civilian or military life, tend to render human existence abstract and bureaucratic, at the expense of experiences of belonging and meaning. It may be partly as a consequence of this loss that images of disintegration, which seem most appropriate to extremely traumatic situations such as war, enter so often into the metaphorical talk of everyday life. We speak of a person *cracking up*, or *falling to pieces*, as *scattered* or *flaky*, as *shattered* by a traumatic experience; these expressions represent failure as falling apart. Success, on the other hand, is equated with the achievement of coherence and unity, of the "integrated personality" which ego psychology identifies with mental health. Other commonplace remarks also rely on this metaphor: "I hope to get through this in one piece," and "Get it together!"[14]

Popular expressions that rely on the metaphor of things falling apart – the "*disintegrating* nuclear family," the "*crumbling* of confidence in political leaders" – suggest an unsettling and weakening of family and community ties, a loss of coherence and centeredness that also subverts individual identity. Continuity of tradition, reliability of expectations, and consistency of values and commitments are essential supports of the self; when these are perceived as having come undone, the self falls prey to dissolution. As Peter Berger has observed:

> Conceptions of the self are related to experiences of self, and these in turn take place within the context of specific social institutions ... As the individual becomes uncertain about the world, he necessarily becomes uncertain about his own self ... Put differently, as the social identification processes become increasingly fragmented, the subjective experience of identity becomes increasingly precarious.[15]

Stable personal identities presuppose stable contexts in which they can develop and receive support. Whether or not everyday life is more "fragmented" for people today than it was in the past, the *perception* of an unraveling of social ties – associated with global and domestic economic transformations and dislocations and with a loss of coherent moral or political ideals in terms of which people can situate themselves – helps to undermine the security of "personal identity" as it has traditionally been understood in the West.

Issues of identity and fragmentation enter into the arts as well as into everyday life. Psychoanalyst Heinz Kohut argues that artistic representation is in advance of scientific understanding in the matter of recognizing a culture's psychological condition. For artists in the past, Kohut suggests:

> [T]he triumphs and defeats of basically strong people were their subject matter. But now a good many artists have begun to deal with a new set of issues. This set of issues, to speak of it in the most gross terms, is the falling apart of the self and of the world and the task of reconstituting the self and the world.[16]

For Kohut, the contemporary human predicament is epitomized in these lines from Eugene O'Neill's play, *The Great God Brown*: "Man is born broken. He lives by mending. The grace of God is glue." In the visual arts no less than in theater and literature, loss of coherence and identity has become a prevalent theme. Traditional styles of figurative representation, aiming to mirror well-defined individuals and their environments, are no longer found compelling. No less "real" than the world of Michelangelo's Adam (Figure 2.3), the classical individual fashioned in God's image and given the Creator's special blessing, is the reality experienced by painters such as Karel Appel, whose *Nude* (Figure 2.4) is alone, abandoned, and scarcely recognizable as human.

WOMEN AS INDIVIDUALS

Western individuality has typically been regarded as an attribute of men, as in Michelangelo's *Creation of Adam*. Yet it has also been at issue in the lives of women. In Genesis, when Eve tempts Adam away from God, she distances human beings not only from the Creator but also from one another. Expulsion from the Garden is, in a way, an initiation into an individuality, including sexual self-aware-ness, that men and women share.

But they do not share in it in the same way. Differences in gender representation bring out the variability of forms of individuality, and of its loss. During the Renaissance, individualism was a lifestyle available to males belonging to aristo-cratic and bourgeois families; yet female members of those families could to some extent also shape their identities in terms of its ideals. Conceptions of women, no less than of men, were influenced by the Renaissance "discovery" of the individual. In Giotto's art at the beginning of the fourteenth century, we can see a transforma-tion in the way that members of both genders are portrayed. Compare Cimabue's *Madonna Enthroned*, painted in the late thirteenth century (Figure 2.5, p. 32), with

Figure 2.3 Creation of Adam (Michelangelo, 1508–12)

Figure 2.4 Nude (Karel Appel, 1986)

Giotto's representation of the same theme (Figure 2.6, p. 33). In Giotto's work, Mary has become a powerful figure who occupies a space of her own, recognized by angels and saints who admire her from both sides through the apertures of her throne. While Cimabue's "holy family" is cross-generational, linking the New Testament to the patriarchs of the Old Testament at the bottom of the painting, Giotto's is more "here and now," situating family members (excluding Joseph, interestingly) and admirers within a unified physical domain that more clearly delineates solid, corporeal individuals.

Compared to Cimabue's figures, those in Giotto's painting are observed in greater detail and are held by gravity to the earth; no longer do they float up and down the left and right margins of the painting, as in the works of artists using the Byzantine style. Whereas in Cimabue's version, Mary's left hand directs our attention to the Son of God, in Giotto's that same hand rests on the child's knee, no longer deflecting attention away from herself. Note as well that in the Cimabue, the clothing of the Christ child merges with that of His mother, who leans in His direction, in a gesture of unity. Giotto, in contrast, visualizes clear boundaries between Mary and Jesus. Mary even "recoils" slightly from her child, establishing a distance that individuates both figures.[17]

Mary provides a model for all women. They receive an identity by virtue of their roles as mothers, wives, and homemakers, and these roles are anchored in their nature as bearers of children. Although in Giotto's representation Mary gains in individuality, the throne that encloses her with her child defines her permissible roles. Fulfilling the duties associated with motherhood is the *only* way that she can be an individual. Indeed, restriction of women's opportunities to familial roles was a prominent subject of Renaissance debates on the "woman question" (*querelle des femmes*) addressed by many writers, women as well as men. In the name of their "dignity" and "honor," women were denied access to identities as magistrates, artists, merchants, theologians, writers, etc. But aspects of this sexual division of labor were vehemently contested. Christine de Pizan (1364–1430), for instance, reasoned that there is no inherent defect in women that can justify their exclusion from the public domain.[18]

In late twentieth-century industrial nations, Christine de Pizan's argument that women's lives should not be confined to the performance of familial duties is winning the day, as women are drawn into the paid work-force in increasing numbers. Despite this, many women find that neither their public nor their domestic roles provide a sufficient foundation for a secure personal identity. Consequently, women are not immune to the experiences of fragmentation and loss of identity that affect men, although the character of those experiences is shaped by gender-specific circumstances.

Because women have traditionally been more closely associated than men with "nature," with their existence as physically embodied beings, their loss of identity is often perceived as a breaking of this link. Ellen West, a patient of the existential psychoanalyst Ludwig Binswanger, used imagery of fertility and harvest to

Figure 2.5 Madonna Enthroned (Cimabue, 1280–90)

Figure 2.6 Madonna Enthroned (Giotto, 1310)

describe her sense of herself as separate from a body that no longer provides nurture or support:

> The earth bears grain,
> But I
> Am unfruitful,
> Am discarded shell,
> Cracked, unusable, Worthless husk.[19]

West's poem, written almost four decades ago, expresses issues that are commonplace today. Due to recent developments in reproductive technologies, women's capacity to give birth has become more amenable to the social/technological rationalization that dissociates the fetus from its female "carrier" or "environment." Genetic information encoded in DNA is what determines parenthood, a California Superior Court Judge has ruled.[20] A fetus developing from an egg that has been fertilized *in vitro* and then implanted in a woman legally does not belong to her. She provides only the "surrogate uterus" for the information-defined individual growing inside her. Legally and technologically, then, a woman's body can be divided and alienated from her. Such cultural appropriation of the body disallows any simple identification with nature that, in keeping with older stereotypes of femininity and maternity, might anchor women as human subjects.

CONTEMPORARY NARCISSISM AND THE PROBLEMATIC SELF

The discussion above suggests that "individuality" is a culturally relative notion. Yet classical psychoanalysis tends to regard the psyche as formed in isolation from larger social and historical circumstances, making it impossible to account for the ways in which personality and identity vary from one cultural context to another. Specific historical conditions need to be taken into account if we are to understand, for instance, insecurities about the self that are so prevalent a theme in contemporary experience. Christopher Lasch has argued that:

> Every age develops its own peculiar forms of pathology, which express in exaggerated form its underlying character structure. In Freud's time, hysterical and obsessional neurosis carried to extremes the personality traits associated with the capitalist order at an earlier stage in its development – acquisitiveness, fanatical devotion to work, and a fierce repression of sexuality ... The growing prominence of "character disorders" seems to signify an underlying change in the organization of personality, from what has been called inner-direction to narcissism.[21]

Michael Beldoch views the new pathologies as illnesses of the self:

> Today's patients by and large do not suffer from hysterical paralyses of the legs or handwashing compulsions; instead it is their very psychic selves that have gone numb or that they must scrub and rescrub in an exhausting and unending effort to come clean.[22]

Not only those labeled "mentally ill" are afflicted by the transition that Lasch and Beldoch describe. A diagnostic category like "narcissism" not only names a mental illness, but points as well to "normal" features of everyday life. Lasch traces the origins of contemporary self-absorption to an environment that nurtures narcissism. In the family, traditional authority structures and ways of raising children have been transformed. We inhabit a social world that devalues traditional roles and no longer fosters secure child–parent identifications. Nor do such institutions as schools, workplaces, and government agencies offer models of respectable authority or personally gratifying and reliable social ties. Narcissism, on this account, attempts to fill an internal void, to consolidate a sense of oneself in surroundings experienced as devoid of meaningful and identity-affirming relationships.

Those who diagnose contemporary culture in terms of narcissism and anxiety about the self offer ample evidence to support their analysis. But is our "me-first generation" historically unique? Lasch, Kohut, and others who argue that narcissism is today the central character structure in Western societies view this development as unprecedented: humans used to be tradition-respecting, moral, community-oriented beings; today they have become post-traditional, amoral, and self-oriented creatures. This simplistic formulation of "before" and "after" will not work. The problem becomes evident when we try to specify just when the historical transition in question is supposed to have taken place. Those who argue that we have entered an age of narcissism and crisis of the self do not agree with one another (and are sometimes not even consistent within their own work) about the birth date of this new pathology. Is it post-industrial society that inaugurates the "crisis of the self"? Or, was it following the First World War that the self became problematic? Should we locate the watershed, instead, a couple of decades earlier, understanding contemporary conditions of anomie and uncertainty as originating in turn-of-the-century modernization, including the growth of large-scale bureaucratic institutions at the expense of smaller, more personal forms of association characteristic of "small town America"? Or, was it the urbanization and industrialization of Europe, centuries earlier, that, by creating the impersonal capitalist metropolis and driving tradition aside, threatened the identity and security of the self?

Anxiety or obsession about the self is not an illness only of the contemporary age. Rather, human beings tend to turn inward and become self-preoccupied whenever the framework of social relations disintegrates to the point that people no longer experience themselves as associated in meaningful and empowering ways. If we look at the philosophical questioning of life's purpose during the decline of Classical Athens; at stoical and skeptical responses to the eclipse of Roman civilization several centuries later; at the Mannerist deconstruction of form and content associated with challenges to the hegemony of the Italian Renaissance city states in the sixteenth century; at the lamentations of Northern European humanists about the fragmentation of human identity during the Eighty Years War that spanned the sixteenth and seventeenth centuries, we can see that the contemporary "crisis of the self" has plenty of antecedents in the history of the West.

TWO NARRATIVE STRUCTURES: MASTERY AND IDENTITY

The "new narcissism" theorists might reply that although insecurities about the self are nothing historically novel, the particular contemporary forms that these insecurities take are unprecedented. Whether or not we agree with this view of the difference between past and present, it does draw attention to a significant distinction between two dynamics, interwoven but distinct. One concerns the establishment of personal identity, the other the achievement of mastery. The former is inward-oriented, emphasizes self-exploration, and is centered on the question "Who am I?" The capacity for such self-reference is essential to the acquisition of language and to becoming a person in one's own right: a child learns to distinguish "I" not only from "you," "she," and "he," but also from "me."

Mastery, on the other hand, focuses more attention on the skillful handling of one's surroundings. The issue is "What can I achieve?" The goal is control, the capacity to direct and shape objects and processes to meet one's needs. For children, mastery includes control of basic social and material aspects of their environment. The thrill of taking first steps on one's own two feet, tying one's own shoes, reading a storybook – these are experiences of empowerment whereby a child gains a sense of her or his effectiveness and ability to cope.

In the dreams I have collected during the past decade, I find it striking that uncertainties about personal identity are so often expressed. For instance, a young man, Edward, reported this dream:

Friends want to use my computer, so they type the letters "b2" to begin. But what happens is that the printer starts to print out garbage. Irritated I rush into the room and abort the process, explaining that the start-up command is "b," not "b2." The "b" stands for "boot the system." I tell my friends I could write a simple front-end program that would intercept the command "b2" before it gets executed. This way the trouble would get headed off before it had a chance to make everything go haywire.

Associations: Yesterday I visited my brother. His wife is expecting. I found myself envying their good fortune. They are initiating a new life, while the only thing I can set into motion is a computer. "b2" means "I want a baby too." But in the dream I abort the process – a thin disguise of my resentment? You could even say that the garbage from the printer is a miscarriage.

We had a family reunion recently. I am the second born, "b2." Had there been no "b2," there would have been no me.

As far back as I can remember, I don't know who I am in the family. When Mitchell and Lara [dreamer's brother and sister-in-law] have their child, they'll have that much less time for me. One more reason to abort the program!

Although mastery is at issue in this dream, identity is its underlying theme. Edward had for many years been struggling to "locate himself" within his family as well as in the larger social world of his peers.

While identity and mastery are analytically distinct concepts, they are always dialectically linked. Psychoanalytic theory sometimes assumes that a child handles only one of these issues at a time: first the child establishes its own identity and sense of self (pre-Oedipal stage) and only thereafter goes on to develop skills for mastering internal and external objects and events (Oedipal stage). This chronological division tends to overlook that both self-identity and mastery are simultaneously at issue for children, and remain so for human beings throughout their lives.

"Universal" human aims assume culturally variable forms, however. Certainly, mastery is at issue for human beings in every society, since children and adults alike inevitably experience the world as resistant, in one way or another, to their will.[23] But the socially sanctioned ways of overcoming this resistance are enormously diverse. Personal identity, too, is not a fixed ideal, but is historically constructed, in ways that are never entirely unproblematic in our culture or in any other. What characterizes the contemporary moment in the development of industrial societies is an explicit and widespread acknowledgement that the "self" is imperiled. As if to shore up the self, it is submitted to the countless forms of scrutiny, management, and healing that preoccupy so many of us.

This does not mean that mastery – the focus of traditional psychoanalytic theory and practice since Freud's invention of psychoanalysis – has vanished as a human aim in the contemporary "culture of narcissism." On the contrary, there is an ongoing relationship between self issues and mastery issues, although questions about the self often predominate. A programmer, Robert, dreamt that:

> *Two boys are playing in the backyard, near a pile of logs. One wants to vie with the other to see who can stand at the top of the pile. The other thinks it's risky to stand on the pile at all; for all you know, it could tumble down and you would fall, you might get covered with wood.*

In his associations to this dream, Robert saw the two boys as parts of himself. He is, on the one hand, adventurous, virile, ready to compete. But he also feels afraid of a disastrous accident in which, unnoticed by anyone, he could perish. Both of these aspects enter into Robert's work situation: he is professionally ambitious and fairly confident of his own abilities; yet he feels isolated and regarded by others "as if I didn't exist." He speaks ironically about seeming invisible: "The program talks to the user; its designer is neither seen nor heard."

These feelings have analogs in childhood experience. In Robert's dream, the first boy has successfully separated and individuated himself (from the mother, a psychoanalytic interpreter might say) and feels secure about his own identity; he is prepared to take on a traditionally male, competitive role in the world. For the second boy, identity/merger remains at stake; to fall to the ground and be "covered with wood" would be to lose one's identity as a distinct individual, to become invisible and die.

Robert is a "high achiever"; he is the boy clambering to the top of the wood pile. But he identifies also with the fearful boy in the dream, occupied by his own self-preservation. He describes himself as subject to a "mild compulsion": immediately upon arriving at work in the morning or returning to his office after lunch or any other "outside" activity, he feels compelled immediately to "log in" (another allusion to wood?) to the computer to see if anyone has sent him electronic mail. On weekends and holidays, too, he is apt to telephone the computer from home several times a day to "check in" and see if there are any messages waiting for him. This is another of his dreams:

> *I was seeing my mind as a vast empty space, subdivided by an interface or membrane. The dividing surface was absolutely still, still as ice and hard, like the surface of a pond in the dead of winter. I felt trapped. I had to break through, or suffocate and die.*

Both the compulsion and the dream admit of sexual interpretation: logging into the computer, like breaking through the "interface or membrane" in the dream, might represent penetration. But this is not all that the compulsion or the dream are about. The dreamer will "suffocate and die" if he does *not* break through to the other side. This suggests a logic of escape, of an effort made from within an enclosed space to get out. It is noteworthy that the compulsion to log in to the computer takes a similar form: Robert enters the computer, usually only to leave again a few seconds later. Exiting, escape, re-establishing his distance, proved to be a theme that recurred in many areas of his life.

The computer serves Robert as a convenient vehicle for expressing a theme of individuation/identity that is by no means exclusively modern. In every culture, forms of personal identity are worked out in mythological and ritual practices as well as in the realms of material production and reproduction. Robert's life experience reflects his unique surroundings, including the world of information technology to which he belongs professionally. But that experience connects to others remote in time and setting from his own. In certain North American Indian tribes, it is believed that a dream must be re-enacted at once upon awakening. For example, a Jesuit author living among the Iroquois reports that: "Whatever it may be that they believe they have done in a dream they feel absolutely obliged to carry out immediately."[24] This compulsion affects not only the dreamer but also those who learn about it. The Iroquois tell this story:

> One night not long ago a man from the village of Oiogoen while sleeping saw ten men diving into the frozen river, going in one hole in the ice and coming out by another. When he awoke he immediately prepared a great feast and sent invitations to ten of his friends. They all came happily and rejoicing. When they arrived he told them about his dream, without dismaying them apparently, since all ten immediately offered to carry it out. They went to the river, broke through the ice in two places about fifteen feet apart. The divers stripped, and the first man led the way; leaping into the first hole, he very fortunately came up through the second; the second did the same and so did the others until the tenth man, who paid for all of them since he was not able to pull himself out and perished miserably beneath the ice.[25]

Nine men go beneath the ice and re-emerge. The tenth perishes below it. Represented symbolically is de-individuation, the return to (the potentially fatal) initial condition of oneness with the earth/mother, followed by reaffirmation through a ritual repetition of the original separation/individuation. When Robert, whose work environment is about as far removed from the world of the Iroquois as can be imagined, logs into the computer, the unconscious determinations of his actions are not entirely unlike theirs. It is interesting that an ice barrier seems to play the same role in his dream as in that of the Iroquois. They mythologize and enact their dreams collectively, however, whereas Robert experiences his in isolation he has only his own mind to keep him company in his dream, in keeping with his loneliness at work. (The therapeutic session serves, as with the Iroquois, to bring the dream experience into the social realm. A therapist too might be a diver into the unconscious.)

The process of self-formation, in which human beings overcome, as best they can, their initial helplessness and total dependence upon adult caretakers, is never fully consolidated for any of us, in this society or any other. Unconsciously, human beings never forget the traumatic recognition of otherness, and never reconcile their contradictory wishes for both separation and union. Yet for Freud, mastery, rather than individuation or identity is the characteristic idiom of the unconscious; his interpretations concentrate on conflicts that presuppose already existing individuals whose powers and achievements are at issue. The prototypical conflict is Oedipal: within the nuclear family, a male child wants free access to the mother. The father stands in the way. As a consequence, the child passes through a sequence of developmental stages, culminating in the castration complex and its resolution.

The narrative structure here is not Freud's invention, as his acknowledgement of antecedents in Greek mythology makes clear; it recapitulates that of countless legends, parables, and rituals whose subject is human striving and achievement. The exploits of a Prometheus or Hercules, the "pioneering spirit" that conquered the Wild West, Horatio Alger's proverbial rise from rags to riches – these are narratives of the male adventurer and hero aiming to establish mastery through the exercise of his powers and enforcement of his will. This is the dynamic whose unconscious dimensions Freud mapped. Yet he had certain reservations about this will-to-power, and understood in depth not only its psychological origins but also its illusions. The neo-Freudian analysts, however, especially the founders of ego psychology, tended to identify "normal" psychological development with an achievable subordination of experience to reason's mastery. The "healthy individual" has the "ego strength" to organize and master his or her surroundings, including not only external material nature but also others and oneself.

SOCIETY WITHOUT THE FATHER

In the orthodox psychoanalytic model, mastery is the aim that drives human development. For boys, becoming a man entails battling other males in a competition for power over nature, over women, over one another. To be a woman, in turn, is to compete with other women, and to envy the power of men. Indeed, the professions that many of us have taken up give expression to this narrative structure. Science and technology, in particular, represent a quest for control and mastery, the stereotypic goals of men, though shared by women also.

Yet, beneath this narrative, there is another story whose meaning eludes the classical psychoanalytic categories. This story is not that of Oedipus or Electra, of the son's or daughter's competition against one parent to win the other. It is exemplified, rather, in the story of Isis searching the world for the body fragments of her brother Osiris and then piecing them together so that he might be resurrected. Its theme is wholeness and integrity, not mastery. Where this narrative does allude to paternal authority, the reference has more to do with connection and identity than with rivalry, with having a male figure in one's life rather than doing away with him.

At a time when Robert was recalling his relationship with his father, he reported these dreams and associations:

> 1. *I am with some friends ... sporting them around town, seems I have borrowed my father's Cadillac from years ago. It used to be so shiny and new, but not any more. I see that this huge white dinosaur is unlikely to impress. I doubt my friends are taken with it, or with me!*

Associations: Cadillacs had these small, non-functional fins in the later years. [The dreamer's father drove a Cadillac.] These were dangerous, people would get impaled by them. I remember Cadillac was sued and had to tone them down even further. They weren't functional, they didn't provide any guidance or stabilize anything.

> 2. *I was building a circuit with old-fashioned vacuum tubes, the kind that bulge in the middle and then narrow out on top. They were all silvery and opaque inside, as if burnt out. I don't know why I wasn't using transistors.*

Associations: Vacuum tubes sit there on a circuit board like clumsy, old-fashioned stone monuments. Transistors, running on a tiny fraction of the same electricity, form an invisible but much more efficient network of intelligence.

The major themes and preoccupations in these dreams are different in kind from the meanings in dreams that Freud observed and commented on, and not only because of their references to contemporary technological objects. What distinguishes them is that their subject is not a punitive father – an intimidating and dangerous rival in a Freudian scenario – but rather a weak or missing one. The phallic references in these dreams ("small, non-functional fins," "old-fashioned vacuum tubes") no longer carry the aura of power or authority that is given to them in traditionally psychoanalytic dream interpretations.

In the first dream, the Cadillac, which Robert calls a "huge white dinosaur ... unlikely to impress," indicates a father who does not play the formative role in a child's life that Freud projected. In Robert's eyes, his father falls far short of the competent and authoritative figure whose word is undisputable law, and whose superego the child internalizes by way of becoming a man himself. In the second dream, the vacuum tubes are disempowered phallic signifiers, resembling "clumsy, old-fashioned stone monuments." They are "opaque inside, as if burnt out" – again a likely allusion to an ineffective father, "opaque" to his son, perhaps even to himself.

An orthodox Freudian may object that these dreams do indeed attest to the power of the father, through their very minimizing and ridiculing of his role: the dreamer uses this dream material to cut his father down to size. If we remain within this orthodox framework of interpretation, then indeed, whatever Robert dreams or says about his dreams, we can always say that, unconsciously, he wants to do away with dad. But adhering faithfully to traditional psychoanalytic doctrine in this way requires that we deny what clearly is in these dreams: Robert would have liked a *more* powerful father; what he suffered from is not a threatening, domineering father, but, as suggested by the words of the first dream, a father who "didn't provide any guidance or stabilize anything."

The negative consequences in men's lives of weak or absent fathers is a theme that the poet Robert Bly and other writers have popularized. Two decades before Bly, Alexander Mitscherlich wrote about what he called a "fatherless society," in which paternal authority is widely called into question.[26] These authors tend to identify authority as a male function, thereby neglecting the role of women in providing models of discipline and mastery as well as nurturance for children and adults.[27] Yet there is something to their observation that fatherhood, with its traditional associations of omnipotence and indisputable authority, has been par-tially eclipsed in Western societies where educational, corporate, and government agencies assume law-giving roles that fathers previously occupied. (In Robert's dream, the Cadillac, instead of representing power and authority, looks dated and falls under the jurisdiction of an externally imposed legal system that clips its fins.)

Children need men and women to look up to as models of strength, generosity, and intelligence, with whom they can develop relationships of intimacy and closeness. Individual identity develops on the basis of such relationships, first with parents or other caretakers, and later with teachers, religious figures, and other authoritative persons with whom the child, and later the adult, identifies. This process of identification and internalization is a source not only of moral sensibility, but also of one's very sense of oneself as a subject.

Of course, structures of authority have today not simply disappeared. But the forms they assume, such as the rules and procedures that govern economic, government, and state institutions, tend to be impersonal, bureaucratic, and without ethical import. The voice of moral conscience, which Freud viewed as exercising a tyrannical control over the psyche, tends to be discounted or dismissed altogether in post-industrial settings, for reasons that we will explore later. Paternal authority, embodied in mass media representations such as Archie Bunker and Homer Simpson, is routinely ridiculed. Even the righteously masculine and admired fantasy figures of ultra-conservatives – Oliver North and Rambo – resemble dutiful sons more than authoritative fathers.[28]

The problematic status of paternal authority in contemporary society is echoed in the dreams above; one of their most striking features is a symbolic link between the declining role of traditional father figures and the transition from industrial to post-industrial technological structures. This link partly can be understood as follows: a traditional father is an autonomous individual who creates and sets down the law. The older technologies, developed in the context of Western industrializing societies, supported this imagery of individualism and authority. Information technology, on the other hand, occupies a new cultural terrain, in which external and internal authority seem to be detached from the values and interests of particular persons.

To be sure, "intelligent machines" continue to serve the traditional ends of mastery and control. Yet the significance of this technology reaches beyond its merely instrumental value. While remaining wary of facile "correlations" between technological developments and the formation of social character, and of the tendency to exaggerate the differences between old and new technological forms, we may nevertheless note affinities that connect the Information Age with both the "fatherless society" that Bly and Mitscherlich talk about and with the "Age of Narcissism," characterized by insecurities about self-identity. Contemporary pre-occupations with the authority and well-being of the self are bound up with a logic of institutional rationalization and deployment of new technologies that, paradox-ically, both mirrors and effaces the human subject.

Three dreams

There are many respects in which our information-based social order differs from the industrial order it is replacing. Patterns of economic production and consumption; technological and scientific "revolutions"; birth, marriage, and divorce rates all testify to what has changed, and what remains more or less the same. If our aim is to understand how our contemporary world is *experienced*, however, then we need to know how such objectively ascertainable conditions are perceived and interpreted. People drive cars and operate computers – what is the *subjective* import of such activities for their apprehension of themselves and their surroundings? Evidence of this import includes, of course, what people say and write about their everyday conscious involvements with information technologies. In addition to these sources there is another that guided Freud's explorations of the unconscious: the study of dreams.

Dreams are as diverse as any other form of human expression. A single image in a dream may give expression to several levels of meaning, to multiple and contradictory ideas and wishes. Throughout this book, I interpret dreams lifted, and to some extent isolated, from the lives of those who dream them. This is hazardous. A dream is a clue or fragment of a kind that is intelligible only in the context of the life history in which it plays a part. Understanding a dream, in the ideal case, calls for entry into a dialogue with the dreamer, in the context of a free and open-ended exploration. Some of the dreams I shall discuss – those of Descartes, for example, dreamt more than three centuries ago – fall far short of satisfying this condition.[1] Yet they are capable of helping us to understand the lives and the times of those who report them, if taken in conjunction with other kinds of knowledge available about the dreamer.

FREUD'S DREAMS AND OUR OWN

A dream, like any other experience, is a form of social expression, at the same time that it characterizes the uniquely personal history of the dreamer. The "language" of dreams draws on figures of speech and images articulating unconscious meanings not only of individuals, but also of cultures. Contemporary dreams are often different in kind from the dreams of, say, the patients whom Freud analyzed in turn-of-the-century Vienna. Indeed the unconscious is not as timeless as Freud and Jung believed. No less than our conscious beliefs and attitudes, it has a social history; interpretation of that history may reveal aspects of our lives, including the changing nature of our technological involvements, that we might otherwise overlook. The interweaving of personal and cultural circumstances will be illustrated in the following pages by comparing the dreams of three dreamers, whose lives span the period between the early seventeenth and late twentieth centuries.

Freud delayed publication of his work, *The Interpretation of Dreams*, until 1900, the first year of the new century, because he wanted to distinguish his "scientific" discoveries from the speculations about dreams of past centuries. Indeed, Freud's work in this area was pathbreaking, although the world of dreams that was contemporary for him is no longer contemporary for us. As previously noted, the wishes that inform the dreams that Freud analyzes are typically aimed at mastery or external achievement: sexual conquest, medical cure, career advancement. In contemporary dreams, on the other hand, reflecting a cultural setting significantly different from Freud's Vienna, identity rather than mastery is likely to be at issue.

Literary fiction also exemplifies this historical transition.[2] Mastery is central to the narrative form of the traditional novel, with its clearly delineated characters and plot trajectory. An omniscient narrator, who typically does not himself appear in the story, observes the characters and follows their paths through the literary space he or she creates. Faced with certain opportunities and obstacles, these characters try to make their way toward their aims, to master the situation that confronts them: a detective seeks to apprehend a criminal, a lover to win the beloved, a hero to defeat the enemy. In narrative of this kind, the identities of the protagonists are taken for granted. The question is principally whether, and by what means, they will succeed, not who they are or are becoming. A hero may be a changed person by the time the drama concludes, but this development is relatively incidental and subordinate to the unfolding of the plot. The model here is that of mechanical motion. Someone or something with given qualities $Q_1, Q_2, Q_3 \ldots Q_n$ moves from point A to point B. While these qualities may change somewhat over the time-span that a work of fiction covers (a character marries, divorces, becomes wealthy or dies impoverished, etc.), it is a narrative of actions, specifying relationships among the actors whose pre-established identities are given, that is the focus of attention. Freud describes this writing style in "Creative Writers and Day-Dreaming" when he talks about fiction in which "we can immediately recognize His Majesty the Ego, the hero alike of every day-dream and of every story."[3]

An alternative to narrative of this kind might be called "identity narrative," parallel to the distinction between "mastery" and "identity" drawn in the preceding chapter. Here, achievement of an external goal is no longer of primary importance. More essential than what a fictional character *does* is who she or he *is*. "Character" no longer signifies a fixed unity of traits or roles but rather the internal structure, coherent or fragmented, stable or in flux, that the fictional subject is or becomes. Relationships and pathway remain important, but are subordinate to identity, as in novels whose central subject is the formation/disintegration of the self.

In Freud's *Interpretation of Dreams*, the dreams he examines typically assume the form of a mastery narrative. Dreams that express issues that do not fit easily within this framework tend to pass unnoticed. For example, one of Freud's patients, a young chemist, dreamt:

> He was supposed to be making phenyl-magnesium-bromide. He saw the apparatus with particular distinctness, but had substituted himself for the magnesium. He now found himself in a singularly unstable state. He kept on saying to himself: "This is all right, things are working, my feet are beginning to dissolve already, my knees are getting soft" ... Then he put out his hands and felt his feet. Meanwhile (how he could not tell) he pulled his legs out of the vessel and said to himself once more: "This can't be right. Yes it is, though" ... He was positively frightened of the solution [Auflösung, which has the same double meaning as the English equivalent] of the dream.[4]

Freud reads the dream in terms of masturbation, sexual conquest, and the patient's perception of the effectiveness of his psychoanalysis. Dissolution symbolizes, Freud suggests, the elimination of certain barriers that get in the patient's way. That the patient's identity and fear of his own decomposition might be at issue is not considered in this interpretation (perhaps because Freud identifies scientific inquiry so closely with goal-directed adventure).

For classical psychoanalysis, the traditional male paradigm of mastery is sexual intercourse. The objects that turn up in dreams – household items, bodily parts, and the like – inevitably play a role in this drama: things are hard or soft, like the human genitalia; they pierce and penetrate, or they get pierced and penetrated. When teeth appear in a dream, for example, their meaning is typically sexual; functioning as phallic symbols, Freud observes that their falling out of the mouth represents castration.[5] Teeth may also symbolize, according to canons of orthodox psychoanalytic interpretation, instruments of a woman's sexual aggressiveness (*vagina dentata*). But consider this contemporary dream:

> I've written a [computer] program that revolves nicely about itself. When you get to the end, you stand at the beginning and the program is ready to run again. "This program has teeth," I say to myself, thinking of the way in which the molars on both sides of the mouth, like tall guardians, contain a semi-circle of smaller, simpler teeth – like the two "t"s in the word tooth itself, which surround the "o"s. Tooth is symmetrical about itself, as are the individual letters t and o about themselves. But then I recall the h dangling at the end of tooth, spoiling the palindrome at both the letter and word levels. I'm disturbed and wake up.

Associations: As a child I felt uncontained. My parents were too busy to look after me. I was permitted to do almost anything. Remember the song "Don't fence me in"? I never could relate to that because I knew no fences. And no protection either. My parents weren't exactly "tall guardians." I grew up not belonging much to anyone. Like the *h* at the end of *tooth*, I dangle, the odd man out.

This dream's references to teeth bring up issues of aloneness, absence of boundaries, and neglect by parents that would be overlooked if only its Oedipal symbolism were considered. We can find classical Freudian motifs in this dream, and in all of the others cited in this book. But new meanings emerge as well, linking the lives of dreamers to historically specific cultural conditions.

The circumstances of this dreamer's early family life would have been less likely to obtain in the Victorian families analyzed by Freud, where individuals were more intensely involved with each other. It is not that issues of isolation, belonging, and containment were entirely foreign to Freud's dream interpretations, but they were nearly eclipsed by the attention given to Oedipal, mastery-oriented conflict. Freud was certainly resourceful in discovering meaning in his own and other people's dreams. He found affinities and metaphor at every level, drawing freely upon the domains of everyday life, literature, drama, history, and science so that the unconscious might speak. Yet there are unacknowledged relationships, paths that Freud did not explore. The dreams that he dealt with have a certain "coloration," if you will, determined by the psyche of the dreamer, but also by that of the dream interpreter and by the cultural setting that encompasses both.

"Coloration," though, is too mild a word, here. Dreams give expression to different *worlds* of experience, each with its own logic and its own understanding of how human reality is put together. I consider here three of these "worlds": that of Descartes, of Freud, and of the contemporary dreamer, Edward, mentioned in the preceding chapter. Spread across three and a half centuries, their dreams say something both about their personal lives and about the times they live through. I do not intend these examples to be taken as proof that the unconscious is historically and culturally conditioned. Each dream represents only one person's experience, filtered in the very process of its verbal formulation by the one who reports it, and subject to multiple interpretations. A dream can be viewed in countless ways, like a forest, city, or work of art. The discussion of dreams that follows aims only to illustrate, not to demonstrate, what I take to be an historical shift in emphasis from mastery to identity issues.

Although the three dreamers whose dreams I discuss are men whose capacities, personal circumstances, and accomplishments differ widely, comparing their lives will help us trace the formation and then the unraveling of a certain ideological account of human identity. Basic to this account are notions of individuation, autonomy, and mastery that during the past several centuries have been elaborated by philosophers, religious and political leaders, and artists, almost all of whom were male. Today these notions, previously hegemonic, are coming undone. The consequences of this ideological disintegration may of course be experienced differently by women – we shall look more closely at such differences in Part II of this book.

DESCARTES' NIGHTMARE AND REDEMPTION

On November 10, 1619, in a small room he had rented for the night, Descartes had three dreams. His manuscript describing them has been lost, but was copied by Baillet, his biographer, whose transcription is as follows:

1. *Phantoms appeared before him and so terrified him that as he walked through the streets, he was forced to tilt over to his left side in order to reach the place he wanted ... Ashamed of walking in that way, he tried to straighten himself but was suddenly caught up in a kind of whirlwind which made him revolve three or four times on his left foot. What frightened him most, however, was that the difficulty he had in dragging himself along gave him the impression he was falling at every step. Finally he noticed a college with an open gate which he entered, hoping to find a refuge. He tried to reach the church of the school in order to pray, but perceiving he had passed a man whom he knew without greeting him, he tried to retrace his steps to make amends and was thrown violently against the church by the wind ...*

2. *He was visited by a second dream, which consisted of his hearing a piercing noise, like a clap of thunder. He was so frightened that he awoke instantly and, having opened his eyes, saw a great number of sparks all around his room ... wishing to turn to reasons drawn from philosophy, he drew conclusions that satisfied him ... In this way he dissipated his fear and a few moments later fell asleep again.*

3. *He noticed a book on his table ... he was delighted to find that it was a dictionary he thought might prove useful. At the same moment he discovered another book ... a collection of poems entitled* Corpus Poetarum. *Prompted by curiosity, he opened the volume and chanced upon the line* Quod vitae sectabor iter? *[What path shall I take in life?] ... He judged that the dictionary represented all of the sciences gathered together, and that the* Corpus Poetarum *signified the union of philosophy with wisdom.*[6]

Many have tried to interpret these dreams. One obvious issue is that of mastery of one's circumstances and of oneself. Descartes writes of his "extreme desire ... to walk with safety in this life"[7] a safety that is endangered in these dreams. In the first, he finds himself walking through the streets with difficulty and tries "to straighten himself," but a wind revolves him and later throws him against a church. He has difficulty "dragging himself along" and feels himself "falling at every step" his own body is beyond his control. A moment later, the dream, if interpreted psychoanalytically, turns classically Oedipal: Descartes tries to "reach the church [the mother] ... but perceiving he had passed a man [the father] whom he knew without greeting him, he tried to retrace his steps to make amends and was thrown violently against the church by the wind [the dreamer's own, disavowed impulses, perhaps]."

The second dream consists only of a "piercing noise," which frightens and awakens Descartes. In the absence of what Descartes regarded as the "natural light" of the mind – pure, coherent, steady, and a guarantor of the truth – he experiences "fiery sparks" whose meaning he cannot ascertain. Recourse to philosophy brings an end to this perceptual disintegration and, calmed, he falls back to sleep.

In the third dream, mastery is intellectualized; Descartes finds a dictionary that "might prove useful" and a book of poetry representing "the union of philosophy with wisdom." In that book, he is taken with one passage in particular which begins with the thought: What path shall I take in life? And on the day following the dream, Descartes says that he prayed to God "to guide him in the search for truth."[8]

Within this dream sequence, Descartes seems the epitome of the striving individual, pitted against forces that would impede his progress, but insistent on finding his way and confident of his capacity to dominate his circumstances and determine his own destiny. The world is there to be grasped by human reason and shaped to meet human needs. Descartes proclaims that

> a practical philosophy can be found by which, knowing the power and the effects of fire, water, air, the stars, the heavens and all the other bodies which surround us, as distinctly as we know the various trades of our craftsmen, we might put them in the same way to all the uses for which they are appropriate, and thereby make ourselves, as it were, masters and possessors of nature.[9]

Mastery, for Descartes, involves the structuring of one's experience as well as control of the environment. "The whole method consists in the ordering and arranging of the objects on which we must concentrate our mind's eye if we are to discover some truth," Descartes asserts, referring not so much to the world outside himself as to the coherent and secure formation of self-certainty, which is above all mental and conceptually independent of one's surroundings.[10]

While Descartes' arguments address issues central to Western philosophical tradition since Greek antiquity, his particular approach to those issues may reflect his personal circumstances. His lifelong psychological project involved the construction of a fortress of reason and order that would distance and shelter him from painful experiences of unhappiness and powerlessness. Descartes' unhappiness had been of two kinds. A delicate child – he said he had inherited from his mother his cough and pale complexion – he had been vulnerable to physical suffering. Second, his mother died when he was only 14 months old, from a lung disease caused by "certain sadnesses."[11] This loss may have contributed to his lifelong skepticism about the dependability of the environment. Reason, Descartes' *mathesis universalis* (universal mathematics), which he held would enable humanity to understand and to control all of nature, represents a structure more reliable than any other that life, with its innumerable and unavoidable uncertainties, could ever offer.

Descartes describes himself as wanting "to establish something firm and constant in the sciences"; it is only within the realm of the mind, insulated from an everyday contingent existence, that these qualities may be secured. He draws a sharp boundary between thinking being (*res cogitans*: the pure, unattached, and therefore totally free "I" of individual subjectivity), on the one hand, and material being (*res extensa*: external and unpredictable), on the other, and he affirms his identity with the former, to the point that he disassociates even his own body from himself:

> I shall consider myself as not having hands or eyes, or flesh, or blood or senses, but as falsely believing that I have all these things ... it is certain that I am really distinct from my body and can exist without it.[12]

Descartes' "I" affords protection and control, but also establishes identity. Exercise of the intellect, in his second and third dreams, is an antidote to the "whirlwind" that tosses him about in the first, preventing him from drawing near to the man he had passed and with whom he was now trying to "make amends." Oedipal rivalry is bound up with the desire of the male child to identify with a paternal authority promising freedom and certainty. Following the death of his mother, Descartes was raised by other women: a grandmother, elder sister, and nurse. Yet, alluding to himself, he remarks that "the first subject of some people's unhappiness at the outset of their life was that they did not receive enough nourishment." Possibly the substitutions for the mother he lost were unsatisfactory (Descartes never married). This may have contributed to his radical repudiation of a disappointing material reality in favor of total identification with the "I, who am nothing but a thinking thing" – a pure ego to which, he believed, feelings and relationship to anything outside itself are essentially foreign. "I have been nourished on letters from my infancy," Descartes remarked; it is above all the life of the mind that sustained his existence.[13]

FREUD'S IRMA DREAM

In late July 1895, Freud had a dream whose interpretation provided him with a theoretical basis for understanding the dynamics of the unconscious. The "dream of Irma's injection" is the first that Freud reports in *The Interpretation of Dreams*:

> *A large hall – numerous guests, whom we were receiving. Among them was Irma [one of Freud's patients and a friend of the family]. I at once took her on one side, as though to answer her letter and to reproach her for not having accepted my "solution" yet. I said to her: "If you still get pains, it's really only your fault." She replied: "If you only knew what pains I've got now in my throat and stomach and abdomen – it's choking me" – I was alarmed and looked at her. She looked pale and puffy. I thought to myself that after all I must be missing some organic trouble. I took her to the window and looked down her throat, and she showed signs of recalcitrance, like women with artificial dentures. I thought to myself that there was really no need for her to do that. She then opened her mouth properly and on the right I found a big white patch; at another place I saw extensive whitish gray scabs upon some remarkably curly structures which were evidently modeled on the turbinal bones of the nose. I at once called in Dr M., [who] looked quite different from usual; he was very pale, he walked with a limp and his chin was clean-shaven ... My friend Otto was now standing beside her*

as well, and my friend Leopold was percussing her through her bodice and saying: "She has a dull area down on the left." (I noticed this, just as he did, in spite of her dress.) ... Not long before, when she was feeling unwell, my friend Otto had given her an injection of a preparation of propyl, propyls ... propionic acid ... trimethylamin (and I saw before me the formula for this printed in heavy type) ... Injections of that sort ought not to be made so thoughtlessly ... And probably the syringe had not been clean.[14]

Several psychoanalytic interpreters have seen elaborate sexual allusions in this dream.[15] Surprisingly, Freud's own interpretation does not emphasize the dream's sexual connotations, but concentrates instead upon issues of professional status and competition. On the day before the dream, he writes, he had been visited by a colleague who had annoyed him by remarking that a woman in treatment with Freud had apparently remained uncured. The underlying subject of the dream, Freud believes, is his own effectiveness and integrity as a healer. The dream seeks to establish his "professional conscientiousness," Freud suggests, by attributing responsibility for Irma's sufferings to others. First of all, Irma is to blame for her own condition because she has not accepted his "solution" (his evaluation of her illness). Furthermore, "If Irma's pains had an organic basis, once again I could not be held responsible for curing them; my treatment only set out to get rid of *hysterical* pains." Finally, if there has been medical malpractice, it has not been that of Freud: "The conclusion of the dream ... was that I was not responsible for the persistence of Irma's pains, but that Otto was."[16]

There is a strong resemblance between "Irma" in the dream and one of Freud's patients in waking life, Emma Eckstein. She suffered not only from hysterical anxiety but also from pains and nosebleeds. Fearing that her symptoms might be organically based, Freud asked his close friend and colleague, Wilhelm Fliess to examine her. Fliess promptly decided to operate on the woman, with disastrous results. Emma did not recover as planned. It turned out that the operation had been bungled – Fliess inadvertently left a length of gauze in her nose, which caused severe hemorrhaging and Emma nearly died. Freud was stricken with guilt, because he had recommended Fliess to Emma and because he had attributed her post-operative problems to psychogenic origins. But shortly thereafter, as if to exonerate his friend, he returned to his psychosomatic diagnosis: Emma Eckstein's symptoms were "wish-bleedings."[17]

If "Irma" in the dream is indeed Emma Eckstein, then the dream may express Freud's wish to exculpate both Fliess and himself of responsibility for her condition. This reluctance to view himself as responsible for Emma's suffering takes on a special significance in the context of Freud's own ambitions, which were, in his own eyes at least, called into question by her failure to respond well to his and Fliess' treatment. Freud's expectations for himself were high: to make a fundamental contribution to scientific knowledge, to win recognition from others in his profession, and to establish a successful career. He remarks that when he was a child the following anecdote was often repeated about his birth: "An old peasant woman had prophesied to my mother, happy over her first-born, that she had given the world a great man." Freud downplays the importance of this episode but mentions another that made a greater impression: when he was 11 or 12 years old, a man had declared that "I should probably grow up to be a Cabinet Minister."[18] Freud's father seems to have been more ambivalent. He apparently shared these great expectations for his eldest son; yet Freud remembers that on one occasion when he misbehaved, his father remarked:

> "The boy will come to nothing." This must have been a frightful blow to my ambition, but references to this scene are still constantly recurring in my dreams and are always linked with an enumeration of my achievements and accomplishments, as though I wanted to say: "You see, I *have* come to something."[19]

In *The Interpretation of Dreams*, hardly any male figure appears in Freud's dreams who is not a rival. In the dream of Irma, Freud calls upon three of his colleagues to assist in her diagnosis, but he then goes on to pit them against one another and by the end of the dream he has demolished the stature of two of them, while elevating his own. One of these colleagues, Otto, who had called into question Freud's cure of Irma, is accused in the dream of "thoughtlessness in handling chemical substances" and of being "too hasty in his medical treatment." As for Dr M., the senior colleague whom Freud consults in the dream, he is an "ignoramus" whose "far-fetched explanations" are worthy of ridicule.[20] Dr M. is Freud's pseudonym in the dream for Joseph Breuer, who had been a father figure to Freud. A renowned physician, mentor, and research collaborator with Freud, wealthy and respected in the community, Breuer gave to Freud not only intellectual encouragement but also financial support. At the time of Freud's Irma dream, though, his relationship with Breuer had reached breaking-point, the ostensible reason being that the older man balked at Freud's hypothesis about the sexual origins of psychopathology.

There is a third figure in the dream with whom Freud is dissatisfied: Irma herself. Freud says he would have liked to exchange for Irma one of her friends, who also suffered from hysterical symptoms but who would have been more amenable to treatment: " ... either I felt more sympathetic towards her friend or had a higher opinion of her intelligence ... Her friend would have been wiser, that is to say she would have yielded sooner. She would have *opened her mouth properly*, and have told me more than Irma."[21]

Substitutivity defines the structure of the Oedipal triangle – the child seeks to substitute him/herself for a parent – and is the organizing principle for handling nearly everyone who appears in Freud's dream:

> Indeed I seemed to be appealing from him (Dr M.) to someone else with greater knowledge (to my friend [Wilhelm Fliess] who had told me of trimethylamin) just as I had turned from Irma to her friend and from Otto to Leopold. "Take these people away! Give me three others of my choice instead! Then I shall be free of these undeserved reproaches!"[22]

These dream relationships can be represented as follows:

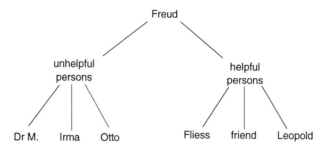

The dreamer's wish is to replace the three members of the unhelpful group with their counterparts in the helpful group. Ultimately, only one individual remains unique and irreplaceable – the dreamer, Freud himself.

The hierarchical structure above resembles that of the chemical formula for trimethylamin, in which the dream culminates and whose visual character Freud emphasizes, "I saw the chemical formula of this substance in my dream ... printed in heavy type."[23] Diagrammed, the methyl groups of the compound would have appeared like this:[24]

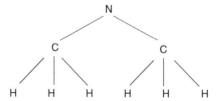

With people as with atomic elements, one may substitute items within the same category – in chemistry, one 'H' (hydrogen atom) for another, for instance. On the evening before the dream, Freud says that the odor emitted by a liqueur given to him by Otto had "stirred up in my mind a recollection of the whole series propyl, methyl, and so on."[25] In the dream itself, he elaborates the chemical chains: "propyl, propyls ... propionic acid ... trimethylamin." Subject to a chemist's control, constituents chain together to form stable compounds much as the symbols in a dream join to create coherent meaning. Freud is this chemist, the 'N' in the formula upon whom the subordinate chains depend. The compound visualized at the end of the dream, together with the dreamer's concluding assessment, "Injections of that sort ought not to be made so thoughtlessly," represent a reinstatement of Freud as knowledgeable and fully in charge once again.

EDWARD'S DREAM OF THE PROGRAMMED KEYBOARD

At the time of our meetings, Edward had recently graduated from college and was working in a corporate environment as a computer programmer. He reported this dream:

1. *I am attending an economics lecture at a conference in a European capital. The amphitheater slopes down steeply from the back of the room to the front, as if the whole thing could collapse. Down below, the prominent lecturer stands and tells us emphatically that "Europe must learn to stand on her own two feet."*

2. *Everything suddenly changes! Image of a head – it might be of a cat, or human – and behind it is suspended a computer keyboard. The keys are being depressed, you can see them going up and down like the keys on a player piano, but no one is there operating them. Attached to the head is a network of wires and tiny lights as if it were a Christmas tree – a light near an ear, another on the nose, one on the mouth, etc. As the keys depress and release, the lights wink on and off to some banal programmed music:*

'Twas Xmas Eve
and all through the house
Not a creature was stirring,
not even a mouse.

3. *I have to leave the lecture to make a call. I pick up the phone but I have the wrong number. Someone gets woken up, and is sleepy and irritated. I put down the phone and wonder if I should go back to the lecture.*

Associations: Part 1 – The lecturer appears in full control of his audience. Standing on his own two feet, he admonishes Europe that she should do the same. I was thinking of the proposed integration of Common Market economies.

Part 2 – I'm this programmed head! Controlled from outside. I am also the Christmas tree, observed by others. Naomi [the dreamer's lover] likes trees a lot. Here I am trying to make myself what she wants to see. Parts of my face – ear, nose, mouth – feel as if they're not mine. The "lights wink on and off" – the joke's on me.

'Twas Xmas Eve – I'm Jewish, so Christmas was not my holiday. The teacher just had us sing these Christmas carols; some administrator, I suppose, had set the program. Be a good student, be a good Christian.

Xmas – 'Twas we who Xed out Christ, the gentiles' hero. I remember *Kristallnacht* and a film of the Christmas Eve parade in Berlin in 1938, the marchers singing "Silent Night." X marks this moment in German History when the pogrom began, signaling the beginning of the end for European Jewry.

Part 3 – Language comes on the scene to save the day – but fails. I don't even know who the hell I'm calling. The lecturer's words at the beginning of the dream were being heard by his audience; mine reach no one's ears. I wonder whether to return to the lecture and rejoin the passive listeners. Full circle.

In this dream I guess I was viewing myself in various disguises. First I was a lecturer, forceful and commanding; then a programmed head, thinking other people's thoughts, and finally a telephone caller, a would-be speaker. But a programmed head is really no one at all – although David Byrne's "Talking Heads" can at least scream, if nothing else!

I'm the second of three sons. The eldest is my brother Paul, self-assured and professionally successful, like the economist in Part 1 of the dream. The youngest, my brother Mitchell, student and English language teacher-to-be, will rescue people through the Word. Me in between with no identity at all. Let's make the best of it and take up Zen!

Three parts to my dream, three sons in our family. Everything comes in threes, that's the way the universe is put together. I remember a few lines from [the astronomer] Stephen Hawkings' book: if space had more than three dimensions, the earth would either spiral away from or crash into the sun; "We would either freeze or burn up." The sun wouldn't remain stable, but would either explode or collapse into a black hole.

DREAM INTERPRETATIONS

Comparing the dreams of Descartes, Freud, and Edward, we can see the different ways that narratives of identity and mastery are expressed in each. Descartes' universal mathematics, which he took to be his fundamental discovery, discloses the essential structures of reason and of the world we reason about. This disclosure is placed in the service of mastery: a potentially unruly, threatening environment (which for Descartes includes the human body itself as one object among others) is ordered, tamed, and made useful for the subject's purposes. The ordering of his dream sequence echoes the same theme:

Part 1: Forces seemingly beyond his control buffet and terrify the dreamer

Part 2: Chaos, total loss of control

Part 3: Control regained, thanks to reason

Reason affirms, moreover, the coherence of the individual. "A lifespan can be divided," Descartes writes at one point, "into countless parts, each completely independent of the others, so that it does not follow from the fact that I existed a little while ago that I must exist now."[26] Against the prospect of this disintegration of the self, the integrative power of logic is the antidote. In the second dream, it is reason that dispels the "fiery sparks" and reintroduces order into Descartes' experience, thereby re-establishing the boundaries between illusion and reality.

It is not accidental that the second dream, in which the boundaries between the self and its surroundings dissolve, is so abbreviated. Descartes' writings allude only rarely and indirectly to the dissolution and chaos that a failure to find internal order and unity would imply. Unlike the material realm, characterized by passivity and disorder, the mind for Descartes is defined as active and unified: reason connects, integrates, and individuates, providing a firm foundation for the self that one is. That this self could come apart and lose itself is a possibility that Descartes does not countenance.

In Freud's dream, too, mastery is spotlighted. At stake is the effectiveness of his treatment of Irma, one of his patients. Is he or is he not capable of curing her illness? As philosophy is the foundation of Descartes' power, so is medical and psychoanalytic science the basis of Freud's – although Freud is much less optimistic than Descartes about the power of science to improve the human condition.

In Freud's dream, as in those of Descartes, identity issues are subordinate but not absent altogether. Freud indicates his identification with Irma in several ways. First his illness resembles hers: "The scabs on the turbinal bones recalled a worry about my own state of health."[27] Freud looked inside Irma's mouth; his own, too, was diseased and he died eventually of cancer of the jaw. At the outset of the dream, Freud's role is active – he is the examining physician – whereas Irma is the passive patient. But Freud soon joins her, calling in consultants to continue the examination, in relation to whom he is as passive as she. There may be an association here to Freud's own medical treatment as a patient: Irma occupies the position of Freud in relation to Fliess, who treated Freud's nasal problems. About an observation that Leopold makes of Irma's condition, Freud remarks "I noticed it in my own body."[28] If Irma is in danger, then, so is Freud. He is concerned about his own identity in the literal sense – his survival as a biological being. But just because the issue of identity is displaced into the biological realm, it fails to arise as a *psychological* issue.

Freud came to psychoanalysis from medicine – it had been the integrity, the wholeness of the body, not of the mind, that first concerned him. Even following his discovery of the psychodynamics of the unconscious, it was for the most part mastery – the relation of an already existing individual to his or her objects of desire – not identity, that he thematized and explored in his theoretical work and his analyses of himself and others. Reading Freud, one rarely gets the impression of any fundamental sense of dislocation or doubt about who he is. On the other hand, achievement is often an issue. We know, for example, that Freud's career path was far from secured in the 1890s. In his biography of Freud, Peter Gay points out that Freud had been appointed *Privat-docent* in 1885. The average waiting time between this appointment and professorship was eight years.[29] But Freud had to wait seventeen – his anxieties about this appear in some of the interpretations he made of his own dreams.

In the pace of Freud's work and his sense of intellectual isolation, in the endless and exhausting hours spent thinking and writing and worrying about his career, his patients, and his family, we can see a kind of desperation that Freud scarcely acknowledged and that might be interpreted as an underlying uncertainty about his own identity. But Freud did not understand himself in these terms, although his chronic medical symptoms, including a nasal infection, rheumatism, migraine headaches, and cardiac problems, might be interpreted as somatic expressions of a fundamental anxiety about identity.

Similarly, in Freud's dream about Irma, the emphasis upon physical suffering occludes issues having to do with the self. These played a lesser role in Freud's theory and practice, not necessarily because his patients did not experience insecurities of identity as severe as those attributed to contemporary "narcissistic" individuals, but because it was not in keeping with the presuppositions of the times to attribute symptoms, medical or psychological, to such insecurities. Freud's female patients, especially – subject to a turn-of-the-century Viennese environment that deprived middle-class women of any substantial place in the world, maintaining them in a "completely sterilized atmosphere," as Stefan Zweig[30] put it – did not suffer only from the Oedipal problems (penis envy) that he postulated as primary. Hence he could scarcely understand them, as he himself remarked:

> The great question that has never been answered and which I have not yet been able to answer, despite my thirty years of research into the feminine soul, is "What does a woman want?"[31]

Freud was far more confident about his elaborations of the psychology of men. Here Oedipus provides the key metaphor, expressing the fundamental dynamic of male rivalry. The primordial history that Freud offered to explain the human condition is the struggle of the sons against the father of the tribe in *Totem and Taboo*; as a consequence of this battle for power and prestige, the father is killed and replaced with a totem, establishing a rule of law and prohibition.

Remembering his own early years, Freud thought of himself as a child with hostile feelings toward his father. Later he viewed himself as the patriarch, some of whose students, the "sons" of psychoanalysis, wish to "kill" their father. Although relationships within Freud's milieu – first his family and thereafter his professional surroundings – were conflictual in this way, he did not experience that milieu as unstable or foreign. On the contrary, as Freud worked out the theory and practice of psychoanalysis, while seeking to move his career forward, the terrain he traveled remained always familiar and secure beneath his feet.

This terrain becomes problematic for those whose sense of direction and of themselves – of their own "groundedness," to speak in the contemporary idiom – has become unclear. Confusion of this kind enters into many contemporary dreams, including that of Edward cited on p. 53. His is a radically private dream reality: there is no *terra firma* that the dreamer shares with others or that supports even his own existence. In contrast to an amphitheater possibly on the verge of collapse in Edward's dream, the setting in which Freud and his wife receive their guests in his dream is not itself problematic. In the middle of the dream, Freud stages a collegial consultation, whereas Edward introduces an isolated brain whose only relations are to a programmed keyboard. In Edward's dream, the passive tense in phrases such as "behind it is suspended ... " and "Attached to the head is ... " dispenses with the need for a personal noun. Things, not human subjects, are agents: the keys of a player piano "depress and release," "lights wink on and off," programmed music plays.

If Freud were to send a letter or telegram in a dream (roughly equivalent to the phone call that Edward tries to make), he would at least get through, there would be someone at the other end of the line, although the intentions of that someone might be at odds with Freud's. For Freud as for Descartes, access to language affords mastery of a kind. For Edward, on the other hand, language "comes on the scene to save the day – but fails."

Nor would Freud, at the end of his dream, consider returning to the beginning, as Edward does in his. Circularity is a theme also in the following dream that Edward reported:

I find myself disagreeing with a chemistry teacher about a formula. "No, it's N_3O_2," I insist, "a variant of nitrous oxide." I picture in my mind a compound made of 3 nitrogen atoms, attached to 2 oxygens.

Associations: The chemistry in the dream is probably unsound. It's an imaginary compound of 3 nitrogens, 2 oxygens – not unlike the air we breathe. Our oxygen supply is being depleted, though, as the world's rainforests are being cut down. The *N*s – human nothings, although oh so proud – are killing the *O*s, the basis for their own sustenance!

A compound like that is mainly space, an energy distribution in which, quantum mechanics assures us, none of the electrons is ever going to find a stable home. The tinker toys go together one way today, another tomorrow. "N_3O_2" is nice-sounding, but inside at the sub-atomic level it's a buzzing confusion.

Its structure would be something like this [Edward drew the following diagram]:

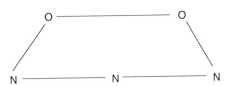

The *N*s are like me and my two brothers – *N* is a jagged, aggressive letter – and the *O*s like our parents – nurturing, whole, supposedly. The *O*s are kind of distant from one another. When I was a child, my mother and father slept in separate bedrooms. My older brother was more closely attached to my dad, the younger one to my mother – with me suspended in the middle.

The differences between this dream and the conclusion of Freud's Irma dream are captured in the image of the chemical structure in each:

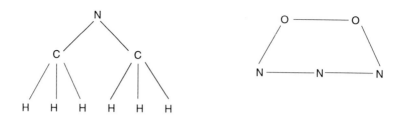

Freud's diagram forms an open tree, Edward's a closed figure. The nodes and branches in Freud's diagram represent relationships between himself and the many people in his life whom, like an accomplished chemist, he combines in various ways, replacing one with another to elaborate and advance the project of self-exoneration that the dream-work articulates. The tree form in Freud's dream might represent other structures as well: the system of neuron pathways that Freud, during the same period in which the Irma dream occurred, was postulating as equivalent to the psyche; the social hierarchy in terms of which Freud's professional life was organized; Freud's own family, including himself in the role of *pater familias*.

The chemical series that Freud elaborates in his dream succinctly symbolizes modern ideas of exploration and progress. Freud's formula is the extending structure of a plant reaching its roots into new territory, of a nation-state's enlarging its foreign empire, of a merchant's pursuit of new markets, of a virus that invades and takes over the body. This logic is one of expansion, proliferation, divide-and-conquer. It is also the logic of psychoanalysis: the unconscious, as Freud conceives it, represents that private and unknown territory that psychoanalysis aims to enter and chart. He writes in a letter to Fliess of those "unexplored regions of the mind in which I have been the first mortal to set foot." In other letters to his closest friend, Freud refers to himself metaphorically as a mountain climber, an explorer of new oceans, an adventurer who enters the dark forest.[32]

While such images aptly describe the ways in which Freud and his professional contemporaries typically regarded themselves, they do not capture Edward's reality. Whereas Freud's preoccupations are the extension of the reach of knowledge and his own career advancement, Edward's are more circular than linear. Edward's model of science is not turn-of-the-century neurology – the science of an evolving brain elaborating neural pathways in response to internal and external stimuli – but rather relativity and quantum theory in which space and time fold and unfold into one another, and particles and waves, matter and energy, are complementary ways of being the same thing.

The physics from which Freud borrowed the concepts of energy and drive is Newtonian: well-defined objects interact within a homogeneous and continuous space of three linear dimensions. The modern science with which Edward is familiar, on the other hand, conceives of an expanding–contracting universe in which stars implode and explode, and black holes capture individual trajectories.

The self-enclosed chemical formula in Edward's dream suggests an anxiety about containment and stability that is far removed from the self-assurance of forward-marching Newtonian science.

TECHNOLOGY AND IDENTITY

Although the specific images and associations in Edward's dreams are unique and express his particular life circumstances, the questions that come up in his dreams are asked also by many of his contemporaries. I belong to a generation preoccupied with Hamlet's dilemma: "To be or not to be ... " For reasons that we will explore in the following pages, today's self tends to revolve about itself. Establishing an identity for oneself overshadows more traditional ambitions of mastering or changing one's surroundings.

I do not mean to exaggerate here the differences between the past and the present. A post-industrial order does not do away with traditional ideals of progress, innovation, and mastery. Yet these become problematic for us in new ways. How are we to square the proclaimed ideals – of ever-expanding opportunities for the individual, unlimited access to information, and unfettered emotional and personal growth – with the realities of a chronically stagnant economy, a pillaged environment, and technological/bureaucratic systems that exclude individual self-determination? Conflicting images of ourselves – as autonomous actors but evidently dependent in many ways, as presumably free subjects but also objectified and fitted into prescribed social roles – make it impossible to view ourselves coherently. To be sure, the conventional values remain in place; progress is still the prescribed mission, and technology its favorite instrument. As much today as in the past, it is expected that we will become better informed, increase productivity, advance our careers. Yet many of us are no longer so enthusiastic about this glorious future.

Although technology organizes, entertains, and fascinates, it is associated as well with depersonalization, unemployment, and isolation. The rationalization of everyday life that technology facilitates may amount to a regimentation that we did not anticipate and do not necessarily want. Improving the technical means at our disposal for satisfying our desires seems reasonable. Yet we cannot help but ask the questions: Who is the person whose desires are to be satisfied? What will become of subjectivity in a social world that submits everything to analysis, measurement, and surveillance? It would be naive to believe that the structure of desire, and the very identity of the one who says "I want," will be untouched by the vehicle that promises to take us to our happiness.

Chapter 4

Individualism: the perplexing project

Every culture allows for at least a minimal distinction between persons. That much is entailed by the use of names and "shifter" pronouns in all languages; in English, for instance, "I" refers to the speaker, "you," "he," or "she" to specific kinds of others. The particular ways in which individuality is structured and interpreted, however, depend on culture-specific norms; not every society defines or deifies the individual as Western societies do. Anthropologists and sociologists have pointed out that "the individual," endowed with personal liberty and autonomy, is a European invention.[1] Balinese culture, often cited as an alternative, does not disassociate personal identity from its milieu.[2] For the Balinese, it is not the possession of certain rights and freedoms that defines persons, but their placement within an all-embracing and timeless social order. The community is fundamental; persons receive an identity via their social involvements and recognized status within that community.

This understanding contrasts with Western traditions that exalt the detachment of the individual from the collective. Since the early formulations of the Greek philosophers, the notions of "individual" and "individualism" have been given diverse and often conflicting interpretations, in an effort to cope with their ambiguities and internal contradictions. Individualism has been identified by its critics with greed, exploitation, and isolation. On the other hand, individualism has also been taken to include belief in the intrinsic worth and dignity of every human being. Today, it is unclear whether individualism in any of its traditional forms, elitist or egalitarian, rational or romantic, associated with the pioneering spirit of the American West, the enterprise of nineteenth century "captains of industry," or more recently with middle-class professionalism, is culturally viable any longer.[3] Nietzsche, who proclaimed the "Death of God," foresaw another "death" as well, that of the unified, self-initiating, and self-determining human subject, and he conjectured that eventually we would fail to recognize ourselves in this self-image.[4]

Loss of confidence in the status of the individual has been a major theme of literature and art in the nineteenth and twentieth centuries. We may admire, but it is questionable whether we can expect to model our lives after, say, the Renaissance ideal of the individual; the centered, grounded subject depicted for example in Giotto's painting of *Mary Enthroned* (Figure 2.6, p. 33) or in Michelangelo's representation of Adam (Figure 2.3, p. 29). Adam rests securely and confidently upon the Earth and sees his own resemblance reflected in the figure of the Creator (who also is quite adequately supported). Adam is born to create, to form his surroundings and himself. Michelangelo alludes here also to his own creative powers. Artists, philosophers, and statesmen of the Italian Renaissance regarded their own individuality and brilliance as patterned after this divine model.

Compare Michelangelo's image of the individual with that of the Dutch artist Karel Appel about 450 years later (Figure 2.4, p. 30). No one mirrors this abandoned figure, whose features have been effaced. Unlike Michelangelo's Adam, he floats in an uncertain space, passive and alone. The raw, streaked quality of the painting of his body is suggestive of anatomical dissection, the body stripped down to the bone. This is a representation of someone bereft of power and individuality, bereft of a self. Appel's art, like that of many of his contemporaries, expresses a sense of isolation and loss of being that is totally out of keeping with the optimistic conceptions of the European Renaissance and Enlightenment.

At the time Michelangelo painted the Sistine Chapel, art was a medium of expression patronized and esteemed by a social elite who regarded certain individualist values as appropriate for themselves but not for others. As a way of organizing and conducting one's life, individualism has always been the prerogative of a limited population; its goals of independence and self-determination have been scarcely within the range of most women and working people, past or present. Moreover, even those for whom an individualist credo might make sense do not always find that it delivers what it promises. Doctors, lawyers, engineers, and other professionals often remain remarkably vulnerable to feelings of emptiness, fragmentation, and other symptoms of a failing self. Edward, the computer expert whose dream was compared in the preceding chapter to those of Descartes and Freud, is quite "successful," in conventional terms; he has achieved a respectable career as a systems analyst and computer programmer. Nevertheless, his identity, his sense of himself as an integrated person, remains very much at issue. The traditional ideals of autonomy and self-sufficiency scarcely work for him at all.

The social world, as perceived by Descartes and Freud, was one in which human beings could locate themselves as individuals who were relatively clear about their own identities. For Edward, on the other hand, as for so many of his contemporaries, personal identity falls out of focus; when he turns the microscope of self-observation inward, a well-defined, stable image does not appear. The events of Edward's personal history are relevant to explaining this, but a larger historical transition is involved as well. A certain construction of social reality has been coming apart at the seams. That construction, which admits of many variations (and enjoys for the time being a resurgent popularity in Eastern Europe and the former Soviet Republics) represents the human domain as consisting of interacting but separate and sovereign subjects, each the master of his or her own destiny. The automobile provides one of the key metaphors here: each person has his or her own destination and is driving to get there; other people represent obstacles; the less traffic, the better.

TECHNOLOGY AND INDIVIDUALISM

Why has the Western individual, whom Iris Murdoch describes as "free, independent, lonely, powerful, rational, responsible, brave, the hero of so many novels and books of moral philosophy,"[5] become a problematic ideal? Part of the difficulty arises as a culmination of the internal logic of what we might call the "technological project." We human beings are born into a world that is in many respects more powerful than we are, that frustrates us in countless ways, preventing us from getting what we believe we want. But we come up with an ingenious idea for handling this situation: we shall take a part of the world and make a tool of it; using that tool we shall establish *ourselves* as the powerful ones, compelling the world to fall into line with our desires. We begin with hand-made artifacts – a clay pot, an arrowhead – and evolve toward more complex devices. Along the way, we discover that the many methods we have devised for making use of the material world can be assembled and systematized into what we call "scientific and technical knowledge." Constantly adding to and revising this lore, we are able to turn the tables on nature, as it were, and harness its mechanisms and energies to our own ends.

This subordination of nature is linked to the role models of individualism: the scientist or engineer is Prometheus stealing fire from the Gods; Archimedes demonstrating the mechanics of the lever; Agricola explaining how to extract precious metals from the earth; or – in modern times – Hausmann paving the streets of Paris; Edison dispelling the darkness with his light-bulb; Orville and Wilbur Wright defying gravity at Kitty Hawk. Eventually, however, the masters of nature, the individuals who have achieved all of the above and more, fall themselves within the scope of the framework of objectivity and technical control. Given the limitless ambition of scientific/technological systems to explain and master virtually everything, and the ever-widening scope and depth of its investigations, ranging from the microphysics of the atomic nucleus to astronomy's accounts of the origin and make up of the universe, such mid-range objects as human beings are inevitably drawn into the domain of empirical inquiry. The irony is that this empirical appropriation undermines the ideal of the masterful individual, of the subject as autonomous knower distinct from and outside of the object of knowledge, which inspired the quest for scientific and technical knowledge in the first place.

This subversion is a consequence not only of the expanding explanatory power of scientific/technical theoretical frameworks but also of the constraints on everyday life imposed in part by the very technologies that in past decades symbolized the liberty of the individual. Again, automotive technology, which in the past provided the strongest ideological support for the free, self-sufficient male-identified individual, is not perceived as the unmitigated blessing that it seemed decades ago. Detroit is no longer one of our most admired cities, and as for automotive travel itself – traffic congestion and pollution are as likely as unlimited liberty of movement to be the associations that come to mind (see Ron Cobb's cartoon, Figure 4.1).

Figure 4.1 *Trail-Blaze a New Destiny!* (Ron Cobb cartoon)

PREMISES OF INDIVIDUALISM

What about information technology? Might this "leading edge" of the economy restore the sovereign subject? Or is an information-based social order all the more likely to call the status of this subject, the "Western individual," into question? Information technology seems to offer new vistas of freedom, of a world in which our own unimpeded action may flourish. But when we reflect upon the character of the contemporary social order, I believe we can see that information-processing technology, as incorporated into our current social institutions and culture, is unlikely to breathe new life into the individualist ideal.

The classical "individual," as conceived within the rationalist philosophical tradition, is autonomous, self-sufficient, self-contained – one who "masters" the "external world." But as we shall see, the very boundaries between subject and object are called into question by the new technologies. On a social level, it is evident today that every one of us is dependent on links – networks of communication, transportation, education, collegiality, etc. – that sustain us. This dependence has always been the case, though advocates of individualism often have pretended that it was not there. Today, even the pretense falls away. Yes, the "independent professional" still represents an attractive ideal. But the conventional models of this ideal – doctors, attorneys, scientists – find increasingly that their work is bureaucratized. At the same time, traditional roles outside of the workplace, in families, neighborhoods, and local communities – roles which in the past supported to some extent the identities of individuals and located them within meaningful face-to-face social relationships – are not as central to our lives as they once were, and therefore often contribute little to the sense of coherence and stability that are hallmarks of the individual.

I will argue that information-processing concepts and practices play an important role in this subversive historical process. As noted above, not everyone who talks or writes about "individualism" would agree exactly on what it is. We can nevertheless delineate a set of core assumptions upon which traditional notions of the "individual" have depended. These assumptions overlap, and none can be understood in isolation. As a consequence of this, considerable cross-referencing occurs between the chapters in the next part of this book. In each chapter, I'll discuss one of the following premises about human beings that have been influential within the Western individualist tradition:

1 **Boundary.** Individuals are defined in part by the boundaries, socially formed as well as biologically given, that exist between them. Historically, the establishment of individual autonomy has always been associated with the consolidation of boundaries, as in the dividing up of common land in England into separately owned parcels, which signaled the end of medieval communal relations. Psychological boundaries are no less crucial to independent persons than those of economic property; part of what it means to be an individual is that one sets up one's own housekeeping, both literally and figuratively, apart from everyone else.

2 **Centered subjectivity.** The autonomous individual is a "command central" of a kind, a subject from whom thought and action project outward to grasp and master the environment. The internal source of one's unique personhood may be regarded as divine (the "spark" or "soul" that passes from God to Adam in Michelangelo's representation) or, in more secular terms, as the ego or self; that agency within the psyche, capable of self-awareness and self-reflection, that is the essence of the person.

3 **Ethics.** The human subject, as conceived within the Protestant tradition for example, is a moral individual – responsible not only for self-formation but also for establishing and maintaining ethical relationships with others. One achieves an identity through the ethically committed "calling" or "vocation" one lives. The value-laden character of the unity that constitutes personal identity is

suggested also by the concept of "integrity," which signifies at one and the same time wholeness and virtue.

4   **Recognition.** Individuality turns upon interpersonal recognition. It is to some extent the product of our believing in it: I am the person I am inasmuch as I am recognized by others and myself as a distinct subject, with my unique personal history, particular interests, beliefs, and relationships with others. In the Italian palaces of the fifteenth-century Renaissance as in today's corporate boardrooms, a distinguishing feature of the individual is that he or she is recognized by others.

5   **Identification.** Individual identity involves social and physical identification. I am *this* person, with *this* body and *this* name. You are *that* person with *that* body and *that* name, distinct from mine. We "locate" ourselves through identifying relationships, including role models. In the conventional nuclear family, parents serve as a "transmission belt" of a kind, whereby gendered identity is conferred upon their children, enabling them to establish a sense of themselves as persons in their own right.

THE SOCIAL LOGIC OF TECHNOLOGY

An information-based social order tends to negate each of the above premises of individualism. These premises are normative as well as descriptive: the boundaries, autonomy, values, and identifications of individuals *ought to be* respected. Yet there is a structure, or *logic* if you will, of information technologies that tends to efface ethical considerations in favor of technical ones, to collapse the boundaries between persons and their surroundings, and to disembed the self from traditional contexts of its identification and recognition. This logic is simultaneously in the machines and in those who use them. The philosopher and social critic Herbert Marcuse argued that technical reason validates certain social and psychological structures:

> Today, domination perpetuates and extends itself not only through technology but *as* technology ... In this universe, technology also provides the great rationalization of the unfreedom of man and demonstrates the "technical" impossibility of being autonomous, of determining one's own life.[6]

Marcuse wrote this in 1964, before information technologies had become essential to the functioning of advanced industrial societies. At that time, one could still think about reversing the relationships between machines and people; the machines have gotten out of control – we need to assert that control again. But what happens when technology is no longer only mechanical but also symbolic, when technical devices simulate thinking, organizing, and managing – activities that interweave or merge individual, institutional, and technical capacities and purposes? My aim in the following chapters is to explore the structural relationships between information technologies and the character of the human subject who both shapes and submits to them – a subject whose unity or even coherence cannot be taken for granted.

Part II

Technological objects and divided subjects

Chapter 5

Boundary

Boundaries play an essential part in our experience of ourselves as individual persons. They are not simply given to us at birth, however, but are constructed. Infants are not consciously aware of a distinction between what happens to them and what happens to others. This has a technical name: "transitivism." For example, when one baby in a nursery falls, several others begin to cry, as if they were saying, "If it happens to you, then it happens to me too."[1] That the experience of ourselves as separate, bounded beings is a result of psychological development was noted by Freud at the beginning of *Civilization and Its Discontents*. He recognized that this experience is not limited to awareness of one's physical embodiment. Boundaries are also essential to knowledge of oneself as an occupant of a social field involving connection with others as well as distinction and separateness from them. In addition to the boundary that "encloses" the individual person, there are many others. Countless are the networks of legal, moral, material, religious, geographic, and bureaucratic boundaries into which human affairs are parceled. Wherever we make a distinction, we draw a boundary of some kind. There exist conceptual boundaries, property boundaries, the edges of physical objects, and so forth.

While such boundaries may contribute to the stability of the lives contained and governed by them, they may also be experienced as constraint or even imprisonment. "Something there is," wrote the poet Robert Frost, "that doesn't love a wall, that wants it down." Well, yes and no. Something in someone must also want walls, or else they wouldn't go up. What a wall, like other kinds of boundaries, seems to provide is protection. A wall means, "This is where you end and I begin. Keep out." Or less militantly, "Enter only with my permission." What falls within the walls or fences, material or imaginary, that we build around ourselves belongs to our domain, is under our control. By the same token, what falls outside these boundaries is foreign and possibly threatening.

Boundaries prevent what is outside from coming in, but also what is inside from falling out. Multiple boundaries surround and contain me as an individual, helping to define the family to which I belong, my neighborhood, circle of friends, community, nation. These boundaries contribute to identity: this is *my* family, *my* neighborhood, *my* nation. Any threat to their integrity threatens me. The powerful appeal of boundaries is nowhere better illustrated than in the rhetoric of politicians.

In the 1980s, President Reagan, for example, encouraged by a coterie of nuclear strategists and scientists, promised a star wars barrier that would encircle the continental United States and protect its citizens from penetration by incoming Soviet nuclear missiles. The form of the Pentagon building in Washington, like that of the "nuclear shield" so dear to military planners, expresses the idea of an enclosed interior, impenetrable from the outside and therefore made safe. According to the Monroe Doctrine, "foreign influence" is to be excluded from "our" hemisphere, regardless of what our Latin friends south of the border might wish (for example, the 1980s image of Sandinista Nicaragua as a Trojan Horse concealing the Soviets). When it comes to immigration, though, suddenly the border between Mexico and the United States firms up again: *they* are alien wetbacks, *we* are "Americans" (as if "*Latin* American" were an oxymoron).

Boundaries, then, are ideological as well as psychological constructions. They cut not only between hemispheres or nations but, notoriously, between social classes. At the bottom of a tiered social order are the homeless, bereft of boundaries in a literal sense; they are not surrounded by four walls. Perhaps we imagine that their wants, too, know no boundaries. So if we become involved with them, we too might lose our boundaries. The *haves* are reluctant to share with the *have nots*, for fear that this process will have no limit – one could easily give everything away – with the consequence that the distinction between "us" and "them" would dissolve.

The irrational aspects of boundary reasoning – its capacity to sweep aside considerations of logical consistency, empathy, and social justice – derive partly from its association with the earliest issues in our lives. Imagery of an unbroken, protecting circle, surrounding the United States or surrounding the Americas, keeping out the bad and holding in the good, is effective in part because it appears to fulfill fundamental human fantasies of being safely held, encircled within a mother's arms, perhaps even of the warmth and security of the womb. Children learn early that the world, including other human beings, has an existence apart from themselves. Margaret Mahler speaks of a process of "separation/individuation" in which a child, during approximately the first two years of life, develops a sense of its own identity.[2] Although the specific ways in which personal identity and personal boundaries are understood vary from one cultural context to the next, human ambivalence about boundaries may be a universal phenomenon. Part of what it means to a child that her parents are distinct beings is that she cannot always count on them to know or to satisfy her needs. There exists a "line" between self and other, however culturally defined, that a child must learn to cross in order to communicate what she wants. The person on the other side of this boundary may stubbornly ignore or even repudiate the demands she makes. On the other hand, the absence of boundaries is also intolerable. Total unity or fusion would mean a terrifying loss of self.

Children's preoccupations with shielding and containment, definition and limit, are continuous with corresponding adult anxieties. Boundaries are elaborated and renegotiated throughout our lives. Where does what is me or mine leave off and what belongs to the other person begin? To answer this question, we shape and adjust what we take to be the rights, responsibilities, and jurisdictions of ourselves and of others, always within a social context whose shifting boundaries, within and between institutions, affect our own.

TECHNOLOGY AND BOUNDARIES: AUTOMOBILE VERSUS COMPUTER

What roles does technological innovation play in boundary formation and transformation? At first glance, technological structures seem to contribute to the establishment of boundaries. The Ancient Greek technologies of measurement made it possible for civil engineers to delineate property boundaries. Technologies of edifice construction, ranging from pyramids, castles, and fortresses to modern houses, produce bounded spaces. Abstract boundaries, too, are generated by technological devices. The descriptive categories of a computer database, for example, establish locations – "bins" they are sometimes called, emphasizing their quality of containment and limitation – into which data are placed.

It can be argued that the very structure of technical instruments entails boundary formation. Even the simplest implement or tool carries this implication: at one end is its user, at the other is the object it operates on. A fork, for instance, marks a distinction between the eater and the eaten. Other instruments, for lifting, moving, holding, crushing, and so on – whether small as a thimble or large as a steam shovel – similarly introduce boundaries between subject and object. Insofar as information technologies enhance our capacity to label and group things, they too create new boundary definitions or sharpen old ones. Ironically, though, information technologies also exert exactly the opposite influence; they tend to efface boundaries, even those that define and contain the self.[3]

Comparing automotive and computer technologies will clarify this point. An automobile is a compelling metaphor for the bounded, self-contained individual. In typical urban environments, car travel reaffirms a separation between a comfortable realm inside and a somewhat alien or hostile world outside, between the suburb and the city, between the private and public domains of our lives. In an automobile, as at home, I am by myself or share with one or several others an intimacy that contrasts with the world outside – the street, exposed and possibly hazardous, that I am merely passing through on my way somewhere else.

I describe all of this in the present tense, although to some extent this view of ourselves and of our surroundings is going the way of Detroit's auto industry. The boundaries that secured the Western "autonomous individual" can no longer be taken for granted, and the machine for which Silicon Valley is famous is making a significant contribution to their dissolution. Unlike an automobile, whose material shell separates an internal space from the external world, a computer does not affirm this dualism. Of course the technologically sophisticated rectangular box sitting in front of me is a visible and tangible material object like any other. But the physical properties of the machine – its hard edges, physical contours, metallic luster, and internal electronics – are not central to the experience of its user. For a computer is above all mental, an invisible organization of a kind. Moving about within a word-processing or spreadsheet program, or playing a video-game, I am drawn into the technology, so to speak, and no longer encounter as such the physical parameters of the device. A computer could more easily be compared to an automobile in the ways it structures experience if, somehow, one were to operate it from inside, from within its physical structure. But this is not the way we use computers, whose dimensions are comparable to or smaller than those of a human body. The "world" of experience that information-processing devices open up to us articulates a mental, rather than a physical terrain. Within this "virtual" space, the distinctions between "inside" and "outside," "subject" and "object" tend to collapse, as technologies are developed that render consciousness continuous with its surroundings. (Virtual reality simulates these distinctions, but, under software control, they become entirely arbitrary.)

Although the automobile is only one kind of mechanical instrument, its metaphorical functioning is typical; whether as simple as a hammer or as complex as a motorized vehicle, mechanical devices extend and/or replace only a peripheral appendage of the human agent. The hammer concentrates the focus and magnifies the impact of the arm's striking power. The automobile extends/replaces our physical means of locomotion. An information-processing system and its user, on the other hand, share in a cognitive, symbolic process, and since we tend to identify our thinking closely with ourselves, the distance between the thinker and the thinking instrument diminishes. Presumably, we know perfectly well that there is a distinction between ourselves and the machine. Yet we may also experience a kind of symbiosis of our thought processes with those the machine carries out. The program is mental, extending and simulating the functioning of the mind, and thus becomes integral to the thinking self. In short, the boundary between the self and the technical system with which it interacts is a far more tenuous and abstract demarcation than the borders of material objects.

Advertisements for information technologies boast their capacity to merge with the mental functioning of their users. These technologies are touted as adjuncts to intelligence, continuous with the mind, as in the illustration, "Friendly Superpower" (Figure 5.1). Computational power, represented here by the circuit board, joins inside and outside, subjective and objective. Instead of remaining a mere instrument, inanimate as a hammer or other simple tool, the merchandise has come alive, advertised as a kind of partner ("Friendly ... on Speaking Terms with You") that unites with whomever it assists. Although the caption, "Friendly Superpower," borrows from the domain of global politics, geopolitical boundaries are nowhere in evidence here. A "superpower" is represented as limitless intelligence, and global rivalry has become an affair of the mind.

Human/computer integration is an attractive prospect in academic as well as corporate circles. Technology is no longer regarded simply as an educational adjunct, a tool appropriate merely for facilitating learning. In the future, human cognitive capacities may literally be joined to that of the technical apparatus. Proposals in this area include "linking the nerve cells of teachers and students with

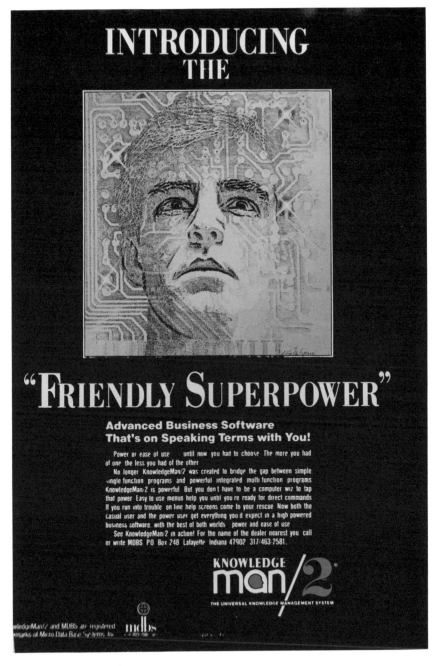

Figure 5.1 Friendly Superpower
Source: Byte: the Small Systems Journal (August 1983)

circuitry in the computer, thereby multiplying the intelligence of both learners and teachers," and "implanting computer chips in the brain to augment intelligence."[4] Terms such as "biochip" and "virtual reality" facilitate talk about the integration of human capacities with artificial intelligence.

The idea of a unified human/machine, or "cyborg," remains in the realm of fantasy; such creatures are unlikely to be created anytime soon. Yet the popularity of this notion suggests that it captures certain features of contemporary reality. Consider terms like *word-processor* and *data-processor*. They refer ambiguously both to an electronic device and to the person who uses it. Blurring or effacing this distinction, information technologies call into question the traditional boundaries between human subjects and their technical environment. When writing a program at a computer terminal, keying in one's identification to an automatic teller at a bank, or accessing an information service from one's personal computer at home, there is a sense in which the subject, in the process of conforming to the algorithm of the program, joins her or his intelligence to the logic of the technical apparatus.

INTERNAL COLONIZATION

The processes cited above are simultaneously psychological and technological, mediated by changes occurring also in the fundamental structures of the economy. Post-industrialism dissolves organizational boundaries of the past. Smaller firms merge into conglomerates or cartels. Capital is integrated vertically as well, uniting enterprises involved in various stages of production. Corporate operations encompass activities of nearly every variety; foundations, museums, university research facilities, city orchestras, youth programs, and libraries are beholden to and sometimes virtually belong to the firms that sponsor and fund them. Government, corporate, and banking apparatuses interpenetrate to steer the economy as a whole. The "military–industrial complex" President Eisenhower warned about has become a military–industrial–government–university–media–medical complex whose previously distinct components increasingly overlap or join.[5]

Yet boundaries are by no means becoming anachronistic. Information technologies contribute to forming them in new ways, by making telecommuting possible, for example. In some post-industrial settings, there is no longer a technical rationale for bringing workers together under a single roof. They can stay at home, using a microcomputer or telephone link to a central system. Human activities other than labor are subject to a similar dynamic of privatisation. Banking and shopping, for instance, may be done from one's home. The consequence is an increasing fragmentation of relatively public domains that people previously occupied together.

Computer technology, then, does not only merge and incorporate; it also distinguishes and segregates. The introduction of information technology into a work environment typically involves a restructuring of social boundaries: new roles are created – programmer, word-processor, system administrator, to name a few – and new authority jurisdictions define locations within the organizational hierarchy. Contemporary boundary formation exemplifies the "colonization of the lifeworld" Jürgen Habermas talks about.[6] When a colonial administration enters a new territory, it aims to establish new boundaries and jurisdictions. This rationalization is imposed "from above": its aim is efficiency measured in colonial terms, not compatibility with the pre-existing culture of those whose lives are reorganized by the colonial regime.

During the past century, for example, Western colonial powers parceled Africa into administrative regions with little regard to the previously existing associations of the inhabitants according to their diverse languages, ethnic communities, clans, states, and kingdoms.[7] Boundaries delineated by indigenous peoples themselves – in keeping with their kinship relations, customs, and natural environment, including its configurations of rivers, mountains, and rainforests – were of relatively little interest to colonizing powers, except in so far as they got in the way of the colonial mapping of the continent for the purpose of exploiting its natural and human resources.

A somewhat analogous "internal colonization" reorganizes forms of life within the borders of industrially advanced countries. The reshaping of boundaries that goes on within and between institutions affects the everyday experience of the people involved in them, but typically not at their behest and not necessarily in keeping with their priorities or values. New technologies introduce new boundary discrepancies and conflicts – new "interfaces," a term that expresses at once separation and integration, not only within computational devices themselves but also within the settings of their deployment. Interfaces are not boundaries of the traditional kind; they do not delineate reliable or durable social roles. A module belonging to a machine, or a person belonging to a project, may "interface" with one counterpart today, and with another tomorrow. Front-line personnel must constantly be adjusting to reshuffling of this kind, although they typically have little say over its direction or outcomes.[8]

Such rationalization is apt to have unsettling consequences for its participants, who recognize that their responsibilities and boundaries have been arbitrarily contrived and may be displaced or dissolved at any moment. This description by William, a programmer whom I interviewed, of his work situation vividly expresses the sense of impermanence and boundary-loss that characterizes many contemporary environments:

About every six months or so there is a personnel reorganization and work teams are juggled around. Someone from the other side of the building is suddenly working in the cubicle next to mine or has even joined my group, and someone from our group – who could be me! – has gone to other side of the building. You rearrange the pieces of the chess game and start all over. The rules might change too. In the new setup, some people will end up higher, with a promotion, and others lower. You know what it's like? If you have a jar full of candies and you shake it up good, then you'll see that they're all rearranged, some have risen, others have fallen. Ones that were neighbors get separated to opposite ends of the jar.

That's why you never get too close to the people you're working with. You'll probably be at a different place working on a different project before too long. You have to be friendly to get the job done, but then later you go your way and they go theirs. I prefer it that way, I suppose; you don't accumulate entanglements.

The glass jar is actually a good model, because everything is always visible to everyone else. The partitions that separate our offices are these thin, pathetic things. You can see over and under them. In the "open office," there's no secrets, no privacy. What others do, I know; what I do, they know. What's in their heads can be linked into mine, and vice versa, just like shared files under Unix [the name of the computer operating system]. There is one body of information, with plural representations in us. We become, in a sense, branches or extensions of the project that animates us all. [I asked: Is management separated off, to some extent?] Yes and no. In our system the directories under which files fall are themselves files – shorter ones, in fact, than the others. In my last project, managerial personnel were shifted in and out constantly; the programmers had more longevity! The only thing that stays around is the project and then one day that too goes to heaven – meaning that the user receives the system we've built – or to hell, the whole thing fails, a few heads roll, and you move on. Usually it's somewhere in between – the customer gripes and wants revisions and enhancements. There are few clean breaks in this business.

The workplace is organized in such a way that traditional boundaries scarcely exist: "the partitions ... are these thin, pathetic things." This dissolving of boundaries is abetted by the integrative character of the technology: "What's in their heads can be linked into mine, and vice versa ... There is one body of information, with plural representations in us." Compare this human/machine relationship to another, taken from the realm of mechanical technology: the worker as cog-in-the-machine, immortalized by Charlie Chaplin in *Modern Times*. The difference is that the cog, although literally "driven" and tiny in comparison with the large machine to which it belongs, retains its permanence and individuality – it does not merge with its surroundings. Whereas mechanical technology is affiliated with the apartness of the individual, information technology – as William perceives it – has more to do with fusion.

William finds no coherent perspective from which to view his situation; he shifts between objective and subjective perspectives. On the one hand, he identifies with the detached and impersonal agent of rationalization: "About every six months or so there is a personnel reorganization and work teams are juggled around ... You rearrange the pieces of the chess game and start all over." This "you" represents corporate authority that makes policy decisions about job classifications and other kinds of boundaries in the company hierarchy. On the other hand, William identifies also with a more subjective "you," referring to personnel like himself, as in "you never get too close to the people you're working with. You'll probably be at a different place working on a different project before too long." A detached resignation prevails here: when boundaries shift within the corporate architecture, one adapts to the new contours.[9]

BOUNDARY LOSS

For William, the network of impersonal relations that characterizes his work environment is tolerable. The distance from others that he experiences is compensated by bonding elsewhere in his life – to family and friends. For others, corporate life has more disturbing consequences. Antonio, a systems analyst, finds that when he is working alone, he feels as if he might disappear, "A photo could be taken, and I wouldn't even be there." Antonio dreamt:

An atomic particle occupies a closed box which is otherwise empty. The particle moves in a straight line and keeps bouncing off the walls of the box – mathematically predictable, like the motion of a billiard ball. Nothing interferes with this particle, for a long time. Perpetual motion.

But then a slot in one wall slips open and the particle shoots outside the box, traveling in a straight line into empty space. A camera follows, moving at the same speed as the particle so that the box is left behind and all that you see is a round dot at the center of the field. Since there is no longer a reference frame for noticing the motion, it just looks as if the particle is stopped dead center. This doesn't change – until I wake up.

Associations: In a way this is not my dream, but the camera's dream.

Antonio feels isolated in his professional and personal life, in part because of his Mexican-American background that he says sets him apart from others. In the dream, the particle in the closed box is contained and its trajectory is "predictable," reminding him of the way he is at work. Talking with people reassures Antonio; he feels secure as long as it is possible to "bounce ideas" off others. They reflect him back to himself, like the walls in the dream. But when there are no longer boundaries to hit up against, the dreamer himself perishes; "the particle is stopped dead center ... this is not my dream but the camera's dream." The dream camera sees, but the human subject has vanished. A thin line separates the technological *augmentation* of human capacities (the camera increases the capturing power of the eye) from *replacement* of the subject (the camera no longer needs the photographer). The meaning of technological metaphor in Antonio's dream is virtually the opposite of that which inspired such seventeenth- and eighteenth-century thinkers as Descartes, Bacon, and the philosophers of the Enlightenment. For them, technology means domination of nature, enabling human agents to claim a status as masterful and self-reliant individuals. Technology belongs to a rationalizing project that will liberate humanity; it signifies the opening of the world to practical understanding and transformation, as well as the freedom of the individual to pursue a course in life unconstrained by restrictions of religion or tradition. These early enthusiasts of science and technology took for granted their existence as distinct individuals; at issue, rather, was Descartes' question *Quod vitae sectabor iter?* (What path shall I take in life?).

I am not suggesting that this enthusiasm has ebbed in the late twentieth century, but a change has occurred. Even those who celebrate technology are usually aware to some extent or another of its depersonalizing consequences. These are experienced by Antonio, whose dream expresses isolation and absence of boundaries – absence above all of people. He noted that the automated camera in his dream resembles a computer, that it functions without his intervention, even without his presence. When he is logged into the computer at work, he says, "there's nothing tangible to push against, you lose sight of where or who you are."

Although Antonio's experience is bound up with the particular circumstances of his life, some of those circumstances are shared with his contemporaries. In the past, role boundaries typically enclosed the individual as an automobile does its driver. In the traditional nuclear family, for example, there is a defined place and clear expectations for each actor: father, mother, children, and a grandparent or two. Automotive technology echoes and reaffirms this logic; the man of the family occupies the driver's seat, mom is at his side in front, with the kids behind or between them, as in the Norman Rockwell painting of the motoring family on holiday (Figure 5.2). At the end of their trip, these family members have been exhausted by their fulfillment of the American dream, but each retains his or her place in the scheme of things. The family that motors together stays together, each of its members true to his or her assigned role.

As the character of family life has changed, the boundaries between roles have lost their clarity and consistency. In Antonio's Mexican-American family, everyone occupied fairly traditional roles; but now in his own roles as husband, father, and software engineer, he experiences ambiguities and ambivalences that are incomprehensible to his parents. Mothers work, fathers mother, individuals feel freer to change their roles and social relations – their jobs, church affiliations, hobbies, friendships – as often as it is advantageous for them to do so. Information systems, which admit of infinite reconfiguration both internally and in relation to their social contexts, exemplify on a metaphorical level the variability of boundaries that characterizes perpetually changing personal identities.

BOUNDARIES MADE BY WHOM?

We tend to think of a limit or boundary as a line put around or between things by an *external* agent. A corral does not corral itself, nor does a box box itself. The very idea that something might create its own limits or boundaries is paradoxical: wouldn't they have to be already in place in order for the "something" to exist in the first place? That boundaries are imposed on human beings, rather than determined by them, is certainly the experience of children. For them, "boundaries" – the wall of a crib, the limitations imposed by a parent – have a quality of coercive constraint. Adult experiences confirm this observation. In the instances discussed

Figure 5.2 Motoring family
Source: Norman Rockwell, *Saturday Evening Post* (August 30, 1947)

in this chapter, boundaries are experienced as lying beyond the determination of those whose activities they limit, as in "About every six months or so there is a personnel reorganization and work teams are juggled about."

Not only the transience of boundaries, but the absence of control over the manner of their formation and alteration contributes to experiences of isolation and disempowerment. If boundaries were subject to the decision-making powers of those whose lives they shape, then our perceptions of them might radically change. Changed also would be the meanings of individuality, property, rights, and community, all of which are defined in boundary terms. In so far as information technologies become involved in the ways we form boundaries, or experience them as formed for us, they are likely to influence nearly everything else about us as well.

Chapter 6

Subjectivity

Built into the classical Western notion of the individual is a distinction between an internal realm, private to oneself, and an external, public realm beyond the self. There are many ways of construing this private realm – as an enclosed landscape of a kind, or perhaps a home whose windows and doors permit exchange with the world outside. Presumably, there must be as well an "inhabitant" of the internal world, an occupant of the private landscape, of the home that is oneself. Our view of the human subject turns upon a premise so basic and so much taken for granted that we scarcely notice how essential it is: there exists within each of us a "command central" or agent of some kind in charge of integrating our experiences and initiating our actions.

FOR AND AGAINST THE "SELF"

Western tradition views this agent, whether called *subject* or *self* or *soul*, as the core person, complete with essential qualities of inwardness that make each of us distinct and unique. Presumably, inanimate objects, including machines, do not have this inwardness. We observe a distinction between dead instruments and live humans. However "smart" an information-processing device may be, we balk at attributing subjectivity to it. Surely, there is not anyone "at home" inside the computer enclosure on one's desk. But what reason is there to believe that there is a subject or self inside the "enclosure," or body, that is oneself? When "communicating" with a computer, we do not assume that there literally is a center of subjectivity inside the machine who is holding up its end of the conversation; perhaps we should not make this assumption about humans either.

An argument can be made against the very existence of the subject or "self" that parallels skepticism about the existence of God. David Hume, eighteenth-century English philosopher and atheist, reasoned that we do not need to postulate a divine agent to explain what goes on in the world. For somewhat similar reasons, he also disbelieved in the unity presumed to lie behind our experiences that we call "the self." Hume's words are as unnerving today as they were at the time they were written:

> For my part, when I enter most intimately into what I call *myself*, I always stumble on some particular perception or other, of heat or cold, light or shade, love or hatred, pain or pleasure ... The mind is a kind of theatre, where several perceptions successively make their appearance; pass, re-pass, glide away, and mingle in an infinite variety of postures and situations. There is properly no *simplicity* in it at one time, nor *identity* in different [times] ... They are the successive perceptions only, that constitute the mind.[1]

This picture of a human being as a "theatre" of perceptions, without any "perceiver" or "subject" to whom they belong, receives contemporary support from the development of information technologies. What we regard as the subject or self might amount to nothing more than the extraordinarily sophisticated command and control apparatus of a "human computer": a program or system of programs exceedingly complex but not fundamentally different in kind from the software that operates "intelligent" technologies.

"But surely," one may object, "a computer is merely an instrument. The program and the machine on which it runs are products of human agency. That's not 'live' speech you see displayed there on the video-screen, not an authentically human response at all – notice how inflexible are the machine's 'replies' to whatever is said to it by the user." Here we seem to have found a basis for denying subjectivity to machines and for reaffirming our own: whereas they are merely inflexibly functioning objects, we are spontaneous and creative subjects. But consider: how flexible and free are we, really? Man is but "a poor player that struts and frets his hour upon the stage," says Macbeth. Do we write the scripts of the various roles we play? We are biological creatures, formed originally at the behest of the DNA inside us, and subsequently by family and other cultural influences not chosen by ourselves. This wet protoplasm that each of us is – what *hubris* to attribute to it "personhood," "subjectivity," "self."

Freud reports three wounds to the narcissistic pride of human beings: Copernicus' discovery that our planet is not at the center of the universe; Darwin's that we are merely the latest step in an evolutionary chain, one rung above our primate ancestors; and Freud's discovery that we are subject to unconscious processes and therefore not even masters in our own house. There remains perhaps a final, radical step to be taken in this historical process of deconstruction: the human subject – the one to whom actions and experiences, whether conscious or unconscious, are attributed – does not exist! The "crisis of the self," on this account, rests upon a fundamental misunderstanding of what human beings are.

The attribution of selfhood to experience is no more warranted, according to this view, than hypotheses about sun-, water-, or tree-gods to explain the workings of nature. In words like "myself," "himself," "self-understanding," "self-esteem," the syllable "self" plays an innocuous role. Where we go wrong is in detaching this syllable from the expressions to which it inextricably belongs, as if, "self," standing alone, refers to something. If this assumption is mistaken, it is no wonder that the enormous effort devoted to pursuing and understanding the self is so frustrating.

The innumerable hyphenated expressions that attach to the word "self" (-discovery, -development, -fulfillment, -concept, -image, -involvement, and so forth) are like satellites circling a void. One "looks inside" and finds, ultimately, nothing. Anxiety about the self, then, proves incurable because the self is nothing more than an illusion.

BUILDING A SELF

Although a case can be made for the non-existence of the self, as we have seen above, we are not dealing here simply with a fiction. As Steven Toulmin has pointed out, if the notion of the self were to be eliminated, there is much that we could not say. It is significant, however, that the use of "self" as a free-standing noun in English and other Indo-European languages is etymologically recent.[2] In American middle-class culture (which so much of the world seems currently to want to imitate) the "self" is what one develops by way of constructing a personal, individual identity. As noted in Chapter 2, the project of "making something of oneself" is one that American profession-bound children take up at an early age.

But this project is problematic, if not impossible to realize. The conventional ideal placed before us is that of a unified and autonomous self. Yet certain features of contemporary life, including our involvements with "thinking" machines, are apt to undermine our confidence in the assumption that such an entity as a self exists at all. The project of self-formation divides its human subject in two. When "I work on myself," the "I" who undertakes this labor is split from the object, "me" or "myself," the one worked upon. The self, produced and presented like any other object, becomes thinglike, something to be observed and manipulated. Such hyphenated expressions as "self-development," "self-observation," and "self-regulation" point to activities in which people take themselves as the objects of their own attention and are engaged in shaping and reshaping the human material they are.

This managerial relation between "I" and "me" has to negotiate constantly changing and sometimes even conflicting demands that are brought to bear upon one's self-formation. Contemporary role identifications for both men and women – as husbands or wives, students or teachers, as bureaucrats, manual or mental workers – are difficult to live out consistently. From women, qualities of softness and receptiveness continue to be expected, but these virtues contradict the qualities of efficiency and initiative required of them as housewives and as mothers, and are incompatible also with the assertiveness required for them to compete in the workplace. Many men face similarly inconsistent expectations; self-sufficiency and competitive drive are valued, but so are cooperation and sharing. Men are responsible for going out into the world and succeeding economically, but are also asked to devote their time and attention to their families in their roles as devoted husbands and fathers.

The tension between the professional and the personal is reproduced within the workplace itself; social workers, nurses and other service providers are expected to "process" each case objectively and efficiently, according to prescribed rules and procedures, but also to take a personal interest in the well-being of their clients. Even those with minimal direct contact with a public they serve find themselves subject to contradictory requirements: a programmer with high-blood pressure is urged by her therapist to slow down and relax, but she must meet next week's deadline. A clerical worker employed by a company that builds nuclear power plants believes that they endanger humanity and that their production should cease. These contradictions are exacerbated by the chronic recessionary tendencies of post-industrial economies.

In these examples, there is typically a conflict between impersonal "system" obligations and the world of everyday lived experiences and associations with others. Moreover, the alleged obligations are themselves mutually inconsistent, making it all the more difficult to establish a coherent personal identity that unifies the divergent roles one plays. Technological involvements do not alleviate this predicament, but instead articulate and mirror the contradictions. Consider this dream told to me by Dorothy, employed in a scientific research institute:

> *I'm helping Maggie (a co-worker) with a problem she's having on the computer and I'm having a hard time figuring out what needs to be done. Bob (a new member of the organization) says that he can help and I'm astounded that he's already used what I've taught him as a foundation for knowledge I don't have myself ... He says, "You're a little thick when you're late, aren't you?" I hear this as a reference to my having come to work that morning around 10:00 ... I do feel thick, like I'm incapable of holding ideas.*

Associations: Bob's comment in the dream, "You're a little thick when you're late ... " is a pun on pregnancy. [When I spoke with her about my dream] Maggie said, "Funny that you should say that. I'm over two weeks late now, and I'm terrified that I'm going to have to have another abortion." Often when I have dreams that seem to invade other people's private lives, they involve pregnancy and abortion and marriages unmade ... [The dreamer had been pregnant and had undergone an abortion fourteen years earlier.] When I first joined that office, I had a dream about a computer that was also a freezer that contained pieces of information about the future. It exploded and I found out that one of my employers was pregnant with a son.

Computer technology in this dream mediates relationships that partake of the procedural and systematic on the one hand, and of the personal and private on the other. Dorothy's job engages her intelligence within a system organized around an abstraction: scientific truth. Her work is subject to criteria and procedures of scientific method, as interpreted by a research team. The computer, an instrument of this methodology, processes and stores the empirical data that supports the researchers' claim that their findings are to be regarded as scientifically warranted.

On a more personal level, the computer symbolizes concerns about identity. Years earlier, Dorothy had been attracted to a man whose "ideas about the world were so solid and certain that for the first time in my life I felt utterly secure, and within his point of reference began to develop what felt like a base of operations from which to launch a self." Information is apparently a source of being; sharing her male partner's ideas, Dorothy wanted to believe, might help her to establish her own existence. Dorothy elaborated:

> Even my earliest memories – mostly surrounding my mother being pregnant with my brother when I was not quite two, and the months after his birth – involve the sense that reality is so malleable as to be near-arbitrary and always in imminent danger of falling apart ... I can't remember a time or a place in a social sense where I actually felt concretely there, wholly part of something real and of value.

When I asked Dorothy whether being "real" has something to do with feeling effective or adequate, she explained:

> I'm not sure that I mean by "not feeling real" that I feel inadequate. It's more like feeling unstructured, as though the bases from which I operate are never strong enough to support anything worthwhile or consistent.

Mental work helps to build structure and support. In Dorothy's dream, the information she has given Bob functions as "something real and of value" that provides him with a "foundation." The body, on the other hand, is more problematically related to personal identity and security. Dorothy's mother, and other women of her mother's generation, typically found their calling in the traditional way: by becoming housewives and mothers. For these roles, involving the bearing and raising of children, a woman's body is essential. But in Dorothy's world, pregnancy no longer automatically carries meanings of family and traditional motherhood. Rather, the subject of pregnancy is introduced into a new symbolic discourse where it signifies not only biological but also mental "conception." About her own capacities as a technician and editor, Dorothy remarked, "I always think of the skill as midwifery." In this new discourse, attributes of pregnancy also carry negative associations; Bob, one of the researchers with whom she works, remarks in her dream that "You're a little thick when you're late, aren't you?" and she agrees: "I do feel thick, like I'm incapable of holding ideas." "Thick" for Dorothy means "with child," but also: dense, opaque, incompetent.

Dorothy also associates pregnancy with the unpredictable and disruptive: she dreamt of "a computer that was also a freezer that contained pieces of information about the future. It exploded and I found out that one of my employers was pregnant with a son." When Dorothy was a child, her mother would get angry and occasionally "explode." Not only anger is at issue here, however. Dorothy has not had children, the "information" contained within her – DNA, the foundation of biological reproduction – remains as yet "frozen." Giving birth is an information explosion of a kind, one for which the dreamer is not yet prepared. I am reminded of the ways in which other women of Dorothy's generation sometimes represent their birth-giving potential in technological and economic terms: aware that their "biological clock" is ticking, they realize that one day the "window of opportunity" will close.

What the theoretical abstraction, "internal colonization of the lifeworld" (a phrase whose meaning we will look at more closely in Part III of this book), means concretely is just this intervention of system concepts, many of them taken from the realms of computation and biological engineering, into everyday contexts where they rearticulate human identity and relationship. Even Dorothy's personal concerns are swept up in a vortex of information-processing imagery. One of her goals has been to establish an existence for herself outside of the technological system that engages and seems to assimilate not only her intelligence but her very being.

That system reappears in the dreams of many of those whose work life involves them with information-processing technology. A programmer, William, dreamt:

I am caught between two rows of teeth that are sawtooth shaped, resembling the staccato sound of my printer. At the center of each tooth is an eye. The rows come together in silence, so that each eye now has a partner. I am nowhere to be seen.

Associations: Yesterday, at home, I was printing out a file [on the computer]. I have a parakeet and it was mindlessly echoing the rasping noise that the printer makes. I felt that now that the file was finished and was printing out, there was no longer any need for me. After weeks of painstaking attention, I could be as empty of consciousness and purpose as the machine or this dumb bird.

William was soon to come up for review by his peers and supervisor. He sometimes noticed them looking over his shoulder, watching silently. They were, he feared, critical of his work. Now they would meet in his absence and "decide my fate," as he put it. At the end of the dream: "The rows come together in silence, so that each eye now has a partner. I am nowhere to be seen." Once assembled, his evaluators would not have much to say, he suspected, since the verdict would be self-evident. His very existence seemed to depend upon their approval. Their function was to keep an eye on those under their jurisdiction and to decide, in his words, "who shall live and who shall disappear."

This dreamer felt quite angry about the way he was being judged. Anger, however, is a forbidden feeling within professional contexts. If this irrational feeling does arise, it must remain contained. Even in dreams, anger is apt to assume disguised forms, as in the exploding of the computer in Dorothy's dream. In William's dream, he "is caught between two rows of teeth that are sawtooth shaped like the staccato sound of my printer." His double bind was this: how to express his feelings of frustration and aggression without putting people off by acting "unprofessionally." The "rasping noise" of the printer raps out his own stifled protest.

Another programmer dreamt:

A woman from Latin America owns a dog which she is very attached to ...

Meanwhile, I'm part of a team automating the operation of a government veterinary facility. The dog barks noisily, as dogs are wont to do – you can see it is harmless. But its yapping and running about get in the way of our program, so when it is run, the dog gets put to sleep. That way, everything goes smoothly.

The dog lies there and someone guesses that it's dead. But I see its stomach rising and falling, just a little motion but it's unmistakable proof of life. I exclaim that the dog is by no means expired. The Latin American lady is happy and chatters on.

Associations: My own chattery emotions have to be put on ice when I'm working. Whether I'm in a good mood or alone and miserable, building the system requires my full attention. Then later, after I exit from the screen, I'm a little surprised that I'm still alive, maybe even human! I can yap noisily and happily once again.

Will the dog survive all that is done to it? When I'm sitting at the keyboard, I might be motionless too, but I'm still breathing.

I hope that a veterinary facility will take care of a veteran dog like me someday. Enough of this morbidity. Better go connect up with that Latin American lady and her dog!

The dreamer identifies with his professionally defined role as a programmer, which organizes much of his life. The Latin American woman and the dog represent aspects of the dreamer himself, unorganized and spontaneous, that have to be "put to sleep" so that he can function effectively. But he has his doubts about this arrangement. The rational system signifies stillness and death; will it "take care of a veteran dog like me someday"?

This dream expresses a traditional association: male = rational, female = irrational. Getting closer to women signifies, for this dreamer, getting closer to the irrational or non-rational aspect of himself. Today, however, this symbolism may be in the process of breaking down. In Dorothy's dream, and in other dreams reported in this book, women no longer perform only the traditional female roles: lover, mother, homemaker. They, no less than men, are thinkers, related in complex and problematic ways to their own rationality. Women enter into many contemporary dreams (of both women and men) not only as sexual objects, but often as teachers and managers – as authority figures of one kind or another. This may reflect shifting occupational roles and cultural attitudes (see Chapter 12).

In the following dream, technical rationality closes off the realm of the senses:

I want to know whether my room is cold or warm. So I log into my computer to find out. Suddenly millions of symbols splash on to the four walls of the room and I'm lost. I don't know for sure the symbols for hot and cold. I am aswim amongst them but cannot decipher any, and am reminded of Coleridge's "Water, water everywhere, but nary a drop to drink." At the same time, each symbol is also a beautiful Chinese calligraphy – flowing not binary. I would like to learn more about that.

Associations: I'm using expressions – "aswim," "amongst," "nary" – that sound like old English. I might be just making up these words. They are not my usual vocabulary; I don't feel I'm myself in the dream. I could be making fun of someone who puts on airs – my English teacher in junior high school, for example. I could never be like him, English lit. was never my thing.

I cannot feel warm or cold but have to read the temperature out of the machine. As if someone had to consult a table of numbers to know whether they are hungry or thirsty. At least the Ancient Mariner knew that much about himself! I too am thirsty, thirsty to understand these symbols. I might be hot or cold and not know it. Either extreme and you perish. Flowing Chinese calligraphy. Not like the bytes and bits I work with that chew the mind. In school I could never draw anything. Another identity that I could only observe from afar.

The divorce of rationality from sense experience in this dream is so complete and the subject's identification with his mental functioning so total that he depends entirely on the computer for contact with his surroundings. An intellectual system filters all the input that crosses the interface between self and world. The dreamer's reminiscences call up alternative identities that he perceives as never having been available to him. "Calligraphy – flowing not binary" suggests a dialogue that literally might return the dreamer to his senses. Possibly the dreamer is also referring to his conversations with me, uncertain as to whether he feels "warm or cold" in our sessions. I am like the English teacher in his dream, an unavailable identity. Yet, might our talk help him to become someone?

What these four dreams share is a profound misgiving about the identity of the dreamer. Each includes the dreamer as "I," but it is as if the pronoun is searching for a referent. The first dreamer "can't remember a time or a place in a social sense where I actually felt concretely there, wholly part of something real and of value." In the second dream, "I was nowhere to be seen." In the third, the subject remarks that "I'm a little surprised that I'm still alive, maybe even human." In the associations to the fourth dream, two possible personal identities are mentioned, that of a junior high teacher and another of someone who draws well, but the dreamer is unable in his own eyes to fill either. He repeats the word "I" over and over, as if saying it often enough will somehow guarantee that it names something.

What accounts for such insecurities? These dreamers are not "failures" in any obvious sense. All are well-educated, "accomplished" individuals. Yet it seems that a secure identity cannot be counted among their accomplishments. Although the personal history of each of these dreamers is absolutely unique, their dreams share certain themes, one of which is a dissociation of thinking from lived experience. The genesis of this phenomenon is both cultural and individual. Institutional involvements, with parallels reaching back into early family relationships, are often abstract and impersonal in ways that tend to render identity abstract and impersonal, "insubstantial" in a psychological sense. The computer provides a perfect metaphor here: as a model of detached, ownerless cognitive processing, the machine symbolizes an *absent* subject.

THE ULTIMATE SELFLESS INDIVIDUAL

This symbolism may seem surprising, given the influence traditionally attributed to technology. Doesn't technology help to affirm the existence of those it serves? Machines, after all, leverage our power, our mastery of nature. And where there is leverage there is presumably someone who applies it; where there is mastery there is a master. The problem with this logic, mentioned earlier, is that the computer is an instrument not so easily distinguished from the person who uses it, since it extends not just physical capacities – as a hammer amplifies the striking power of the arm, for example – but mental capacity as well. Artificial intelligence not only augments human thinking power, but *joins* or even *replaces* it. Inasmuch as we identify mental functioning as something that is essential to the individuals we are, then it is we ourselves whom the computer merges with or supplants.

What is most disturbing, then, about information-processing devices is not the fact that in certain limited areas they can or might someday outperform human beings. A computer carries out mathematical operations fast. So what? We regard this as a mechanical assignment and need not feel threatened by its efficient execution. One day a chess program may defeat the world champion. Achievement of this kind could bring us to devalue our own accomplishments in realms where computers excel. But I doubt that it is from competition of this kind that our deepest misgivings about computers originate. More threatening is the conjecture that all of our cognitive functions might in principle be carried out by a computer, and, moreover, that whatever a computer does, it does without there being a subjective center or self from which (we believe) our own thoughts and actions arise. Regarded in this light, a computer resembles an egoless and selfless individual of a sort. In the process of following the steps of a program, it seems less like a kingdom in which orders from a single ruling agency mobilize a chain of actions spreading down a hierarchy, than like a bureaucratic apparatus over which no one appears to be in charge.

Of Oakland, Gertrude Stein is said to have remarked "There's no there, there." Apocryphal or not, the saying does capture a truth about computers. Granted, one can point to the central processing unit (CPU) inside the computer and say *that* is where agency really resides, while the other functions of the device only carry out the instructions that the CPU issues. The trouble is that the CPU itself has an "inside." There is in the microprocessor a logic that operates it from within, just as the microprocessor, in turn, operates input–output devices, storage units, and other peripherals located logically and physically external to itself. The CPU, no less than the larger system to which it belongs, has an "outside" (extending outward from the pins of the microprocessor chip that are used to communicate with its surroundings) and an "inside" (logical circuits within the microprocessor itself). A tiny microprocessor chip, viewed under magnification, looks like the plan of a city, with its elaborately differentiated and interlinked functions.

As we peer into the computer, moving from the observable macrolevel into the hidden microelectronics, we find ourselves in a "worlds within worlds" cosmology reminiscent of alchemy and early modern Christianity's "Great Chain of Being" – but with entirely different implications for the way we view ourselves and others. When Christian theologians became aware of the endless mystery of biological processes, of pyramiding levels of hierarchy extending from humans down through other forms of animate and eventually inanimate life, they could take this to be the most glorious confirmation imaginable of God's design. The intricate beauty of nature served to escalate their attention to its divine origin: the topmost link in the "Great Chain," the sovereign Creator. In this universe, human beings occupy a special place. Created in the image of God, each soul partakes of the divine and is separated by a metaphysical divide from "lower" forms of being.

The nesting of levels of reality within a computer system, on the other hand, represents organization of a very different kind, for it does not seem to require subjectivity or consciousness at all. The model of the computer as capable of performance without a performer clashes head on with our view of ourselves as ultimately being in control. If we need not postulate an agent within the computer that is responsible whenever a computer does something, then might there not exist also *human* action without a personal agent who directs it? We might say that the real actor, standing behind everything the computer does, is the human programmer or user. But inasmuch as human behavior, too, is viewed as caused by (to be sure, very complex) information-processing operations, shifting our attention from the computer to the human being does not get us any closer to establishing the existence of a human self or subject who organizes/directs our thoughts and behaviors "from inside."

An emphasis upon individual subjectivity and agency lies at the heart of the Judaeo-Christian project, Auerbach argues.[3] This project is endangered by cognitivist accounts that regard human beings as information-processing systems. For it is possible to describe such a system fully without referring to any subjective center of experience/agency that accounts for the order or coherence of its behavior.

NARCISSISM AND SELF-PATHOLOGY

Questioning the ontological status of the subject is not a preoccupation only of cognitive scientists and academics. In less erudite forms, it pervades contemporary culture. The self-absorption attributed to the "me-first generation" represents not just a compelling interest in self-gratification, but more fundamentally, the search for a self to gratify. Narcissism and related disturbances of the self may be replacing the traditional neuroses – the obsessional and hysterical disorders that were the focus of Freud and his successors – as the characteristic psychological illnesses of our time. Heinz Kohut, psychoanalytic theorist of the self, suggests as much:

Instances of Oedipal pathology are seen less frequently now, whereas instances of self pathology are encountered with increasing frequency ... If it is true that self pathology is now in the ascendance, then we will understand why psychoanalysis, the science that more than any other is in touch with the deepest concerns of the individual, is shifting the focus of its attention away from the already carefully investigated inner conflicts of man (in particular the conflicts about repressed Oedipal and other incestuous strivings) and why it is beginning, however haltingly, to pay more attention to the investigation of the vicissitudes of the self.[4]

Although Kohut's claim that problems of the self are increasingly common is controversial, his distinction between "self pathology" and "Oedipal pathology" has become standard among his followers. The distinction draws attention to two kinds of issues that arise for children (in Western cultures, if not universally), each characteristic of a particular developmental stage. Prior to the onset of Oedipal relations, development moves in the direction of individuation: the formation of an internal coherence and order that may be called the "self."[5] If this formation goes awry, because a child is not sufficiently loved and understood and "mirrored" by its parents or other caretakers, the result may be a lifelong vulnerability to fragmentation or, in less extreme cases, chronic insecurities about identity.

As the self consolidates, at around the age of three, new issues arise about the child's status and power vis-à-vis others. The Oedipal struggle assumes center stage, on the orthodox analytic account, as the child vies against one parental figure for possession of the other. "The presence of a firm self," Kohut argues, "is a precondition for the experience of the Oedipus complex. Unless the child sees himself as a delimited, abiding, independent center of initiative, he is unable to experience the ... desires that lead to conflicts and secondary adaptations of the Oedipal period."[6]

Pre-Oedipal development depends on the child's relation to a nurturing, empathic adult. If such a relation is available, the child is able to form a self and simultaneously to recognize others as distinct persons, as unique centers of experience and initiative in their own right. Under optimal conditions, according to Kohut:

[A] core self – the "nuclear self" – is established. This structure is the basis for our sense of being an independent center of initiative and perception, integrated with our most central ambitions and ideals and with our experience that our body and mind form a unit in space and a continuum in time.[7]

But in contemporary society, Kohut believes, the child's family life tends no longer to encourage the formation of a healthy sense of self. One reason for this, according to Kohut, is that parents are no longer as emotionally involved in their children's lives as they were in the past. This renders self-formation problematic, since parents are less available as empathic figures.[8] Children growing up under these circumstances become adults who remain entangled in the issues of the pre-Oedipal years of their lives. Hence the unmitigated and endless pursuit of self-definition and self-gratification that, on Kohut's account, replays the child's very early, unsuccessful efforts to develop and affirm a secure, bounded, and centered self.

I do not want to minimize the importance of the familial origins of the contemporary "crisis of the self" that Kohut and other psychoanalytically oriented theorists have highlighted (although their speculations about the ways in which family ties have changed historically are questionable).[9] Experience of the self is shaped, however, not only within the "crucible" of the nuclear family but also in relation to a larger social world that includes but also exceeds family relationships. Today, that world is technologically structured. Our evolving relationships with technology, viewed not only as an instrument but also as a model of the human subject, may very well contribute to uncertainty about the status of the self. For information technology, presumed to simulate thinking in the absence of a thinker, reflects back to us an image of ourselves that has essentially nothing at its center.

MANAGING FRAGMENTATION

The view of ourselves as "information processors" isn't entirely unappealing; for it elevates cognition to a masterful role in our lives. "Processing" our emotions promises to make them more manageable. Such self-administration functions quite differently, however, from the repressive "mechanisms of defense" that classical psychoanalytic theory elaborated. The logic of contemporary intellectualization is not that of a Western sheriff who heads off outlaw desire at the pass (in keeping with the traditional psychoanalytic model of impulse control), but that of a bureaucratic apparatus that, from the outset, organizes and monitors desire so that its aims will not be wayward. This shift in defensive structure is evident, for example, in the kinds of presenting problems that clients bring into therapy. Often the complaint is not a difficulty in suppressing sexual desire or other feelings – anger, love, fear – but rather a perceived absence of any feelings to be suppressed. More common than "I don't know what to do about my feelings" is "I don't know what I feel." Emptiness, absence, loss of direction – these are characteristic themes of contemporary psychotherapy. With exploration, these themes, like the kinds of symptoms that preoccupied Freud, reveal an unconscious structure, but one that cannot be construed along the lines of the classical psychoanalytic drive-discharge model.

Addressing the needs of a self in danger of fragmentation, intellectualization provides at least minimal consistency and integration; whatever is confusing, disruptive, or divisive in one's life can be handled within the relatively controllable domain of pure cognition; reason will piece together the fragments and resolve the contradictions.

Freud regarded reasoning primarily as a reality-oriented activity of the ego. Consequently, he tended to overlook reason's defensive roles. Anna Freud, too, in her book on the structures of defense, does not include intellectualization among them, and writes almost nothing about the symptomatic functioning of the reasoning ego. On the contrary, she equates thinking with reality-testing and fantasy (in the psychoanalytic sense) with denial:

> When we compare children's phantasies with psychotic delusions we begin to see why the human ego cannot make more extensive use of the mechanism – at once so simple and so supremely efficacious of denying the existence of objective sources of anxiety and "pain." The ego's capacity for denying reality is wholly inconsistent with another function, greatly prized by it – its capacity to recognize and critically to test the reality of objects.[10]

On this account, fantasy diminishes as cognitive contact with reality increases. The problem is that this postulate makes it impossible to understand contemporary intellectualizing strategies. Involvement with technology, especially of the information-processing variety, provides simultaneous adaptation to, and denial of, reality. More prosaic machines, such as the automobile, serve only to move from point A to point B. The prospects that information-processing technologies promise, on the other hand, seem limitless. The child's fantasies of omnipotence, the sense that "thinking makes it so" and denial of emotional relatedness and dependency upon others, are not only compatible with, but may be encouraged by technological involvements. For this reason, the contradiction between thinking and illusion that Anna Freud assumes, and that is a central dynamic in the case histories she discusses, does not universally obtain. The "micro-worlds" and "virtual realities" that information technologies make possible harness fantasy to adaptation, foster narcissistic grandiosity, and facilitate an avoidance of intimacy, commitment, and vulnerability.

THE ESTRANGEMENT OF REASON

Although intellectualization is functional and adaptive in post-industrial settings, it may exacerbate anxieties about the self. Engaged within abstract frameworks, one may experience oneself as cut off from a meaningful world of concrete relationships that supports personal identity. Reflecting on such life experiences and dreams as those I have discussed above, I find considerable confirmation for the "decline of the individual" thesis of Critical Theory.[11] Inasmuch as rationality becomes technical and furthers the manipulation of things and people, it contributes to an objectified world in which subjectivity has no role to play.

We cannot remedy this situation by restoring the traditional notions of "soul" or "self." I agree with postmodern critics who argue that the belief in a central, unified agency within each person is illusory. Yet this illusion has been central to Western concepts of liberty and individual flourishing. To the extent that it loses its cultural hold and no longer organizes our lives, we shall have to revise our understanding of what being human is all about.

Chapter 7

Ethics

[When I was a kid] I liked to figure out the way things are put together. It might be a watch or a radio. Things are made of parts or processes, you can understand *how* they work, but there's no justification. Wood burns, snow falls, acid turns litmus paper blue – that's the way the world is. You can't ask whether it *ought* to be that way. And when I thought about people, it struck me that it must be the same – you have a biological mechanism there, some information-processing, but it's engineering all the way down. It was of course myself I was thinking about, as well as the reality around me.

Sam's memory

Machines are functional objects, designed to serve as the slaves of their masters. Human beings, on the other hand, cannot simply be used, cannot be treated merely as objects. Or can they? Within a post-industrial order that regards "value-free" information and technical objectivity so highly, we may discover that ethical considerations have little or no role to play. Inasmuch as technical reason is applied to human affairs as well as to inanimate nature, the distinction between manipulable objects and human subjects tends to collapse. I will argue here that the elimination of ethical considerations in favor of being "objective" effaces the human individual, traditionally defined as the owner of certain rights, moral obligations, and dignity.

The association of ethics with individuality has been central to Western civilization since antiquity. The idea is that human beings deserve a special quality of acknowledgement and respect that we withhold from inanimate objects, from machines in particular. This "ethical" quality is somewhat elusive and has certainly been interpreted in many different ways. But in post-industrial settings, we may find that it is excluded altogether. This was one of the issues in Sandy's dream of a dolphin, with which this book began: "I was a dolphin sailing through the waves, pure thought, cutting through the water like a knife, silent and invisible." She explained how the dream might have originated: "I read in a magazine that the military trains dolphins to find and destroy enemy mines and deep-sea divers. Intelligence, like anything else, can be harnessed and used." At work, Sandy said, it seemed sometimes as if her mental powers did not belong to her, but served as instruments applied to tasks assigned to her by others. From this presumably rationally and factually defined world, she was trying to recover a sense of herself as a unique subject, as a person valuing and valued by others.

ETHICS AND HUMAN IDENTITY

Ethical sensibility is vulnerable to various hazards. The traditional hazard, of course, is narrow self-interest; looking out for "number one" explains why someone disregards the well-being of others. When "selfishness" takes command in this way, our first inclination may be to try to understand this at the individual level; we hold responsible the person who, by our lights, is misbehaving. But there may be a more fundamental breakdown than this, a shattering of the shared social context within which the notions of ethical regard and responsibility first make sense: if you and I no longer regard ourselves as inhabiting the same moral universe, then we may very well feel that we can treat one another any way we please. Labeling another person, or group of persons the "enemy" can serve this function; denying their humanity makes it easier to destroy them without suffering remorse.

Militarism, which divides the world into "us" (well-intentioned, freedom-loving) and "them" (evil-intentioned, inhuman) is only one of the ways of breaking down our sense of belonging to a moral community. Another is scientific/technological objectification that calls into question the validity of ethical evaluation of any kind. Under conditions of modern warfare, these two attitudes are linked. The Gulf War was represented by the American mass media as a moral crusade, aiming to punish the evil Saddam Hussein and his followers. But the war was also a matching of "our" technology and military expertise against "theirs" – a game of a kind that played well on television and from which moral restraint regarding treatment of the "other side" could almost be excluded as irrelevant. Treating people in this way does not happen only during wartime, of course, but to some extent characterizes activities as various as market analysis, genetic engineering, and office automation. Early in this century, Max Weber pointed out that bureaucratic institutions handle "cases," not people.

But regarding others and ourselves as objects of technical understanding and manipulation contradicts our image of human beings as free subjects, meriting respect. In the Old Testament we are told that human beings have been fashioned in the image of God. As the "Crown of Creation," they are uniquely valuable beings. Ancient Greek culture and Christianity agree on this idea. A person is not merely a body, passively subject to laws of growth and decay, it is also a soul which, as much for Plato as for Saint Augustine, differentiates us from animals. Augustine's conception of this "soul" or "essence," and of the higher law to which it is subject, is of course not that of Plato, and following in their footsteps, Western philosophers and religious thinkers have elaborated many different accounts. But, as Charles Taylor explains in his review of this intellectual history, these accounts have shared the assumption that human beings are, by definition, ethical beings.[1] If there did not exist relationships of recognition and respect among people – ethical relationships – then it would no longer be possible for them to regard one another as subjects or selves.

Is this traditional conception of the ethical constitution of the subject viable in a contemporary world that views individuals through the lens of scientific/technical objectivity? Today the study of artificial intelligence combines with the biological sciences to draw the human subject within the compass of a purely technical understanding. One of the implications of this process of objectification may be that reality is defined as consisting exclusively of empirical states of affairs ("facts"), so that such evaluative expressions as "virtue" and "evil," or even "good" and "bad," lose their reference. Philosophers have combated skepticism of this kind for centuries, but have never been able to secure a logical foundation for ethical judgment.

ETHICAL SKEPTICISM

The case for ethical skepticism goes something like this: simple factual judgments such as "There is a desk in this room," as well as more complex, scientific judgments such as "Table salt is composed of the atomic elements sodium and chlorine," are empirically verifiable and therefore at least potentially credible. Value judgments such as "Honesty is good," on the other hand, do not describe empirical reality at all, and cannot be judged to be either true or false. Such judgments indicate at most the personal inclinations of those who make them. On this account, it cannot be established that any state of affairs really is objectively superior to any other. Strictly speaking, then, honesty is not "better" than deception, generosity is not "better" than cruelty. The most one can say is that someone, or some group of persons, *prefers* one of these states of affairs to another. Preferences are themselves facts of a kind, on a par with any others, but cannot justify ethical conclusions. The British empiricist David Hume formulated this proposition as follows: it is impossible to derive an "ought" from an "is."

In an industrially advanced social order, such ethical skepticism is supported by technological structures. Interacting with machines, human beings notice certain similarities to themselves. If we can understand and relate to machines without bringing in ethical considerations, might we not adopt the same attitude in our relationships to others? That the human body operates according to technological principles is a hypothesis entertained already by the Greek philosophers of antiquity and elaborated in detail by scientists and philosophers such as Harvey and Descartes in the seventeenth century. The heart is a pump of a kind, circulating blood through the body's "plumbing," the limbs are placed into motion by the mechanical tension and relaxation of the body's muscular tissue, and so on. Today, the brain's activities also seem amenable to explanation of this kind. When we see how apparently "intelligent" computers can be, we can scarcely help but ask whether *our* mental functioning is anything more than a variety, albeit a very complex and sophisticated variety, of information-processing. The American psychoanalyst Emanuel Peterfreund grants that computer functioning is much more primitive than that of human beings. He argues nevertheless that "an understanding of the nature of the information processing in existing computers" provides a framework for understanding "certain fundamental aspects of the activity of the central nervous system, and the psychological experiences that correspond to that activity."[2]

"What about feelings?" we may ask. From an information systems perspective, these too may be regarded simply as empirical events, subject to explanation and manipulation like the other processes that occur in the body. This way of viewing the world is not merely theoretical. On the contrary, the practical assumption that, whatever else may be said about human beings, they are materially constituted, biological creatures, is one of the bedrock premises of our culture. Many of us may never have consciously acknowledged that we accept this premise, but we demonstrate our belief in it every time we take an aspirin or vitamin tablet, or pay a visit to the family physician. We assume that the pill, for example, influences us in some causal, physical way, although most of us are pretty much in the dark about the specific chemical and physiological processes that go on inside us.

This "scientific world view," which most of us accept to one degree or another, expands the range of human control over the physical environment, but may also legitimate the replacement of ethical evaluation by technical reason, and ultimately to render superfluous the very idea of a distinctively human subject.

ETHICS AND COMMUNITY

I do not want to counterpoise any particular school of ethics against ethical skepticism, but rather to cite a distinction that is basic to many of them: we recognize a difference between what is valuable only as a means, only because of its usefulness in producing something beyond itself, on the one hand, and what is intrinsically valuable, an end in itself, on the other. Most importantly, we view human life as an ultimate, intrinsic value. Talmudic commentary speaks of its preciousness: "Whoever takes a single life it is as though he destroyed the whole world, and whoever sustains a single life, it is as though he sustained a whole world" (Mishnah 4:9).

Things, like persons, can receive our "respect," in a manner of speaking, as instrumental values. For example, a bomb may demand our "respect" for the amount of damage it can do. We speak idiomatically of the "respectable" performance of an object or device that serves adequately the functions for which it is intended. In this sense a computer or a racing-car performs "respectably" if its operation compares favorably with that of its competitors, as measured by objective criteria of excellence. Respect for human beings, on the other hand, involves more than acknowledgement of their functional value or efficiency – they are valuable in and of themselves. In the eighteenth century, Immanuel Kant designated respect of this quality "ethical" or "moral." It constitutes a relationship between human beings through which they first become subjects, belonging to a community of other beings like themselves. The dignity of persons admits of no logical proof, yet we must recognize that dignity if we are to regard ourselves as human at all.[3]

Notwithstanding the problems we may find with Kant's ethics,[4] his distinction between what we value for its usefulness and what we value as an end-in-itself is essential to any ethical sensibility. Integrated circuit boards, disk drives, keyboards have a "price," in the Kantian sense – these objects are valuable only because of their utility, and one can be substituted for another that serves the same purpose. Human subjects, on the other hand, are literally priceless. Each is precious in his or her own right, each has an intrinsic and irreplaceable value.[5]

The point here is not that we always treat one another as subjects rather than as objects. Indeed people often treat one another callously or cruelly. But even in these cases, the call of conscience is not entirely stilled. To justify themselves, those who mistreat others typically shut out the consequences of their own actions, repressing them from awareness, or they construe their behavior as necessary. In the war against Iraq, for example, both psychological defenses – denial and rationalization – were employed to make the war acceptable. Western media censorship edited out the massive devastation inflicted by this intervention. The humanity of the Iraqi soldiers and civilians had to be denied in order to make their destruction palatable; objectifying descriptions of "collateral damage" and aerial "sorties" obscured a reality of suffering that, if fully acknowledged, might have experienced as intolerable.

Technical discourse of this kind, whether occurring in military or civilian settings, tends to drive out all others. If I am "seeing" the world technically, from the point of view of a military officer mapping out the deployment of his troops or a business executive planning an allocation of personnel, then I may regard my surroundings in functional terms only. Everyone and everything becomes an object or counter within a strategic game whose goal – defeating the enemy, maximizing end-of-quarter profits – is taken for granted. The "objects" manipulated in this way are no longer human subjects. Hence technical discourse, by supplanting ethical reason, literally de-personalizes.[6]

VIRTUOUS TECHNOLOGY

Industrial and technological innovation has not always been associated with a devaluation of life's subjective, ethical aspects. On the contrary, Max Weber in *The Protestant Ethic and the Spirit of Capitalism*, and many others have pointed out that an ideology of individualism, touting such virtues as frugality, discipline, and self-initiative, thrives in an industrial culture. Although this ideology is used to justify exploitation ("individuals," responsible only for themselves, need not look out for anyone else's well-being), it does not dispense with ethical norms altogether. On the contrary, the mechanical technologies that made industrialization possible are value-laden: the structure of the machine echoes that of the stable, rule-governed, well-behaved worker. During the Industrial Revolution of the past centuries, the comparison between the orderly functioning of machinery and that of the virtuous individual has been made many times. Its antecedents go back to late medieval letters and iconography, as in this early fifteenth-century praise of temperance, regarded at the time as the most important of the seven Cardinal Virtues:

> Because our human body is made up of many parts and should be regulated by reason, it may be represented as a clock in which there are several wheels and measures. And just as the clock is worth nothing unless it is regulated, so our human body does not work unless Temperance orders it.[7]

Visual artists in the fifteenth century also took up this theme; see Figure 7.1, in which a variety of well-ordered clock mechanisms illustrates temperance.

In the United States, a long tradition beginning with the Puritans associates technology with virtue. The assumption that technology exercises a morally enlightening influence helped to legitimate the factory system in towns like Lowell, Massachusetts in the early nineteenth century. Socially as well as technologically engineered to maximize productivity, Lowell's factory system was no less celebrated as a marvel of American ingenuity and efficiency than is Silicon Valley today. In the eyes of the system's admirers, machinery made possible the "good" life not only because it generates material prosperity, but also because it embodies an ethics of discipline and order. In a poem entitled "The Manufacturer's Pocket Piece; or the Cotton-Mill Moralized" (1816), Walton Felch eulogizes factory life:

> Remark the moral order reigning here,
> How every part observes its destined sphere;
> Or, if disorder enter the machine,

Figure 7.1 Clock of Wisdom (fifteenth-century France)

A sweeping discord interrupts the scene!
Learn hence, whatever line or life you trace,
In pious awe your proper sphere to grace.[8]

POST-INDUSTRIALISM AND THE "WANING" OF THE SUPEREGO

Ideologies of production in the twentieth century (Taylorism, Fordism) continued to understand machinery in moral terms; efficiency, in humans as in machines, is virtuous. Today, on the other hand, the very notion of "virtue" is often regarded as suspect, or as relevant only to the private aspects of our lives. Consider the fate of one of the traditional Protestant character traits: discipline. Past advocates of modernization, ranging from Turgot and Condorcet in France to Franklin, Webster, and Carnegie in the United States, ranked discipline among the highest virtues, a vehicle of humanity's moral as well as material advance. In many contemporary settings, on the other hand, "discipline" is stripped of its ethical connotations and implies little more than concentrated, diligently self-controlled behavior. Discipline continues to be associated with living a successful life, but "success" is no longer understood in traditional ethical terms.

A psychoanalytic perspective might associate the change in meaning of a word like "discipline" with the historical decline of the superego. Morality, ranging from the Ten Commandments, to Victorian values, appears to play less of a role in contemporary middle-class lives than in the lives of Freud's contemporaries. One might counter that the superego has by no means been disarmed; it continues to reward or berate the self, but not for the traditional religious or moral reasons, not to satisfy dictates of goodness or God. The aim of self-regulation becomes the management and advancement of the "rational" pursuit of a career, love, wealth, or a slim body. The "high-powered professional" has molded herself or himself, sometimes in quite self-punishing ways, to attain these things. In the "Fatherless Society," then, we may find a harsher and more vindictive, not a weaker, superego, although it is one that no longer expresses the proverbial "voice of conscience."

A study of North American lifestyles entitled *Habits of the Heart* attests to the diminishing influence of shared ethical values that previously linked the lives of individuals within communities, churches, and other social settings. The interviewees tend to view their surroundings strategically, as a means for getting what they want out of life, but without any meaning or value that goes beyond their functionality. For example, Margaret Oldham, a therapist, speaks of the basis for her own orientation toward life as follows:

> It really sort of comes down to the authority I say I give my values ... all those sorts of goals I've set up for myself, that kind of motivate me and tell me which way to go, what to avoid.[9]

According to this study, even when individuals act on behalf of others, they typically do so in a moral vacuum. Interviewee Brian Palmer, a manager in a Silicon Valley corporation, made the decision at a certain point in his career to spend less time at work and more time with his family. But he could justify his judgment only in terms of personal preferences, "I just find that I get more personal satisfaction from choosing course B over course A. It makes me feel better about myself."[10] In Brian's world, there exists no ethical frame of reference capable of legitimating his or anyone else's choices.

The authors of *Habits of the Heart* do not elaborate on the ways that the structure of an information-based social order contributes to the exclusion of moral considerations. The very notion of *information* suggests value-neutrality. Information is something we take to be more or less useful, and its processing, by machines or by people, is measured in terms of efficiency, not according to ethical standards. This implies that, inasmuch as we regard what we do at work, in school, or elsewhere in our lives as the processing of information, traditional value judgments of right and wrong tend to lose their relevance. Constraints of an *ethical* variety get displaced by functional, procedural requirements to which people conform in the pursuit of self-interest. Of course, this displacement occurred also in the industrial contexts of the past. But these contexts were counterposed to such settings as family, church, and neighborhood environments that were somewhat sheltered from instrumental reason. In these "enclaves," people could still regard themselves as subject to traditional moral standards. Such standards were often repressive and aligned with patriarchal authority, yet they provided a basis for mutual respect and support. Viewing their workplace relationships as analogous to the personal relationships in other areas of their lives, working people protested against the conditions of industrial labor partly on the grounds that they violated fundamental ethical standards of human decency and justice.

In post-industrial situations, on the other hand, human beings are linked in ways that traditional ethical codes, oriented toward personal, face-to-face relationships, can scarcely recognize. Post-industrial production, marketing, and communications are bureaucratically organized on a global basis. Information technologies are developed and deployed with little respect for national boundaries or local cultures. A circuit board assembled by women in Manila, using chips manufactured in Kyoto, is inserted into a computer at a facility in San Diego and ends up sitting on my desk here in Berkeley. Such complex structures of production are fairly opaque to most of the participants – as opaque as the internal design of a computer is to most of its users – and therefore escape critical scrutiny. Only in extreme situations does the global character of interaction and interdependence come to light. Referring to one such instance, the worldwide dispersal of radioactivity from the Chernobyl nuclear accident, Ulrich Beck notes that "The most intimate – say, nursing a child – and the most distant, most general – say a reactor accident in the Ukraine ... are now suddenly *directly* connected."[11] Dependence and risk may be global, but ethical responsibility is not. Traditional ethical belief systems, providing for the governance of local, relatively simple and personal relationships, provide little or no guidance when it comes to the complex, technically mediated relationships characteristic of post-industrial settings.

ETHICS AND INFORMATION TECHNOLOGY

The irony of technological innovation, then, is that it links geographically remote cultures, while at the same time narrowing the attention of individuals to matters of technical detail. This narrowing is a consequence of involvement with industrial technologies (with one's attention focussed on the machine, or its product, one scarcely notices anything else) but is carried even further by the introduction of information technologies. Information-processing, by machines or by people, is procedure-governed reason that tends to blot out the larger contexts, including the possible ethical implications, of judgments and behaviors.

At the beginning of this chapter, I quoted a computer programmer, Sam, who already as an adolescent disavowed any non-empirical reality; for him, what is, is factual. Sam recalled that as a child:

> My parents weren't strict with me at all. No ten commandments or anything like that. They let me do pretty much what I wanted. In fact we did little together. They both worked and were gone during the day. So I had the house all to myself for long stretches of time. I remember knocking about the house like a loose atom, going from room to room not knowing what to do with myself. There was plenty of space to do whatever, but not much of anything to do.

These memories do not confirm the traditional psychoanalytic story in which the child, intensely involved in conflictual relationships with other members of the family, internalizes parental authority in the form of superego or "conscience." On the contrary, neglectful parents placed scarcely any boundaries at all, physical or moral, on what Sam was permitted to do.

Without guidance or attention, however, Sam could scarcely appreciate his "liberty" to do as he pleased. There is a continuity between his childhood, as he remembers it, and his life as an adult. At work, too, he is pretty much left alone; he is assigned to certain projects and given certain tasks to accomplish, but no one tells him how to carry them out. He finds his employment intellectually challenging and well paid. Yet he experiences a void at the very heart of this success. Notwithstanding his apparent "autonomy," his feelings of emptiness and depression brought him into psychotherapy.

Sam works in a milieu that directs his attention to the construction of technical means for achieving given ends; one does not ask questions about these ends themselves, about the fundamental purposes that technological objects serve. This situation is not unusual. Work in post-industrial settings tends to amount to fulfillment of a highly specialized function or role. As social contrivances of a kind for the efficient accomplishment of given ends, roles embody what Weber and Frankfurt School theorists like Horkheimer, Marcuse, and Habermas have called "instrumental," "functional," or "technical" reason. Although these notions are not synonymous, they all refer to procedural, means–ends rationality, which these authors agree is formative, but also potentially disintegrative, of modern culture and the individual. Habermas describes the following historical transition:

The life conduct of specialists is dominated by cognitive-instrumental attitudes toward themselves and others. Traditional ethical obligations to one's calling [as in Calvinist Protestantism, for example] give way to instrumental attitudes toward an occupational role that offers the opportunity for income and advancement, but no longer for ascertaining one's personal salvation or for fulfilling oneself in a secular sense.[12]

The distinction here between a traditional "calling" and an instrumental "occupational role" is elaborated by Alasdair MacIntyre in his analysis of the notions of *virtue* and *character*.[13] Virtue contributes to the fulfillment of the human *telos*, a purpose that is simultaneously social and individual, a supernatural as well as a natural good that is realized through, but is not external to, the means that brings it about. The utilitarian, on the other hand, measures action only in terms of advantageous consequences; cost–benefit analysis generates the strategy most likely to maximize the agent's return.

MacIntyre associates virtue with traditional character, which signifies a moral and cultural ideal that integrates human existence within a shared social world. Character of this kind tends to be supplanted in contemporary industrial societies by strategic reason. To the extent that social roles are loosened from any moral nexus and become merely technical competencies, they fail to support the identities of their performers. Unlike a *calling*, in the Calvinist sense, these roles do not confer a stable personal identity enabling one to recognize oneself and to be recognized by others within a community of shared traditions and values.

Some psychotherapists speak of a "healing" or "restoration" of the self, as if at one time there existed a psychic unity that is now damaged or broken. But if it is only within a world of meaningful, non-instrumental relationships that the notion of a "self" makes sense, then the "crisis of the self" is bound up with the crisis of an entire civilization that has lost its ethical bearings, a civilization in which – as Kant might have put it – everything has its price, but nothing has a value.

Chapter 8

Recognition

Human individuality is not simply given but is socially constructed. One's status as an individual depends on recognition, by others and by oneself, of that status. But "recognition" has different meanings in different cultural settings. In the West, it has signified above all a *personal* relationship among selves, on the model of the link between God and His subjects in the Judaeo-Christian tradition. In the past, institutional roles, even when they have been exploitative and demeaning, have given a certain support to such relationships of recognition. In the workshops of medieval European towns, for instance, masters and their journeymen and apprentices worked together intimately. Apprentices typically lived in the homes of their masters and could be considered members of their families. Centuries later, workers in small capitalist enterprises got to know one another, as well as those in authority over them, quite well; human relationships, although oppressive, were personal.

Modern technologies, on the other hand, implement social arrangements that often diminish such direct recognition, together with the individuality it defines. Technological innovation substitutes abstract and anonymous procedural relationships for the more personal relationships of the past. In corporations, schools, and government bureaus, the functional coordination of diverse human behaviors minimizes spontaneous interactions that might interfere with the planned and predictable functioning of the system as a whole. Strictly speaking, formal procedures, those governing a state service agency, for example, apply not to persons at all but to "cases," characterized by abstract properties that a database can store and manipulate. In these contexts, human interactions can scarcely proceed at all in the absence of technological mediation. When the computer goes down, the social service-provider shrugs his or her shoulders and reschedules the client's appointment. Without access to the information stored inside the machine, nothing can be done.

Bureaucratic authority is of course nothing new. But the post-industrial integration of information technologies with productive and administrative functions introduces further qualitative changes into the domain of everyday experience. Tracing the social history of this rationalizing process will help us understand it better.

AN HISTORICAL OVERVIEW

Formal, procedural relationships have characterized Western societies for many centuries. In the past, though, they combined with human interactions based on personal recognition to contribute to the formation of relatively stable, socially anchored human identities. In the Greek *polis*, a legal procedural system defined the formal civil rights of citizens (excluding slaves and women). At the same time, the city-state was small enough to permit a unification of the political and the personal; the legal status of Greek citizens established at least in theory a secure basis for mutual respect and recognition.

Christianity, too, provided a shared framework of belief and expectations that could integrate the procedural, impersonal aspects of institutional life with personal faith. St Augustine conjoined what he calls the "City of Man," the worldly realm in which people look after their diverse worldly interests, with the "City of God," whose members are united with one another in the body of Christ. Roman Catholicism continued this tradition through the Middle Ages. When the Church Fathers of the eleventh and twelfth centuries elaborated a system of canonical law regulating relations among the faithful, they drew upon such classical sources as Cicero's "Of Friendship," and the perfect Biblical friendship of David and Jonathan, to make the point that good Christians understand and love one another. Anselm and Abelard, for example, emphasized that compassion for Christ's suffering not only links believers to the Lord but also unites them in a caring community.

There was, however, a polarizing dialectic at work here. Medieval Christianity acknowledged the role of individual prayer and belief in achieving salvation, but there was a hazard in this: private faith might disengage itself from the procedure-based official doctrines and practices of the Church. The "Imitation of Christ" credo that in the twelfth century attracted a considerable following, consisting of "those who live in Him, that is, imitate his life," bypassed the mediation of the clerical hierarchy and came to be perceived as a threat to its authority.[1]

Similarly, the teaching of St Francis of Assisi about the paramount importance of a personal relationship with the Savior appeared to dispense with the need for any Church intercession. In one of Giotto's paintings of the Stigmatization (Figure 8.1), Francis' encounter with Christ is direct and intensely intimate. But in the middle panel at the bottom of the painting, Francis receives official approval from the Church for the new order established in his name. The deeper wisdom of the Church Fathers was that Francis' emphasis upon the personal quality of faith would serve to strengthen the institutional authority of Catholicism rather than call it into question.

That authority was more seriously threatened by the urbanization and commercialization of late medieval Europe. An expanding market economy coexisted uneasily with the Church. Market relationships evidently obeyed a secular logic of their own, endangering the hegemonic control of clerical administrators. Many expressed misgivings about the trade in commodities of every variety that flourished in late medieval cities. It was critical, they believed, that such activity

Figure 8.1 The Stigmatization of St Francis (Giotto, early fifteenth century)

should occur under the watchful eyes of the Church, as both visual representations and textual sources of the time make clear.

Consider a fifteenth-century artist's representation of a fair in medieval France (Figure 8.2). Notice that the centrifugal tendency of market activity, possibly indifferent or even antagonistic to traditional religious precepts, is held in check by the personal presence and authority of the Church Fathers at its center, serving as the hub about which the wheel of exchange relations is organized and held together. We see in the background the rounded temporary stalls occupied by visiting merchants. The shops of local craftsmen and merchants are depicted in the foreground; hanging above the front doors of some of them are emblems identifying particular trades. The division and specialization of labor represented here played a critical role in the transformation of social relations in the late medieval period in Europe. As methods of commodity transport and exchange between and within local municipalities were refined, it became increasingly profitable for one region to specialize in a particular product: wool, silk, gold- or silverware, wine, wooden artifacts, or another item of exchange. Within the confines of the municipality, a sharpening division of labor differentiated economic trades from one another.

One consequence of this development was the replacement of perennial, face-to-face relations by new and relatively anonymous processes of commodity

Figure 8.2 Medieval Fair in France (fifteenth century)

exchange: local townspeople buy from or sell to merchants and craftspeople with whom they may have no connection outside of the economic transaction. This new reality, including a market mechanism that organizes human activity "behind the backs" of its agents, is only half-acknowledged in the medieval representation mentioned above. As if denying the changes that have taken place, all human activities here, including those of market exchange, unfold in an orderly manner under the jurisdiction and direct observation of the local Bishop and his associates, whose many eyes view everything from on high.

No less challenging to Church authority than the marketplace pursuit of self-interest by anonymous agents was the separation of urban activity from its rural surroundings during the late Middle Ages. This, too, the artist is not fully prepared to admit. The shepherd and his flock in the foreground of the picture are included within the circle of commercial activities. Preserved, in art if not in reality, is the sense that everyone remains a member of a single community, united and ruled through the personally exercised authority of local magistrates and the Church.

One of the main accomplishments of the Protestant Reformation was containment of the secular, divisive tendencies introduced into the traditional *Ecclesia* (the unified community of believers) by economic and political rationalization. The Protestant confessions, like orthodox Catholicism, aimed to join personal faith with reason and religious authority, although they to some extent withdrew that authority from Church practices and located it instead in the conscience of the individual. The Protestant notion of a *vocation* or *calling* signifies at once a worldly role and a religious commitment. In Calvinist Amsterdam in the seventeenth century, jurists, physicians, civil and religious administrators defined themselves in terms of their work, rendering them visible to one another and to the public at large as individuals worthy of recognition and respect. Within such a community, one's *calling* is simultaneously rational and personal; rational inasmuch as it systematizes and formalizes one's everyday activities, personal in that a calling delineates an identity, manifest in one's professional standing, code of conduct, and private life, that is recognized by others and oneself. It is this identity that peers out at us from the numerous seventeenth-century portraits of Dutch burghers, visibly self-confident and at home in a world of their own making.

One of these portraits, Jan Steen's *The Burgher of Delft and his Daughter* (Figure 8.3), illustrates the way in which the public and the personal were reconciled at this time. At first take, there is something odd about this representation. The presumable intention of the picture is to acknowledge the admirable qualities of this administrative official, including his prosperity and benevolence. Yet, there is no indication that he will respond directly to the outstretched hand of the woman who begs on behalf of her child and herself. Instead of alms, he holds in his hand a paper which, one historian has remarked, "may be the license announcing the woman and child to be themselves *of residence*."[2] So licensed, these indigents would qualify for public, institutional assistance. Instead of relying on individual charity to take care of the poor and the sick, the officials of Dutch cities organized public orphanages, almshouses, and hospitals to administer to those deemed unable

Figure 8.3 The Burgher of Delft and his Daughter (Jan Steen, 1655)

to take care of themselves. Indeed the indigent fared better under this rationalized administration than in other European countries where they still relied on hand-outs from the well-to-do. In Steen's painting, it is as if the burgher of Delft is saying, "I need not take care of you personally, because procedures are in place for handling your situation."

TOWARD AN IDEOLOGY-FREE SOCIETY?

Each of these syntheses of the personal and the procedural was founded upon a worldview that encompassed both. In Greek antiquity, *Logos*, the supreme principle of collective as well as individual reason, played this role, uniting the particular and the universal, the private and the public. During the Middle Ages and Reformation in Europe, Christian faith unified Church and State and provided an overarching framework, characterized metaphorically as a "sacred canopy," that blended regard for persons, on the one hand, with regard for institutional authority, on the other.[3]

A similar metaphor was the Christian "Great Chain Being,"[4] linking all things on heaven and earth. This unifying image retained its power well into the eighteenth century; it could be given an evolutionary reading, in keeping with modern ideas of economic "progress" and individualism, by emphasizing the importance of the Great Chain's individual links; these alone make the chain strong. There is some continuity between the "Great Chain" metaphor and Adam Smith's idea that an "invisible hand" guarantees that the pursuit of private interest will benefit society as a whole. Individualism, as formulated by the laissez-faire economists and empiricist philosophers of the eighteenth and nineteenth centuries was thought to contribute to a harmonious and prosperous social order held together by underlying shared commitments to fairness, justice, and responsibility.

In this century, these grand ideologies have lost much of their credibility. Ours is an age of unmasking and cynicism that tends to regard the proclaimed public values of the past – self-sacrifice, community service, patriotism, and the like – as rhetorical devices serving manipulative interests. To be sure, contemporary leaders continue to speak in the name of these values and to draw upon the old ideological allegiances and identities. An occasional military adventure in a Third World country, accompanied perhaps by a speech about a "New World Order," may capture television viewers' attention momentarily, but a few minutes later they will probably be switching channels. While fundamentalist Christianity remains a powerful force in certain Western societies, it persists more as a reaction than as an antidote to the fragmentation and de-personalization of everyday life. We still have our symbol systems and unifying mythologies, elaborated in the mass media and the marketplace; human well-being is linked, for instance, to technology: Apple, IBM, and Microsoft will supposedly usher us into a better organized and more prosperous future. But access to computer terminals – or, for that matter, to television screens – cannot provide, except superficially, such experiences of belonging and recognition as are characteristic of ethnic, religious, and other traditional affiliations.

PRE-INDUSTRIAL, INDUSTRIAL, POST-INDUSTRIAL

Three depictions of family life (Figures 8.4, 8.5, and 8.6), taken from different historical periods, illustrate the processes of secularization outlined above. The first, *The Marriage of Giovanni Arnolfini and Giovanna Cenami* (Figure 8.4) painted by Jan Van Eyck in 1434, is a portrait of a fifteenth-century bourgeois and his new bride. The convex mirror at the center of the painting reflects two witnesses to the marriage, and the painter himself appears to be one of them. He has signed the painting "Johannes de Eyck fuit hic" (Jan Van Eyck was here). He probably played a role as a legal witness certifying the fact of this wedding.[5] The official, procedural character of the event by no means detracts, however, from the mutual and personal recognition that links Arnolfini, the bride, and the painter who witnesses their nuptial union.

The material reality represented in the painting testifies in detail to the Christian meaning of the marriage that is its subject. A "disguised symbolism"[6] gives to worldly objects a transcendent significance. For example, the dog that links the two human figures at the bottom of the work, and the single lit candle in the chandelier designate fidelity. The wooden shoes at the lower left indicate the sanctity of the marriage contract and ceremony by alluding to God's admonition to Moses, "put off thy shoes from off thy feet, for the place whereon thou standest is holy ground."[7] The mirror at the center of the painting, symbol of the immaculate Virgin, is surrounded by ten scenes of the Passion that have been set into its frame and that further elaborate Mary's virtues. The man lifts his right hand to pledge his faith and holds in his left the hand of his betrothed. Everything is solemnly meaningful and connected within a Christian world that unites the visible and the invisible, material affluence and spiritual commitment.

The Arnolfini marriage portrait gives visual representation to ideals of harmony and happiness that continue to shape the way we imagine family life should be. This construction is caricatured by a British artist, Richard Hamilton, in his collage of everyday life in the 1950s, *Just What Is it that Makes Today's Homes so Different, so Appealing?* (Figure 8.5). Here, too, as in Van Eyck's painting five centuries earlier, an entire culture receives expression through the material artifacts of a domestic environment. In place of the mirror with its surrounding Biblical representations, a "Young Romance" magazine (also a mirror of a kind) conveys fantasies of sex and love, suggested also by other media alluded to in the collage: movies and television. As in the case of the Van Eyck painting, various everyday objects contribute to the scene's symbolic meaning: a lollipop, automobile decoration, and a canned ham all signify the "good life." The dog at the feet of the Arnolfini pair has been replaced by a tape-recorder, designating auditory fidelity (the faithful reproduction of the voice) rather than the more traditional spiritual variety. Unlike the Van Eyck representation, however, in Hamilton's there is virtually no human relationship at all. Fantasy no longer points to any reality beyond its own images. A Charles Atlas representation of a man is adjacent to one of a sexually desirable woman. But no recognizable person is visible behind any of the facades represented here, including the efficient, vacuum-cleaning housewife (she comes closest to being "real) and the woman answering the telephone on the television screen.

Hamilton's collage is now nearly forty years old. The most highly esteemed commodities today are not those that entranced us decades ago. At mid-century, there was an aura of specialness about advanced technological objects of that time:

Figure 8.4 The Marriage of Giovanni Arnolfini and Giovanna Cenami (Jan Van Eyck, 1434)

Figure 8.5 Just What Is it that Makes Today's Homes so Different, so Appealing? (Richard Hamilton, 1956)

automobiles, tape-recorders, vacuum cleaners, television. Today it is information technology that impresses. In a collage made in 1992, entitled *The Family that Information-Processes Together* (Figure 8.6), the most significant domestic object is the desktop computer terminal. The crowning IBM logo and McDonald's arch function like icons of medieval Christianity to articulate a culture-wide symbolism. The title of the collage alludes to the Christian adage, "The family that prays together, stays together." Today, however, a user's manual and on-screen help messages prove more effective than a Christian Bible in supplying everyday guidance toward what we believe we need. Lost souls are those who have not yet logged into the Information Age.

All three of these artistic representations take a domestic interior as their subject

Figure 8.6 The Family that Information-Processes Together (Jos Sances and Raymond Barglow, 1992)

matter. In each case, everyday objects articulate an ideology that defines a way of life and provides role models. In the Van Eyck wedding portrait (Figure 8.4), life's procedural and personal aspects are joined by a Christian faith that renders its two subjects visible to one another and to members of the community, including the painter himself. In the collage *The Family that Information-Processes Together*, on the other hand, the personal has been all but eliminated; the domestic information-processing partners represented here are blanked out, as if to suggest that their technically mediated and abstract connection to the world via "personal computers" effaces them as persons.

THE ELECTRONIC OFFICE

Unlike traditional Christianity, a post-industrial culture can scarcely maintain even the pretense of supporting a unified community. Whereas *faith, hope,* and *charity* are evaluative concepts that link human beings in meaningful and personal ways, *information, megabyte,* and *computer literacy* characterize an objectified, presumably value-free world of machine–person relations. Today, people still participate in systems that integrate their activities, but consider the qualitative change that has taken place in the character of their interactions. The modern "electronic" office pictured on the cover of *Byte* for May 1983 (Figure 8.7) represents not just an environment, but an entire, self-contained world. White dots spread randomly across a black expanse, and circuit paths in the shape of comets, suggest the depths of outer space. Information-processors – machines and people – occupy an abstract grid of pathways, receding infinitely into the background and detached from any reality beyond itself. In this automated office, each individual works at his or her own work station, linked only via the network that distributes and collects information. Each is a node, a receiver and sender of information, the representation suggests, like an electronic component or "chip" plugged into a circuit board. As such components are designed to perform preassigned functions within the system to which they belong, so human individuals fill information-processing roles within the office organization.

Human beings who laugh or get angry, whose bodies suffer, desire, and enjoy – these the automated office dispenses with. What is essential for survival is being connected into the information network. Removed from the system, one might become as aimless and lifeless as an electronic component pulled from a circuit board, the only place where it is able to function.

PSEUDO-RECOGNITION

The electronic office is above all clean and efficient. The old-fashioned desk clutter of papers and pencils, files and memos, along with the clatter of typewriters and display of personal paraphernalia have been eliminated. Information relations, not material relations, link consciousness to consciousness: at the office, linked into the institutional system, life makes a certain sense. And when the working day is over, what then? As if imitating the specialized functions of the world of work, private life tends to fragment into "lifestyle enclaves": isolated domains of private activity mediated only by mass media technologies. The model here is the modern apartment dweller, who does not know her or his neighbor on either side, although they watch the same television programs.

Post-industrial settings have little use for the framework of family, religious, and community associations that make people visible to one another in many traditional societies. In the study *Habits of the Heart*, cited in note 9 in Chapter 7, the apparent disengagement of the interviewees from traditional cultural contexts is striking. One of the responses to what might be called "narrative deprivation" –

Figure 8.7 The electronic office
Source: Byte: the Small Systems Journal (May 1983)

the absence of stories or myths in terms of which people can situate themselves and make sense of their lives – is the attempt to reinvigorate customs and affiliations of the past. We take out the family album and trace our genealogy; we embrace the idea of returning to our ethnic "roots," doing our best to recreate meaning and purpose. Fundamentalist religions have proven especially effective in this regard. In Western countries, individual souls are recruited via radio and television channels that disseminate the Gospel message to households isolated from one another, but tuned in to God. The popularity of televangelism testifies to a longing for meaning, community, and personal recognition that current post-industrial environments fail to satisfy.

Fundamentalism's premise is that those who are "saved" recognize the Savior and are in turn recognized by Him. This recognition is intensely personal. Incarnate in Jesus, God is no longer the venerable patriarch of the Old Testament, a stern, invisible, and rather remote father. In the New Testament, God's intimate attention to individual souls becomes paramount. Even in moments of greatest darkness and aloneness, He is there with us, comforting us, and His light illuminates our lives. What is most appealing about this is the personal care and recognition that the Lord gives to each believer. This is the glue that readheres millions to a fundamentalist Christian faith. Jim Bakker who, prior to the scandal that brought about his downfall, was the most popular Christian evangelist on television, concluded his daily broadcasts to the millions in his audience with this sign-off: "Remember, God loves you." His wife Tammy, always at his side, would add "He really, really does."

The message endlessly repeated by televangelists like the Bakkers, Pat Robertson, and Jimmy Swaggart is that the believer is never solitary, but is *personally* looked after, with an infinite love. Christ is, above all, a familiar and devoted friend. A television producer for the Christian Broadcasting Network (CBN) describes Pat Robertson's approach:

> No matter who the guest [on Robertson's talkshow] was, he or she placed extreme emphasis on the personal aspect of a relationship with Jesus. A typical studio interview would include some variation of the question "Have you known him long?"; Him refers to the Lord. The guest's answers would feature the exact date they met Jesus. Jesus was very, very real to both the host and the guest ... Pat would look into the cameras and ask if you, too, would really like to know Jesus as your personal savior.[8]

Religion is not the only enterprise that claims to speak to the contemporary need for recognition. Artificial "recognition" is the gloss that sells wares of nearly every variety: a Duncan Hines cake-mix advertisement empathizes with the predicament of a harried mother who needs to prepare a delicious desert in a hurry. McDonald's slogan is "You. You're the one." At a savings and loan bank, tellers are instructed to remember the names of the firm's regular clients and to address them by their names whenever possible.[9] In the political realm, too, an electoral campaign's chance of success depends on convincing the voters that the candidate is a genuine, caring person. A politician's pitch to the voters, "I understand your problem, and identify with your situation" opens their hearts (even if it closes their minds) and wins their respect and allegiance. Reagan's presidency was "teflon-coated": no criticism could be made to stick, in part because voters felt that Ronald Reagan, like a good (if occasionally absent-minded) father, sympathized with them and recognized their needs.

RECOGNITION'S FUTURE

Recognition remains a hallmark of individualism in Western societies; one is an individual in so far as one is personally acknowledged by others. Yet artificial forms of recognition like those discussed above fail to alleviate people's sense that they are under-recognized, under-respected, invisible. The "disenchantment of the world" (Max Weber) involved in rationalizing processes leaves behind disenchanted, isolated inhabitants. Information technology, incorporated within bureaucratic structures of institutional administration, contributes to this disenchantment. This observation confronts us with a crucial question: assuming that we continue to use advanced technologies, and that society's complex division of labor remains in place, how is interpersonal recognition to be reconciled with the rationalizing features of modernity?

Automation and other applications of information technologies are capable of making our lives more efficient in certain ways, but they may lead as well to new forms of depersonalization, disenfranchisement, and fragmentation. Each of the past configurations of social order discussed above – from the medieval urban commune through the Protestant Reformation to the "consumer society" – attempted to bring together the personal and the impersonal, the abstract and concrete dimensions of human existence. What possibilities are there today for such reconciliation?

Chapter 9

Identification

Personal identity is a process, not a state of being. It develops partly through acts of identification: we form ourselves through imitation and assimilation of the traits of others. Typically, the roles that permit identification to take place integrate physical activity and social meaning. In pre-industrial cultures, for instance, such practices as hunting, gathering, farming, food preparation, and crafts involve visible bodily movement on the part of parents or other adults whom children can imitate and on whom they can model themselves. An industrial civilization, too, provides models of behavior, including manual labor, that can be transmitted from one generation to the next. But in post-industrial settings, the world is literally quieted down, bodies are stilled, and participation in identity-forming interpersonal activities occurs quite differently, and often more problematically, than in the past.

Freud argues that the ego is in the beginning a "body ego." Our first identification is with the embodied beings that we are. A child's originally experienced boundaries are those of the body – this "mortal coil" with which we have a special involvement unlike our relationship with any other object. For many centuries, philosophers have tried to understand the nature of this relationship. St Thomas Aquinas, for instance, argues that what differentiates human beings from angels and also individuates them from one another is their physical nature. He then poses the perennial metaphysical question: how are people related to their own materiality? The human body does not exist as only one more objective entity in the world among others, but is "lived," inhabited by the subject with a quality of familiarity that is not easily put into words. Each person is involved with a specific domain of flesh and bone that "belongs" in an especially intimate way to oneself. Searching for a way to describe the connection of subjectivity to objectivity, Aquinas compares it to that of tool-wielder and tool: the body is the instrument of the soul.[1]

This conception of personhood was further developed several centuries later in the dualism of Descartes, and has been one of the mainstays of the Western philosophical tradition: we learn to identify with the mind, and to regard the body as something that is not quite, or not entirely, us. Yet both Aquinas and Descartes recognized the shortcomings of this model. An instrument may be picked up and wielded or laid down and abandoned by its user. Our bodies are not as readily dispensable. As Merleau-Ponty points out, the body is not just another object external to ourselves:

> If my arm is resting on the table I should never think of saying that it is *beside* the ashtray in the way in which the ashtray is beside the telephone ... my whole body for me is not an assemblage of organs juxtaposed in space. I am in undivided possession of it and know where each of my limbs is through a *body image* in which all are included.[2]

This body image, Merleau-Ponty explains, is not something static, like a reflection in a mirror or a snapshot taken by an observer. It is an experience of the body in actual or potential movement – I move my arm with an immediacy that is not there in my relationship to the ashtray or telephone apparatus. "It is clearly in action," Merleau-Ponty says, "that the spatiality of our body is brought into being."[3]

"Action" here means physical movement. Before farms, factories, and offices were automated, work was centered in bodily activities. Even today, of course, some physical motion is indispensable for the reproduction of everyday life. But what happens when people spend many hours daily motionless in front of a computer or television monitor? According to Merleau-Ponty, "We do not merely behold as spectators the relations between the parts of our body ... we are ourselves the unifier of these arms and legs." When arms and legs are sleeping for long periods of time and mental activity occupies a stationary body, what becomes of this "unifier"?

THE DISEMBODIED SUBJECT

The separation of the mind from the body has become a cliché. The methods for trying to connect with it again are many; body therapies, massage, yoga promise to help us relearn how to touch, to feel, to reintegrate our material nature with ourselves. One of the dreams discussed previously began: "I want to know whether my room is cold or warm. So I log into my computer to find out. Suddenly millions of symbols splash on to the four walls of the room and I'm lost. I don't know for sure the symbols for hot and cold" (see p. 87, Chapter 6). Absent here is the bodily awareness that informs us in an immediate way about our surroundings, about the ambient temperature in this case. Cut off from this access, the dreamer loses his psychological bearings. He pictures himself as an Ancient Mariner, at sea with "nary a drop to drink" and comments that "I don't feel I'm myself in the dream."

Failing to experience oneself as embodied, one's personal identity may appear to vanish altogether. A young man, Samuel, dreamt:

> *I looked in the mirror, but all I could see was an outline, like a metal cookie-cutter with nothing inside. I was a gingerbread man with no ginger and no bread. Then everything was waving, like a video-screen where you cannot tune in anything solid. Suddenly, I'm looking down at my own body, it's like a scaffolding or erector set – all girders, frame, but no substance. "It is this that walks*

and talks and breathes," I thought to myself, "and it could all just fall apart on the floor." Maybe I was just a concept, an organization in someone's head, and if they stopped thinking me I wouldn't exist any longer.

Ever since he could remember, Samuel had regarded himself as, above all, an intelligence. For children as well as for adults, identification with the mind provides a measure of security. One detaches oneself from unpredictable and possibly dangerous situations, which one's reason can then analyze and perhaps disarm. Samuel realized, however, that being what Aristotle called a "rational animal" does not make one invulnerable. For that which is mental is "an organization in someone's head," and therefore possibly transient. The idea behind identification with the world of ideas is escape from perishable matter, from one's own physical vulnerability. The drawback is, in the words of the dream, that abstraction-based identity may leave "nothing inside."

Let us recall, though, that mind–matter dualism is centuries old. We can find it already in Plato. Only under certain conditions does it call personal identity into question. A key factor here is the availability of role models that unify mental and physical aspects of everyday activities. According to the classical psychoanalytic paradigm, babies remain "attached" to their mothers psychologically, without a clear sense of their own separateness. Eventually this attachment is replaced by relationships of identification. "Normal development" signifies that little girls identify with their mothers, little boys with their fathers. We may agree with critics of this orthodoxy in rejecting its specific scenarios of the formation of individual, gendered subjects; yet its emphasis upon the contribution that identification makes to that formation is well taken. Human identity depends on a history of identifications; we become the persons we are in part through identifying ourselves with others.

Identification and gender-formation are closely linked. Girls' conception of themselves as potential mothers involves an awareness of the physical aspects of bearing children. Similarly, boys pattern their own activities and understanding of themselves on the visible tasks performed by men. Robert Bly writes that in most tribal cultures:

> The father and son spend hours trying and failing together to make arrowheads or to repair a spear or track a clever animal. When a father and son spend long hours together, which some fathers and sons still do, we could say that a substance almost like food passes from the older body to the younger.[4]

As Bly notes, sharing of this kind does not occur only in tribal societies. Medieval forms of work, for instance, engaged in by peasants or townspeople, typically consisted of activities that even a young child could perceive and begin to comprehend. Manual labor functions similarly in an industrial society; when a father explains to his child that he is a car mechanic, furniture salesman, printer, plumber, or construction worker, perhaps by showing the child photographs or having the child visit him at work, this will not leave the child utterly mystified. By the same token, girls growing up in traditional households in which the mother carries out domestic chores, sews for a living, or does other manual work, can grasp fairly easily what it is that their mothers do.

Not all roles are equally comprehensible, however. "My mom is a housewife." "Mine is a systems analyst." A child is apt to have a clearer idea of what a housewife does than of what a systems analyst does. The transition to an information-based economy accelerates the replacement of manual by conceptual labor. White collars replace blue ones, and the previously transparent work of many parents becomes obscure to their children. One tells one's daughter or son that one is an accountant, corporate attorney, claims adjuster, or database manager – roles that a child can barely begin to imagine, let alone imitate or identity with.

Even in their roles as parents, many mothers and fathers no longer occupy traditional positions of authority that can be passed on to their children. In many families, the father has lost his status as the sovereign patriarch with whom or against whom a son can identify. The traditional roles of mothers, too, are no longer idealized in the ways they once were. On the contrary, in such television shows as *All in the Family* and its successors, mothers and fathers are routinely ridiculed, often by their own children, as ignorant, inept, and out of touch. In this sense, ours is not only a "fatherless society,"[5] but a "motherless" one also. Parental authority is mediated and mitigated by the subjection of children to various forms of institutional control, including schools and day-care centers, social service agencies, medical and mental care facilities, and television. These institutional authorities treat children more impersonally than do parents, and provide minimal opportunities for identification that enable children to pattern themselves after others.[6]

In the traditional locations where personal identity is formed – families, schools, and workplaces – so-called "normal" role models have been oppressive in many ways. We may nevertheless acknowledge, without romanticizing the conventions and ideals of the past, that these models made possible the formation of the individual identities with which an older generation is most familiar.

FATHERS AND SONS

In contemporary families, children continue to identify with their parents, of course. But this dynamic unfolds in ways that are specific to post-industrial settings. A programmer, Andy, dreams:

> *I'm in my father's house, which has a computer downstairs. He's away on a trip, but my mother and brothers are home. In the middle of the night I hear a pattern of clicks that I can't understand. Unknown to me, there is someone knocking at the door downstairs. The sound is being received by the computer – I hear it reproduced only as a series of clicks, not carrying any of the threat of a loud banging on the door. I wonder why the computer is behaving in this way. The lights in the house go on. I feel drowsy and confused; it turns out that the noise*

is not an intruder after all, but my father calling long distance. He asks to talk to me, so I pick up the receiver. But I hear nothing; either my father has hung up or the line has gone dead.

Computational imagery is interwoven here with Oedipal symbolism: occupancy of the house might allude to possession of the mother, "banging on the door" to aggression on the part of the conveniently absent but threatening-to-return father. But the information-processing mediation between the dreamer and his father raises issues not only of power and competition but also of communication and isolation. The dreamer is literally out of contact with the world; he cannot hear the banging on the door, or the voice of his father calling him. The dreamer picks up the phone to talk, but it is too late (at the time of this dream, Andy's father had already died). The missing conversation with his father will never happen. The dream expresses Andy's childhood experiences of feeling hopelessly distant from his father. Computer clicks are no substitute for what a child needs from a parent. Borne out by this dream, and by nearly every dream cited in this book, is the revisionist psychoanalytic proposition that "The real libidinal aim is the establishment of satisfactory relationships," as Fairbairn argues.[7]

Information technology is an especially appropriate symbolic vehicle for Andy, in part because of the ways in which his situation at work resembles his early family environment. This is another of his dreams:

I'm on vacation with some very smart, computer guru types. They tell me it's desirable to be the main processor on a system. For the peripheral users, logging in via remote terminals, life is slow. I reply that I come in through a peripheral board on the computer. They are incredulous. Why do I do that, when I could be accessing the main processor directly? I review in my mind the reasons why I access the microprocessor indirectly, via the motherboard ... It would be too involved to explain all of this to them.

Associations: I'm with all men. You could say the "motherboard" [the electronic circuit board in a microcomputer that provides the remaining boards with electricity and holds them in place] is a pretty transparent reference to a family; the central processor and motherboard are the parents and peripheral boards are the children. I don't want to play the role of a parent. I'm acting at the same level as an ordinary user, even though I know much more than they do.

I don't have to feel humiliated about this. After all, I'm the insider who knows this system. I've no use for the dubious distinction of entering the system through "the main hallway." A small side window is fine, and allows me to do everything.

In this information world I organize things. It's a small kingdom where I'm not the monarch, granted, but I am the monarch's counselor. I'm the power not behind but to one side of the throne. The monarch may preside over a splendid kingdom or maybe in total disarray but I'm the one who makes everything happen on time and who allows him to impress visitors with the magical efficiency of his kingdom.

As in the previous dream, the subject of this one is access. But access to what? The answer of orthodox psychoanalysis – that the male child wants to do away with the father and have the mother all to himself – does not fit the dream exactly, since in it, the motherboard serves not as a destination point but as a pathway to get elsewhere in the system. Andy's additional associations to the dream clarify this:

> When I [was a child and] went to see my father [a physician] at the office, there would always be patients sitting in the waiting room. They had to wait their turn, which could take longer than an hour. What I did, with the help of my mom, was slip into a side room, bypassing the main thoroughfare, and then just went in directly to see my dad. I was an insider, with special privileges because I belonged to the family.
>
> It looks like I've identified the high-powered computer gurus with the ordinary sick patients of my father years ago. Meanwhile, taking advantage of the help of my humble mother, I use a side-access that gets me to the "main processor," the one who, with the help of the wonderful nurses who worked in my father's office, knew how to heal all the hurt places.

Andy's mother cleared the way for access to his father who, although he remains an authority figure here, is also a potential caretaker and healer.

Andy is a second son, and feels that his father "gave everything" to his older brother. In his dream, he gains access to power by becoming mentally indispensable to it. During one of our sessions, Andy formulated this succinctly, "I am power's knowledge." In the Oedipal constellation, the child wants to remove the one in the power position, and assume power himself. Freud's ambitions as expressed in his own dreams and self-analysis, like those of his male patients, usually follow this pattern. For Andy, too, power is at issue, but is arrived at indirectly; the motherboard in his dream serves as a bridge to the main processor of the computer where the real power resides.[8]

INFORMATION AS THE VITAL LINK

The logic of Andy's dream echoes that of his professional life. In the large company that employs him, Andy can scarcely aspire to be the Chief Executive Officer, but he can find a place for himself within a corporate culture that authorizes his activities. Andy's work situation is like his dream in that status and self-esteem are assured not through identification with a particular person or persons, but through the establishment of a certain *connection* to higher authority by virtue of which one is indirectly empowered.

If one theme stands out in the life histories of the people interviewed for this book, it is that of relationship and connection, and fear of its opposite: isolation. As in Andy's dream, this theme may be articulated in the language of information technologies. When machines were only mechanical, mental functioning tended to be talked about in terms of the containment and channeling of physical power: one gears up, or feels driven, to accomplish something; keeps the lid on or has an explosive temper; accelerates one's efforts; steps on the gas or puts on the brakes; feels energized or suffers an energy drain, and so on. Orthodox psychoanalytic categories, too, draw upon mechanical/hydraulic metaphor: the damming and discharge of libido, impulse, resistance, mechanism of defense, character armor (Wilhelm Reich). Imagery of this kind is compelling and, together with the industrial technology that inspires it, will persist long into the future. But a new set of metaphors built up around information and communication is falling into place. Supervisors welcome *input* from their subordinates, politicians from their constituencies; human sensitivity becomes receptivity to the *feedback* that others provide; one *monitors* the experience and behavior not only of others, but also of oneself.

This different vocabulary implies, among other things, a re-evaluation of human individuality and relatedness. Inasmuch as the individual is regarded as drawing his or her energy from within, from a reservoir of libido, for example, separation from others need not be viewed as deviant or threatening to the individual, so long as discharge of stored instinctual energy is available. For this reason, Freud viewed the nuclear family as a self-sufficient social unit; each partner provides the other with instinctual gratification. When the source of human well-being is no longer energy but information, however, and that information is received not only from experience of one's immediate environment but also from larger institutions and frameworks of meaning, then isolation assumes new forms and signifies new risks. Life depends on access to information; death is severance of the data-link. Space exploration provides a model for this reconceptualization of life's priorities, as illustrated in Figure 9.1; without the information connection to earth, the astronaut is lost.

The changing character of individualism is a subject that German theorists belonging to the Frankfurt School began to explore several decades ago. Their thesis was that industrial societies, at a certain stage in their development, cease to celebrate the "bourgeois individual" and emphasize instead "teamwork" of a kind: high productivity is alleged to require that individuals work closely together under the administration of an agency that organizes and coordinates their activities. The evolution of manned flight, from the adventures of the Wright brothers at Kitty Hawk to the space shuttle voyages of recent years, exemplifies this change whereby individuals become dependent upon a "command central" that understands and guides their activities. Orville and Wilbur Wright were legendary figures, followed by Lindbergh whose solo transatlantic flight in the 1920s became a symbol of how much a single, courageous individual can accomplish. Compare their pioneering achievements to the space missions that began several decades later. We are apt to recall the accomplishments of these missions, but not the identities of their human participants. Who remembers the name of the first American astronaut? Unlike Lindbergh, the self-reliant aviator who had to chart his own course and make his own decisions, the astronaut remains at all times connected into the flow of information from Mission Control. The astronaut's activities do not belong to her or him alone, but are organized and sanctioned by the project administration to which the astronaut belongs. The relation of astronauts to Mission Control is a good

Figure 9.1 Navigating the Internet – a programmer's guide
Source: Unix Review (May 1991)

metaphor for life in a post-industrial social order because in both cases, access and connection, rather than self-sufficiency, are vital for survival. Networking replaces autonomous initiative as the activity that assures success.

COMPUTER AS PRE-OEDIPAL OBJECT

Contemporary language provides concepts that articulate this dependency. Notions such as *input, output, data, feedback, interface*, and *network* characterize not only electronic devices, but also our relations to them and to one another. As I have noted previously, what is novel about this is not the application of technical vocabulary to talk about human beings. Borrowings from previous technologies also served this purpose; think only of all the terms for describing human action that have been derived from our experience with automotive and other combustion technologies – *drive, accelerate, brake, spark*, and the like. But an information-processing vocabulary describes us in a different way, and expresses different issues in our lives, than a mechanical vocabulary.

We can characterize this difference in psychological terms. The key features of information-processing technology (input, output, feedback) are central to the lives of children at birth, and enter into their formation of a sense of self. This sense develops simultaneously with what classical psychoanalysis terms the "oral" stage of development. One of the first challenges that a child faces is to gain control over what enters and what exits from its own body, which is accomplished by learning to open and close the apertures, or "gates," of the body's surface, including the mouth, eyes, and sphincter. At this time, a child's choices are quite limited, consisting primarily of incorporation, avoidance, and expulsion. As a computer regulates the data-flow of bits and bytes at its periphery, so for the infant it is the motion of substances into and out of itself that falls within the scope of its control, not its own motion as a whole. Later on, the child will be able to move away from obnoxious stimuli and toward attractive ones; skills of locomotion eventually enable the child to use its own body as a tool (an arm that reaches toward or pushes away) or vehicle (legs that approach or flee an object or situation) to get what it wants.

Hence the kind of machine that the child's body resembles changes over time. Human developmental history during the first two or three years of life, from incorporation and expulsion in the beginning (pre-Oedipal stage) toward eventual mastery of locomotion and deliberate interactions with objects (Oedipal stage), recapitulates the history of technology, *but in the opposite direction*: from functioning akin to that of a computer, which remains in one place and receives or emits information, toward functioning which is more like that of a mechanical machine capable of physical displacement and manipulation of physical things in the environment. The upshot is that civilization's most advanced technology models a child's most primitive relationships with its surroundings, including interactions and exchange across boundaries between self and other.

DEFENSIVE FUNCTIONS OF LOGIC AND OBJECTIFICATION

Unlike other animals that have complex survival skills biologically "wired-in," human beings are born helpless. A human infant is much more dependent than the newborn of any other species upon the attention and good will of its caretakers. Against this dependency and vulnerability, children, and the adults they become, protect themselves in many ways. One of these is traditional religious belief, as Freud pointed out in *The Future of an Illusion*. Another is objectification of one's surroundings, to bring them under one's control. This strategy seems to liberate us in two related ways: first, it renders the world relatively predictable and manipulable; second, it renders the world emotionally safe: objects do not place demands on us that a human subject might.

In this regard, some people find that a computer is an ideal object, for it is the closest thing one can find to a conscious entity, linguistically interactive with its users, that does not ask of them anything more than an instrumental, technical orientation. (Asked why she was so attached to her video-game toys, a little girl I know expressed her opinion remarkably concisely, "You don't have to share with them, they don't have feelings, and you can make them do what you want.") Even though a computer responds to us in a relatively sophisticated way, we can treat it anyway we please. True, there are technical constraints imposed by the software: one must adhere to certain rules and procedures, but these do not entail the same quality of commitment or vulnerability as engagement with persons. A human being is apt to ask for respect, trust, intimacy, reciprocity – demands that we can conveniently avoid when dealing with inanimate objects.

Although the substitution of objectivity (relatively controllable) for subjectivity (relatively uncontrollable and therefore threatening) has its advantages, this strategy does not necessarily provide meaning and emotional sustenance. Roger, a French emigré employed as a computer programmer in the United States, grappled with this issue. Because his life history interweaves the themes of safety, identity, and technology introduced above, I discuss his experiences in some detail. Roger dreamt:

> *I'm in Paris, seeing a friend off on the metro. I am late and rush up to the subway platform. My friend has boarded the train, which is just now pulling out of the station. I run alongside the train a few steps and ask for the address where we were planning to have dinner together this evening, and he shouts to me "125 rue de l'est."*

Associations: The words "rue de l'est" remained with me as the dream ended. In English, they sound like "rude" "lest": I was being rude by being late. "Lest" is a logical connector, and nicely symmetric:

A lest B means
if not A, then B which is logically equivalent to

if not B, then A, which translates back into
B lest A.

Whereas this logic is clear, direction words in French such as "est" and "ouest" (east and west) make no sense at all. The second differs from the first in adding the prefix "ou" which translates as "or" in English. How can we get "west" by logically or-ing "east"? I am frustrated not only by the traffic in the dream that kept me from arriving at the station to see my friend off on time, but also by the Academie Française that, departing needlessly from the tradition of Pascal and Bourbaki, has allowed the illogic of "est" and "ouest" to stand.

The dreamer is joking a bit, but also serious. Reality falls dismally short of meeting the high standards of logic. Reason had served as a refuge of a kind for Roger, affording comfort and control, for as long as he could remember. But the dream also makes a more recent reference, to someone for whose death the dreamer had been grieving. Roger's further reflections upon his dream were:

The one I loved so much is gone – she has been carried off by the underground [the metro]. It feels as if I am still here, alive, *because* she is absent: if not A, then B ... if not B, then A. There but for the grace of God go I.

Logic, which had sheltered this dreamer for so many years from turbulent and unpredictable surroundings, failed entirely to protect him from experiencing the loss of someone dearly beloved.

Roger had another dream at about the same time as the one above:

I dreamt I was chewing popcorn. I was in popcorn heaven, but at a certain point I couldn't swallow any more.

Associations: Yesterday I read for hours about assembly language programming. Taking a break I looked at a children's book and saw a prank described. You thread popcorn onto a string and then curl it all up into a bowl. When you offer some to a friend, they will be surprised to get quite a bit more than they expected. Returning to my [computer] book, I realized that I had reached the saturation point. Information overload. The word "pop" is an assembly language command. Popcorn is difficult for me to digest, although I like it very much. The computer feeds its users discrete "bytes" or "nibbles" of information, like puffs of popped corn.

Roger suffered from an eating compulsion that began when his lover died. He associated this loss with the dream: bit by bit, two people fall in love; one day, one of them will "be surprised to get quite a bit more than they expected." The connection of food and love here is old hat. But that between food, on the one hand, and information or ideas on the other is less readily recognized, although language certainly attests to it: ideas/information are "food for thought," "half-baked," "warmed-over," "devoured," "digested." Already as a child, the dreamer had learned to take his nourishment from the harvest of knowledge. This did not leave him altogether invulnerable, however, as he learned when he lost the one person to whom he had committed himself as to no one ever before.

These were Roger's additional associations to the dream:

> When I was a kid they sold popcorn at the local department store. The machine was behind a glass enclosure, where a girl from the high school scooped the corn into eagerly awaiting empty bags, selling for 80 centimes each. I would stand there watching, for what seemed like hours. With the fluorescent light reflecting off her cheap make up, she was my mirage of beauty and total happiness!

The dreamer identified himself with the empty bags "eagerly awaiting" to be filled. Emptiness and fullness, with respect to both food and information, became for him metaphors for life's deficits and rewards.[9]

NOURISHING MOTHERS

Of course we cannot generalize from this one case about the psychological implications of involvements with information technologies. Yet the association of nourishment with information is commonplace in post-industrial cultures. Information technologies, although regarded as instruments of male rationality, also assume maternal characteristics; as providers of information, they are bounteous mothers of a kind. (In Figure 9.1, a communications "umbilical cord" links the astronaut/programmer to "mother earth.") Much mythology is built up around mothers: that they are all-knowing, all-powerful, limitlessly nourishing. This childhood fantasy of the perfect mother, whose supply of food, love, and warmth is infinite, is not easily surrendered. "When I was a child, I spake as a child," it says in the Bible, "But when I grew up I put away childish things." Yet as adults we remain as dependent on nourishing objects as ever.

Nourishment has joined sexual gratification as a contemporary paradigm of human enjoyment. (Of human wrong-doing as well. "Sinful" is a word we're less likely to apply to a sexual act than to a rich dessert.) There is abundant evidence for an historical shift here, of which I will offer only a few examples. Sales of cookbooks have skyrocketed in the past two decades in the United States. Newspapers and magazines devote more space to restaurant reviews and articles on diet, food selection and preparation. On television in the United States, Julia Child and look-alikes appeal to a hungry audience.[10] Real-estate agents report that home buyers are especially concerned about their kitchens: "while families may spend less time cooking than in the past, they still want a spacious kitchen with a breakfast nook, a built-in microwave, and lots of cabinet and counter space."[11]

Contemporary preoccupation with nourishment is attested to also by the changing character of psychotherapy. The traditional image of a psychotherapist has been that of a father figure, someone like Sigmund Freud, who may be kind and forgiving but who remains a representative of authority and of the law, however liberally interpreted. As many therapists realize, however, today's clients tend to be looking for mothers rather than fathers. A male psychotherapist is more likely to attract clients if he exhibits maternal qualities. Industrial psychologists have hit upon the same insight. It is a good idea, for example, for a company to give workers bonuses now and then, even if this is to be paid for by reducing their salaries. Whereas a salary is a rule-governed, boring kind of thing, a bonus testifies to the bounteousness and goodness of the employer.

As much as 50 percent of all employment in the United States is now based on abstract information-handling activities of one kind or another.[12] Under these circumstances, might technology also fill the role of the all-knowing and all-nourishing other? Television is the obvious candidate to play this part, but the ways in which a computer serves its users are not entirely dissimilar. To write this book, I am using a word-processor that presents me with a "menu" of options, as if I were in a restaurant. If I try to store too many "bytes," the screen scolds me, "Disk full error!"

Although I have written the above only half-seriously, the interpenetration of nourishment and information vocabularies is by no means superficial. Indeed, information is perceived as essential to the satisfaction of any need. For life seems to confront us at every moment with choices that only someone with the right information can evaluate. Although relatively intangible in comparison to ordinary material artifacts, information is regarded as a life-line. It illuminates the darkness, opens previously closed doors, protects against hazards of all kinds, attracts the respect of others, and is exchangeable for other kinds of goods. It is in terms of information that differences in social power and status are explained and legitimated: what distinguishes the professional from the client is above all that the first is knowledgeable and the second is not.

Information, then, is experienced as empowering, although the power it provides is different from the "domination of nature" that previous technologies afforded. That domination amounted to control over material aspects of the environment – typically the moving or shaping of physical objects by a tool or machine. In the seventeenth century, Francis Bacon portrayed nature as female and receptive, and machinery as a power of coercive, phallic domination. Nature yields up her secrets, he says, only "under constraint and vexed; that is to say when by art and the hand of man she is forced out of her natural state, and squeezed and moulded."[13] Similarly for Descartes, the promise of technology was its ability to make humans "masters and possessors of nature."[14] Technology here is masculine; its aim is pursuit and conquest of the female prize.

Information-processing technologies, too, may embody this logic, but on a symbolic level they express an additional dynamic. Instead of Bacon's "I am come in very truth leading you to Nature with all her children to bind her to your service and make her your slave,"[15] technology, in the form of the computer, becomes a maternal figure that nourishes and sustains its users. What one wants is not mainly to master or even to possess the object, although these motivations may certainly be present, but to interact with or perhaps even to join the object by way of taking in what it has to offer.

What has changed here is, so to speak, the sexual politics of technology. In keeping with the traditional "domination of nature" model, Freud took sexual conquest (the Oedipus complex) as a paradigm of human motivation: one strives against obstacles, consisting typically of people with whom one is competing, to make one's way forward. But there is a satisfaction associated with information technologies that goes beyond coercive mastery of this kind. Having recently bought a personal computer, Anna dreamt:

> *I am wandering through a field not of lilies but of computer terminals, growing out of tall pods like poppies. The earth beneath my bare feet is springy, yet firm enough, as if made of something soft and foamy. As you near a particular terminal you feel yourself drawn in, as into a world of wonder and adventure, a tunnel of boundless exploration and love. Then you emerge again, and as in the beginning the display of cascading colors and harmonies unites all.*

We are within a fantasy world here – that of the child who luxuriates in an exploration of the mother's soft contours. This imagery of technology is organic, maternal, having to do with envelopment and contentment, far removed from the more common associations of machines with aggressivity and goal-driven reason.

HI-TECH NOURISHMENT: "I WANT A COOKIE!"

In Anna's dream, the computer merges with and gratifies its owner. In a different context, a computer may serve to gratify instead its programmer, in potential *opposition* to the desires of its owners or users. A story that has become something of a legend in the software development industry relates that a programmer was working for Hewlett-Packard, writing assembly language routines for an operating system.[16] Months later, after he had completed this project and had left the company, a problem arose. His program worked fine, but every once in a while, the message "I want a cookie" appeared on the screen, and the computer locked up: the cursor would not move. Finally it was discovered that if, but only if, the user typed the word "cookie" at the keyboard, the computer would then resume its normal operations. A few months later, the program would repeat its original request, and the user would have to feed the machine another "cookie" to restore normality. Company management found this situation intolerable, even though it required from the user only a few seconds on a very occasional basis to be taken care of. Programmers were assigned to repair this problem, but since the culprit routine was deeply and cleverly buried in the rest of the code, it was difficult to ferret out. Eventually, though, the "bug" was found and removed.

Programmers familiar with this story sense immediately what it is about. It is intended that their own efforts be invisible to end users when the code they write executes. Those who use a word-processing program, for example, will not want to be made aware of the internal logic of loops and branches that implements their requests. The programmer writes the complex guts of the system, but these are best not seen by those whom it serves. The consequence, often, is that the ingenuity and enormous labor that enter into writing a program go unrecognized. The creator gets overlooked by those who make use of her or his creation.[17] The "cookie" programmer mentioned above resisted this invisibility by building into the operating system a routine that would occasionally require from the user an acknowledgement of his existence. This was unacceptable to management. His need was for recognition, which took the form of a mocking request for nourishment; that of the company, for a product carrying no trace of the personal identities of its makers.

TECHNOLOGY AND IDENTIFICATION

The work of a craftsperson is a personal expression; its literally sensible qualities and design communicate directly and immediately to others. This link between product, producer, and a social world is typically missing from contemporary forms of symbolic labor, much of which is carried out anonymously. Whereas sensation and perception are concrete and particular, "reason," as characterized during centuries of Western civilization, is abstract and general. But individuality, in the traditional sense, comes about through identifications with particular others experienced as personally related to oneself. Rational structures, inasmuch as they displace our relationships to others into a cognitive realm and diminish past forms of intimacy, generate a hunger – for identity as well as love – that more information cannot satisfy.

Part III

Internal colonization and response

Chapter 10

The logic of colonial organization

> Pockets of a deinformationalized society may survive, just as some remote areas have succeeded in sustaining an agricultural society throughout the age of industrialization. But most communities – particularly large prosperous ones – have no choice in the matter. They must opt in. The sooner this fact and its consequences become part of our consensual reality, the better for everyone.
>
> Pask and Curran[1]

One of the first tasks of the colonial explorer is to map out the territory he encounters to locate its mountains and rivers, plot the contours of the coastline, determine tribal boundaries, etc. Driven by an interest in organizing and mastering a foreign geography, the colonial project seeks to bring the dark and unknown to light. Human beings can apply a similar strategy toward understanding themselves. There are striking parallels between the rhetoric of colonial expansion and Western discourses of self-knowledge. Typically the psyche is compared to an internal territory, whose contours self-reflective inquiry enable us to navigate and reshape. The efforts on the part of philosophers and psychologists to achieve this knowledge have traditionally divided the mind into "provinces," so to speak. But the particular divisions that are drawn change over time, as does the way in which their administration is conceived. For Plato and his successors, through Descartes and the rationalists of the Enlightenment, reason is the agency of unification. The world around us and within us, body and mind, is organized and administered by a soul or self or ego.

Along with the modernization and differentiation of social institutions that have taken place over the past several centuries in the West, our views of psychological structure have evolved as well. For contemporary cognitive science, the mind is analyzable into functional "departments" such as perception, abstract thinking, long- and short-term memory, verbal skills, and bodily control. In this catalog of capacities, however, there may no longer be any role for a unifying "soul" or "self" to play.

Parallel doubts arise about the unity of contemporary societies, and with the waning of the Cold War we may expect them to intensify. In past decades, the superpowers were like two individual giants, squaring off against one another, each receiving from the adversity of the other a sense of its own purpose, identity, and self-certainty. Presumably, we were freedom-loving, rational, and moral. They were totalitarian, irrational, and not-to-be-trusted. Today there is only one super-power, and it has a hard time locating an evil other to confirm its own identity. "World-wide terrorism" is a candidate, but it is not as compelling an image of the opposite of Americans as the "Red Menace," centered in the Soviet Union, used to be.

Today, psychological as well as political self-images are apt to lose their boundaries and coherence. Threatened by this disintegration, we may redouble our efforts to shape and reshape our own personalities as well as our social affiliations. We deliberate on our skill sets, needs, relationships, and prospects by way of implementing projects of self-formation that belong to what Habermas calls the "internal colonization of the lifeworld": the intrusion into previously taken-for-granted contexts of daily life by rationalizing systems that substitute formal protocols and organization for informal, more traditional ties.[2]

This dialectic of social administration and self-administration has a historical dimension. In late medieval Europe, processes of rationalization transformed the character of human interactions. Out of the predominantly agrarian matrix of feudalism, urban centers emerged and material production that had previously been handled by craftspeople working at home was centralized and reorganized in factories. The marketing of commodities was submitted to formal procedures governing pricing, interest rates, insurance, double-entry bookkeeping, etc. Feudal economic relationships gave way to a new system for quantifying and coordinating diverse productive activities: each agent comes to the marketplace or workplace driven by self-interest; a system providing for the exchange of goods and labor-power mediated the disparate intentions of the various participants and provided rewards that fueled the machinery of production and consumption.

Processes of modernization were not confined, however, to the factory or marketplace. In the domain of state administration, traditional oral law – unsystematic, fragmentary, and relying on individual precedents – gave way to a formal statutory system aiming at consistency and universality. In other realms, too, rationalization transformed or annihilated traditional practices. The enchantments of magic and alchemy were replaced by the sober, calculated enterprise of scientific inquiry. Religion was also rationalized and depersonalized; Protestant confessions could not abide the seemingly arbitrary pronouncements of a Pope and his priesthood.

I have suggested above that the so-called "crisis of the self" is bound up with the expansion of *contemporary* rationalizing discourses, which work in ways different from the forms of institutional rationalization associated with the emergence of capitalism. Those forms affirmed more unequivocally the identity of the individual. The medieval term *bourgeois*, meaning "city dweller," came to connote those qualities of self-reliance and self-determination associated with urban inhabitants whose identities and status are relatively secure. The very notion of the self-initiating autonomous individual is bound up with the modernization of economic production and exchange, political organization, engineering, science, art, and religion characteristic of early modern Europe. Recall, for example, the portraits of confident burghers, models of reason, that peer at us from Renaissance and baroque paintings, or the definition of the morally and economically righteous individual that Protestantism elaborated in the concepts of *vocation* and *calling*.

Today, however, rationalizing processes have more paradoxical consequences. They continue to introduce order into human affairs, but as we have seen, also call into question the presumption of integrated identity on the part of the individuals whose affairs are ordered. In this context, modernization may be regarded as that historical process in which rationalization first builds up the subject, affirming the subject's autonomy and sense of self, but then turns around and destroys this very unity. A partial explanation is that contemporary forms of rationalization "colonize" consciousness in new ways. Personal identities were traditionally supported by relatively well-defined boundaries between self and other, by conventional role models, and by identifications and commitments binding individuals to their neighborhoods, parishes, and communities. Those definitions and affiliations were often stifling and exploitative; they subordinated women to men. Yet they afforded more or less consistent and stable social identities. Today these identities are subject to scrutiny and "re-engineering," as people construct and reconstruct themselves by way of adapting to the new discourses and shifting requirements of an information-based social order.

We might view industrialization, then, as a centuries-long drama that began with a certain roster of characters: "peasant," "landlord," "capitalist," "worker," "husband," "housewife," and the like. The script provided its actors with well-defined, more or less stable roles, including that of the heroic "individual," enacted within a coherent social order that was meaningful to its critics as well as to its advocates. What the post-industrial *colonization of the lifeworld* signifies is a revision of this traditional drama. The new script resembles that of Pirandello's *Six Characters in Search of an Author*. The characters search desperately for someone to provide them with coherent, identity-sustaining roles that are no longer available. For colonization ultimately rationalizes away the subjectivity of everyone involved in the colonial process.

THE CONTRADICTIONS OF COLONIAL RULE

Although imposed without the consent of the indigenous people that it rules, colonialism involves more than physical coercion; control is exercised administratively, through the organization of information. The Information Age derives not simply from the technical discovery that microcircuits can be etched on silicon, but also from the idea that a bureaucratic system of procedures can organize and manage a subordinate population. Two centuries of British administration in India illustrate this dynamic. The secret of its success was "indirect rule": authority was embodied in a civil code and thereby depersonalized. An apparatus designed to function semi-automatically empowered colonial administrators and native officials to carry out certain formal procedures. The British civil service in India "never had more than 1,000 members to administer the vast and densely populated subcontinent – a tiny fraction (at most 1 percent) of the legions of Confucian mandarins and palace eunuchs employed next door to administer a not-much-more populous China."[3] This organization of so many by so few worked efficiently because of its elaborately codified structure of control.

The order that colonial administration brings into being has disintegrative consequences for the colonized population. It contests for hegemony with indigenous belief systems and forms of life that were in place before colonial penetration began. Once one falls within the jurisdiction of colonial rule, one is required to live the identity of not one but of two people simultaneously: that of "colonial subject," on the one hand, and that of "native," on the other. But it is impossible to superimpose consistently these two images of oneself. As a "native," one remains within the traditional world of the indigenous culture, whose practices – linguistic, religious, familial, vocational – affirm the form and content of one's personal identity. At the same time, as a "colonial subject" one is connected into an administrative system, including formal guidelines, norms, expectations, and rewards that amount to a "second nature." Notoriously, this other nature is at loggerheads with one's identity as defined within the native culture. The colonial subject, divided against himself or herself and "steeped in the inessentiality of servitude," as Franz Fanon puts it,[4] becomes vulnerable to the existential crises that many Third World authors have described.

Although the colonial culture is experienced by the indigenous population as a foreign imposition, over time its ideals may become internalized by individuals and incorporated within the local culture. In those parts of Africa colonized by the French, even those Africans who expressed their opposition to colonialism

> came to do so within the framework of an all too familiar dilemma: they felt part French themselves, having learned the language and the basic ideas of their criticism from the French ... They could never fully bring themselves to reject a political and social culture whose language, ideas, and life style they had in varying degrees made their own.[5]

As a consequence of colonial rule, Westernized Africans were divided between two worlds. Their response to this division and the struggle to form a coherent identity is a predominant theme in modern African thought and art. In the novel *Ambiguous Adventure*, written by the Senegalese author Cheikh Kane, the main character, Samba Diallo, is incapable of identifying fully with his own African heritage against the West:

> I am not a distinct country of the Diallobé [in Africa] facing a distinct Occident, and appreciating with a cool head what I must take from it and what I must leave with it by way of counter-balance. I have become two. There is not a clear mind deciding between the two factors of a choice. There is a strange nature, in distress over not being two.[6]

Samba Diallo reverts here to an external, third-person point of view in describing himself, "There is ... There is ... " The internalization of culturally divided values results in a loss of subjective location. Reflecting on his past, Samba Diallo muses,

> In former times the world was like my father's dwelling; everything took me into the very essence of itself, as if nothing could exist except through me. The world was not silent and neuter. It was alive. It was aggressive. It spread out. No scholar ever had such knowledge of anything as I had, then, of being ... Here, now, the world is silent, and there is no longer any resonance from myself. I am like a broken balafong, like a musical instrument that has gone dead. I have the impression that nothing touches me any more.[7]

Samba Diallo's experiences of self-objectification (seeing himself from an impersonal vantage-point) and loss of feeling are characteristic of the encounter with an administrative system in which the position of the colonizer mirrors that of the colonized. From a system perspective, the personal identities of officials are of little more importance than those of colonial subjects. Of less importance than *who* occupies a particular position within the hierarchy is the set of *procedures* associated with it: personnel come and go; the bureaucratic function remains in place. As an administrator, one falls within the scope of one's own administration: there are protocols governing one's own conduct as well as the conduct of those in subordinate positions.

Of course the colonial officer, occupying a privileged position, experiences the world very differently to the native, on whom the colonial system is imposed without her or his consent. Yet Albert Memmi suggests that even for those who enact their colonial duties willingly and conscientiously, a certain self-interrogation about identification with their roles is inescapable.[8] As an administrator, one is apt to experience one's identity as something objective and alien, becoming, in George Orwell's words, "a sort of hollow, posing dummy ... He wears a mask and his face grows to fit it."[9] Divided in this way, the colonial official does not feel entirely at home, and cannot avoid entirely the realization that the foreign territory he occupies is himself.

One of the sources of this self-estrangement is the commitment of colonial regimes to inconsistent policies and ambiguous or unattainable objectives. Sociologists Ernesto Laclau and Chantal Mouffe argue that we mistake the character of bureaucratic authority if we attribute too much clarity, unity, or consistency to its structure.[10] A colonial regime typically resembles less a closed and smoothly contoured hegemonic edifice than an unstable assembly of partial discourses and practices, within which the administrative official typically finds himself confronting conflicting imperatives and meanings that render his mission as well as his identity problematic, if not terminally incoherent. This theme runs through Joseph Conrad's stories and novels about foreign empire; the internal identity of the colonist tends to self-destruct, regardless of whether the colonial mission appears to "succeed" in establishing control over an indigenous population and in defeating its movements of resistance.

POST-INDUSTRIAL COLONIZATION

The division between colonial authority and the traditional lifeworld it organizes is brought home from abroad, so to speak, in the form of administrative control of everyday life in the mother country. Habermas points out that what began centuries ago as rationalization in the name of Renaissance and Enlightenment ideals of freedom has become a dynamic that appears to operate according to its own logic, regardless of human interests:

> The irresistible irony of the world-historical process of enlightenment becomes evident: the rationalization of the lifeworld makes possible a heightening of systemic complexity, which becomes so hypertrophied that it unleashes system imperatives that burst the capacity of the lifeworld they instrumentalize.[11]

The lifeworld, consisting of bonds linking people within families, friendships, and other informal associations, is as vulnerable to the disintegrative influence of contemporary forms of rationalization as Third World populations have been to colonization. Systemic reason, implementing the norms of an information-based political economy, disrupts lifeworld forms that sustain personal identity. That disruption is made all the more disabling by the internal contradictions of rationalizing discourses ("Be autonomous, but also connected to others;" "Take the initiative, but don't question bureaucratic requirements").

Information technology, no less than prior technological forms, contributes to processes of analysis and objectification that characterize modernizing societies. Machines whose speciality is the handling of abstract representations both implement and mirror a new stage in the rationalization of everyday life by contemporary institutions. Post-industrial settings such as the electronic office (Figure 8.7, p. 116) leave behind the noisy shopfloor of the automobile plant or garment factory in favor of the silence of an increasingly automated system of production. The social logic of the office has merged here with the information-processing logic of a computer circuit board, whose grid forms the connecting network that mediates human relationships. Even where two individuals are located in the same vicinity, on the right-hand side of Figure 8.7, they look not at one another but concentrate instead on the task at hand. The workers represented there might be programmers, data-entry clerks or managers, but irrespective of the specific roles they play, their consciousness is oriented toward and structured by the system. Bureaucracies of the past involved mechanical production and physical traffic: typewriters were used to generate documentation; paperwork and people moved within and between departments, bureaus, and firms. But in the "paperless office" the clutter of documents and clatter of machinery ceases, and minds are linked immediately via the near-instantaneous processing of the computer.

Such linkage requires a quality of attention different from that needed to operate previous kinds of technology. In order to use any instrument, mechanical or otherwise, one must adapt or "attune" oneself to its structure. Driving an automobile, for example, requires that one's arms and hands adapt to the steering wheel, one's legs and feet to the floor pedals, one's eyes to the road. This adaptation calls for a certain mental alertness, yet one can also be thinking about other things at the same time that one drives. Involvement with information technologies, on the other hand, is typically more absorbing; the user's mind must be attuned to the machine on a *symbolic* level. In the case of many computer applications, an abstract structure within the technical apparatus "communicates" with the user: a "dialogue" of a sort takes place, governed by a procedure that coordinates the user's actions with those of the machine. One follows a technically specified protocol in utilizing a spreadsheet program to arrive at a budget projection, interacting with an automatic teller to withdraw money from one's bank account, or retrieving and modifying a record in a database. In each of these cases, one is engaged within a procedural domain defined by the formal parameters and pathways of the program.

"WHAT ARE YOU GOING TO MAKE OF YOUR LIFE?"

The proceduralization of everyday life is as much an internal as an external affair, encompassing not only the education and control of the self, but its very production. It is an axiom of psychoanalytic and Piagetian developmental psychology that a child is a project of a kind, to be closely monitored and administered through its early stages. In all cultures, childcare is an important function, to be sure, but in ours this function is rationalized to an extraordinary degree. Child-raising handbooks are the favored sources of expertise in this area. They supply parents with the information they need to supervise a child's development, until the time that the child is considered able to assume this responsibility. In the United States, Dr Spock's *Baby and Childcare* has outsold any book ever published, except for the Bible.

"Normal" children eventually assume the responsibility for monitoring and working on themselves, taking themselves as the objects of their own construction. This is true especially for children of middle- or upper-class families, although the influence of this view of self-formation is society-wide. Recall Robert Coles' description, cited in Chapter 2, p. 20, of children who think about the processes of their own self-formation "with insistence, regularity, and, not least, out of a learned sense of obligation." Such concentration is a lifelong occupation. Life unfolds as a series of internal as well as external challenges, each of which can be anticipated and planned for. In early years, one prepares oneself within the educational system. This is to be followed by career-building, forming one's own family, and eventually retirement.

These various stages of life may themselves be procedurally subdivided. In preparation for a medical career, for instance, one enrolls in a premed curriculum in college, strives for a high grade-point average, takes the necessary tests, and fills out the requisite applications. Medical school itself is followed by an internship, residency, and then professional employment. For each vocation, there exists a "career ladder" to be climbed. In the area of advanced technology sales, a career-counseling text explains:

Here are two common career paths:

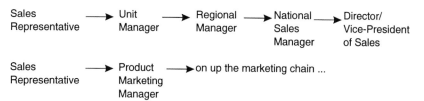

View the goal as a process a series of individual career steps rather than one big move.[12]

Progress within a particular career stage is as procedural as the passage from one stage to the next: "The five basic steps in selling," for example, "are prospecting, qualifying, preparation, presentation, and follow-up."[13]

RITUALS VERSUS PROCEDURES

Procedural activity is, of course, not a recent invention. Its antecedents lie in premodern ritual practices that bind and contain the anxiety of participants at the same time that they organize their behaviors. Rituals, however, are typically *collective* practices that connect individuals within a lifeworld of meanings and values shared community-wide. Contemporary procedures, on the other hand, are formal structures typically employed by agents no longer associated by their activity in traditionally meaningful ways. Executed impersonally and anonymously – more efficiently in many cases by machines than by persons – procedures articulate a social reality where personal identity and personal relationships are irrelevant.

Frameworks of rationalization encompass our private as well as our public lives. Instructions for installing tile in one's bathroom or video-taping a TV program, a Jane Fonda exercise tape, a dietary regimen – all of these are formal procedures. Typically, their logic involves a quantification of human activities: we rise, eat, and sleep by the clock, exercise our bodies by doing X number of push-ups daily and running Y number of laps around the track. We aim to accumulate grade-points in school and dollars in bank accounts. Measured also are salary levels, rents, mortgage payments, miles-per-gallon of our automobiles, the memory capacity of our personal computers.[14]

It is not difficult to understand why so many human activities fall subject to such rationalization. Proceduralization and quantification are useful because they make goal-directed activities easier to master, to repeat reliably, and to teach to others. A formal procedure is efficient because it is detachable from any particular person who carries it out, rendering irrelevant that person's identity. Some effort is typically taken to mitigate the depersonalizing consequences of procedures. At the bank, there is usually a namecard at each service window that identifies the teller. The telephone operator gives his or her name to the caller who dials "directory assistance." But five minutes after the transaction has been completed, how many callers remember the name of the individual who served them?

PROCEDURES, SOCIAL POWER, AND RECOGNITION

There is yet an additional motivation for the proceduralization of many everyday activities: it renders them subject to centralized, administrative control. The classical example of this is the "Taylorization" of industry; the top-down implementation of rationalizing methods and deployment of new technologies not necessarily in the service of productivity, but to reaffirm management's control of the productive process. The formal organization of job tasks removes authority from workers at the shop-floor level and lodges it with management.[15] Several of the procedural systems cited earlier also illustrate this rationalization from above. A medical or sales career ladder, for example, is a program consisting of steps taken in a sequential order, with which one constructs for oneself a career and a social identity. But the ladder itself is built by whom? In the case of medicine, the American Medical Association and other professional and economic institutions establish the path that affords access to a medical occupation. Notoriously, this path restricts the number of persons who are admitted into the medical profession. Do the criteria of admission to medical school permit access to all of those who would be competent practitioners? Are they based on community needs? The norms that many of us internalize as guides for our own behavior interlock with criteria of selection and performance that we ourselves have not chosen.

Procedural frameworks are essential to the governance of many contemporary institutions. But in the absence of democratic participation in determining their structures and purposes, they are apt to be experienced as alien and disempowering. Work in social service agencies provides a classical illustration: a case worker ascertains whether a woman qualifies for aid to single mothers by abstracting from her situation certain facts (marital status, income level, number of dependents, etc.) which are then inserted into a formula that determines her eligibility. The formula itself, however, is determined by bureaucratic structures over which she, her colleagues, and her clients have little say.

In this case as in many post-industrial settings, service providers and their clients remain essentially nameless and faceless, even when they meet face-to-face and address one other by name. An invisible veil of abstraction distances them as surely as if they were separated by a physical barrier. Because input to the relevant procedures consists only of the so-called "objective facts," institutional roles are performed impersonally. Pleasantries exchanged between the parties may contribute to their comfort level, but are incidental to the transaction. Anger and other expressions of strong feeling are excluded from the standard transaction, as aberrant behaviors outside the prescribed norms.

Bureaucratic performance of roles long preceded the Information Age, to be sure. Max Weber described the phenomenon in detail near the beginning of this century. How much of the estrangement associated with these roles can be attributed to unequal power relations that characterize post-industrial settings specifically? To what extent can it be remedied by restructuring our social institutions? "Realists" may argue that a certain anonymity of social relationships is an inevitable and even desirable feature of the modern world, and that we cannot expect to close the gap between institutional reason on the one hand, and personal recognition on the other. The complexity of our economic and political institutions, within urban environments involving millions of individuals, allegedly requires administrative organization and rationalization that go far beyond the personal, face-to-face relationships ("small town America") of yesteryear.

We face a dilemma here, one that was raised earlier in this chapter. Like members of a colonized population, our lives are divided; we operate within various impersonal systems, but also inhabit a more personal, immediately experienced and taken-for-granted world that interacts with and is to some extent shaped by those systems. The rationalization of human affairs that technology affords results in a coordination and integration of social interactions that previously were informally organized or did not exist at all. But in the process it dismantles and reorganizes lifeworld structures, built up gradually over many generations, that served to anchor individual identities.

RETURN TO NATURE?

The consequent malaise, the feeling that somehow human beings have lost their bearings and no longer know who they are, motivates a search for the self that shapes our popular culture. People try to recapture a sense of aliveness and vitality that is excluded from their rationalized routines. Hence the hunger for connection, for roots, for an integral relationship with nature. But how did "nature" become a realm separate from us, with which we experience the need to reconnect? Modernity – in part because of the cultural and physical separation of urban existence from rural, agricultural life – construes "society" and "nature" as opposites: the social world is humanly created, whereas nature is understood as "other," as that which we are not, a realm distanced from ourselves. This distancing signifies, however, an alienation from ourselves, since we are embodied, biological beings. The Marxist philosopher Lukács observes that:

> Nature thereby acquires the meaning of what has grown organically, what was not created by man, in contrast to the artificial human civilization. At the same time, it can be understood as that aspect of human inwardness which has remained natural, or at least tends or longs to become natural once more.[16]

Experiencing a dichotomy between the "artificial" and the "natural," we may long to recover the "aspect of human inwardness" that Lukács talks about. Ironically, though, within the context of contemporary urbanized environments, our very efforts at recovery and renewal typically assume quasi-colonial forms. The fate of animals within these environments symbolizes the problematic character of the project. Animals have in the past linked human beings to their own origins. Judging from the caves at Lascaux in France, animals may have been the earliest subjects of painting. Animals are central as well to many creationist myths and religious traditions. Modern science and industry break with such traditional beliefs about the animal kingdom. In the eighteenth century, the naturalist Buffon remarked that "To the same degree as man has raised himself above the state of nature, animals have fallen below it ... What visions and plans can these soulless slaves have, these relics of the past without power?"[17] As if to re-establish or at least recall a past in which human beings lived within a world of animals, we import them into our homes as pets, or into zoos where they may be visited by the public. But zoo life in particular exemplifies our predicament instead of resolving it. Animals removed from their natural habitats, isolated in cages and fed automatically, become the passive objects of human observation and control. In zoos, John Berger notes,

> The animals seldom live up to the adult's [childhood] memories, whilst to the children they appear, for the most part, unexpectedly lethargic and dull. (As frequent as the calls of animals in a zoo, are the cries of children demanding: Where is he? Why doesn't he move? Is he dead?)[18]

An image of their disenfranchised and deadened selves is sent back to zoo visitors. "Nowhere in a zoo can a stranger encounter the look of an animal. At most, the animal's gaze flickers and passes on. They look sideways. They look blindly beyond."[19]

Living in artificial and imposed habitats, caged animals model a colonial setting: modern institutions remove human beings from traditional and informal associations and organize experience within abstract frameworks that seem to exclude everything tangible and meaningful. Activism on behalf of animal rights or to save endangered species, and the efforts of researchers to talk with and take care of primates, dolphins, and other relatively intelligent animals, involve some degree of identification with creatures who, like ourselves, are vulnerable to processes that exploit all species, not only our own.

THE DISCOURSE LINK BETWEEN LIFEWORLD AND SYSTEM

While acknowledging that modernizing processes assault traditional life forms, Habermas does not romanticize the past. To situate his view of historical development, it will help to outline two views he disagrees with. The first assumes that a continuation of the modernizing processes of the past several centuries, including expansion of human knowledge and control of nature, will allow us to overcome the conditions of poverty and ignorance that retard human flourishing. On this account, we will gradually reorganize the lifeworld so that it becomes less irrational and more efficient. Biotechnology will help to increase agricultural yields and facilitate population control; automation of production will do away with monotonous, demeaning work, etc.

But technological "progress" is so readily harnessed to inhumane ends. Every major technical innovation, including the development of information technologies, has been used to expand corporate and military domination of the world's peoples and habitats. Only by overlooking this history can we anticipate that "reason," in the predominant forms it has taken in the West, will lead us in a humane direction. Disillusioned with technocratic ideologies, we might want to protect the lifeworld against rationalization or intervention of any kind into its traditional structures. One of the reasons that the topic of child abuse receives so much attention today is that people see their own lives mirrored in those of the victims. Living artificially, ensconced in manufactured environments of concrete, steel, and plastic, sitting in front of computer consoles, we sense a psychic wounding of something deep within ourselves, something essential to who we are that has been neglected or lost.

Popular psychology is preoccupied with this predicament. John Bradshaw, the dispenser of therapeutic wisdom to millions via television and his best-selling books, speaks of the impoverished and mistreated "Inner Child" that each of us once was. Animals, too, enter into narratives of manipulation and abuse that express our feelings about ourselves. In the opening shots of the film *Day of the Dolphin*, a dolphin leaps gracefully from the sea to make a beautiful arc in the air, with this voice overlay:

> Imagine – imagine that your life is spent in an environment of total physical sensation, that every one of your senses has been heightened to a level that in a human being might only be described as ecstatic, that every inch of your skin is a perfect receptor, that you're able to see, to perceive with every part of your being – sight, hearing, taste, smell.

Doesn't this description also match our image of a happy infant? A child's sensuousness and spontaneity are what we miss and would like to return to. In the course of the film it gradually becomes evident that George C. Scott, the scientist who has devoted his life to animal research, is himself imprisoned, captive of the bureaucratic organization that funds his work and of the regimen imposed by his commitment to science. He says of the dolphins in his aquarium, "We should be like them – instinct, and energy." His assistant replies, "Then let them go. Send them to the sea." "Afraid it's too late," Scott despairs, "they wouldn't know what to do or where to go. We've changed them." Echoed here is the impasse in his own life. Once a scientist, always a scientist. One cannot simply walk away from this worldview.

This obstacle has always blocked the romantic rebellion against science and civilization. Goethe's *Naturphilosophie* and Rousseau's idealization of the "noble savage" are belied by their own intellectuality and erudition. We human beings have irreversibly altered our ourselves and our environments, to the point that an expression like "back to nature" is difficult to hear as anything more than a commercial sound-bite or New Age cliché. "Natural" characterizes a hairstyle, deodorant, or the contrived prehistorical ambience of *Jurassic Park*, but beyond such representations we can hardly imagine a pristine world we might return to.

Nature exists for us in the first instance only as regarded through culturally and historically relative categories.

The friendliness, gracefulness and spontaneity attributed to dolphins are *human* attributes. Much of what we believe we "find" in nature is what we put there, and our interpretations are as variable as our conceptions of what we are or would like to be. The Marine World representation of dolphins as peaceful, happy go-lucky creatures is only one reading. Other observers have noted that dolphin "communities" are stratified into dominance hierarchies not unlike those that characterize other animal societies, and that adults sometimes subject one another and baby dolphins to a battering that, if these animals are comparable to humans, might well be considered brutal. Popular books like *Dolphins and Their Power to Heal* suggest that these animals have a lot to teach human beings about themselves. But the authors' account reflects as much their own predilections as it does dolphin realities. Describing the sexual play of dolphins, for instance, they report that "In Shark Bay [Australia], pairs and even trios of male dolphins have been seen 'kidnapping' a female, presumably for the purposes of mating." But from a feminist perspective, this practice could also be viewed as gang-rape.[20]

The film *Free Willy* reproduces the standard themes: a whale held captive in an amusement park symbolizes the situation of the film's human protagonists. Jessie, the boy who gets to know the whale, was abandoned by his family many years ago and feels entrapped in his foster home. The whale's caretaker, a Haida Indian, has seen his tribal culture destroyed. Willy's search for freedom is theirs as well, and ours as spectators. I watched the movie with a little boy and girl and something in us responded powerfully to the whale. But this "something," notwithstanding the sentimental script of the film, remains *other*, beyond the scope of our explanations. Nature far exceeds what we could ever say about it. In the evolution of our species, language is a very recent acquisition, one that each child has to make anew, brought into culture by its caretakers. Aspects of our experience hark back to a time long ago when words and thinking did not yet mediate our relationships to our surroundings and to ourselves. Our efforts to represent and assimilate this past, using cinema, poetry, or science, are unending, but inevitably they miss the mark.

DISCOURSE COMMUNITIES

Dolphins and whales, as far as we know, do not pass on a cultural heritage from one generation to another. Although animal skills and relationships are quite elaborate, their structure appears to be biologically given, not taught to them as human children are taught by adults. Human beings, on the other hand, are historical in a radical sense: each generation learns from, but also sometimes repudiates, the experiences of their predecessors. The coordination of behaviors in dolphin societies, exemplified by the famed parallel arcs traversed when they leap in unison from the sea, represents an attunement that, especially in modern settings, is notoriously problematic for human beings. Our modes of interaction, and even what counts as "human nature" itself, are subject to transformation not only because we alter our surroundings materially, but because of the infinitely variable ways we have of perceiving and talking about them.

Habermas's approach to reconciling system and lifeworld builds on this insight. Colonization of the lifeworld is always linguistically mediated, shaped through our conversations. Habermas points out that these conversations go on within contexts of power and domination. Families, schools, workplaces, and the other sites of human self-formation belong to a larger social reality built upon distinctions of class, gender, and race. Habermas envisages a world in which these distinctions and the institutional structures resting upon them could be reflected upon and restructured democratically. Inasmuch as our conversations are not taken over or spoken over by corporate and mass media ideologies, they may lead to more balanced and humane links between "culture" and "nature," prefigured in our very discussions of what they should be. Inasmuch as these discussions are non-manipulative and respectful of differences as well as similarities, they point the way toward less coercive and estranged relationships with our natural surroundings.

We are unlikely to find solutions, however, in any privileging of nature over culture, spontaneity over planning. These dichotomies are historically constructed, and our very puzzlement about them demonstrates that we no longer inhabit a world of taken-for-granted certainties. Again, colonization provides an apt metaphor. When Third World peoples break out of the colonial system, they cannot simply return to their traditional communities. In an economically, politically, and technologically integrated world, local practices have to change. It is not without bitterness and a sense of irony that the colonial administrator, compelled at last to depart from the territory that his laws have governed, predicts that the natives will find themselves required to impose a system of administrative control scarcely less oppressive, and probably more inefficient, than the one they have been willing to give their lives to replace. While this fatalism obscures the ongoing subordination of newly "liberated" Third World nations to multinational economic, political, and military powers, it does speak to a real problem. Pre-industrial ways of life cannot isolate themselves from global structures of technological and cultural modernization.

That modernization, whether in Third World or in post-industrial settings, can take any number of paths, however. Although we have no "nature" to return to, we are still confronted with the question: what kind of world shall we move toward, at whose behest, and in whose interest?

Chapter 11

Information-processing psychology

The real importance of the computer in psychology is that it has created a new and pervasive state of mind. Psychologists have come to take it for granted in recent years that men and computers are merely two different species of a more abstract genus called "information processing systems."

George A. Miller[1]

In the twentieth century, the great colonial empires have been dismantled. Yet international relations of economic and cultural domination remain in place. Although the "New World Order" is not explicitly advocated as a colonial enterprise, its structures are continuous with imperial designs of the past. A possible difference is that today these designs rely less upon the force of arms than upon more purely administrative means. Military action is normally unnecessary within a global system "peacefully" organized by multinational corporate and financial institutions like the World Bank and International Monetary Fund.

Drawing upon the "internal colonization" metaphor, we may observe a similar change in the way the mind is conceived. Freud's push/pull metapsychology, patterned after a mechanics of energy accumulation and discharge, gives way to an information-processing model of the mind's administration of its internal and external surroundings. Internal colonization signifies that life in all of its dimensions, private as well as public, is subject to "reprogramming," we might say. No Third World country is exempt from integration within a worldwide political economy, nor any province of human activity from cognitive reorganization.

An approach to understanding human psychology that compares mental operations to those of information-processing devices is appealing in part because it mirrors the logic that organizes many areas of our lives. Bureaucratic settings are defined in terms of the procedures or "code" that governs them. Family life, too, can be consciously organized and rationalized ("colonized," Habermas would say), down to the details of daily protocol. By the clock, family members know when they are to leave the house and when to return. Activities ranging from meal preparation and childcare to television viewing and sleep are scheduled and coordinated with those of other persons inside and outside the family. Scarcely anything we do seems exempt from a procedural logic. Actions as various as making love, drawing up vacation plans, buying real-estate, or looking for a mate can be analyzed and rationally reconstructed as a set of step-by-step operations.

Given the prevalence of such activities, it is not surprising that the conjecture should come to mind that procedural functioning defines distinctively human behavior and motivation. The development of information-processing technologies supports this conjecture: the computer is not only something that we *use*; as the epitome of procedural reason, it also provides a seemingly convincing model, at least on one level, for what we *are*.

The idea that human beings are similar or perhaps even identical in type to machines is centuries old. What changes historically is not the attractiveness of this analogy but the technology that serves as its basis. In the seventeenth century, Descartes and his contemporaries were impressed with the splendor of the fountains at Versailles and fascinated by their ingenious mechanism. Might not a human being, Descartes asked, resemble such a self-moving hydraulic system? He reasoned as follows:

> You may have observed in the grottoes and fountains in the gardens of our kings that the force that makes the water leap from its source is able of itself to move diverse machines ... Truly one can well compare the nerves of the [human] machine ... to the tubes of the mechanisms of these fountains, its muscles and tendons to diverse other engines and springs which serve to move these mechanisms, its animal spirits to the water which drives them, of which the heart is the source and the brain's cavities the water main ... And finally when there shall be a rational soul in this machine, it will have its chief seat in the brain and will there reside like the turncock who must be in the main to which all the tubes of these machines repair when he wishes to excite, prevent, or in some manner alter their movements.[2]

Many besides Descartes have seen human functioning mirrored in the most advanced technology of their time. A person is like a clock or mill or steam engine or electric dynamo. A new kind of machine cannot be invented without someone conjecturing, "Aha! Human beings work like that!" Taking a relatively recent example, during the Second World War, cybernetic guidance systems were no sooner invented by military engineers than the paradigm of human behavior became, for some psychologists, a feedback loop.

Child development also attests to this apparent fascination with technological objects: children, whose attention span ordinarily lasts no more than a few minutes, readily become absorbed for much longer periods of time in watching machines work. I recall that when my four-year old nephew visited a construction site where heavy earth-moving vehicles were being used, his attention seemed permanently riveted. Was he engaged, at some level, in trying to comprehend not only how the machines work, but also how *he* works? What children learn about themselves in this way may vary, depending on the kind of technology that is being observed. As Sherry Tinkle has pointed out, a computer whose processing involves no moving parts, reflects back to a child a model of his or her functioning that is quite different from that provided by a mechanical machine.[3]

Today, the computer seems to provide the most compelling technological metaphor for characterizing human beings. Among some psychologists and psychoanalysts, the view that people can be understood in terms of information-processing procedures serves as a foundation not only for theories of cognition and perception, but for therapeutic practice as well. On this account, the human body consists of a complex hierarchy of systems and subsystems, characterized by elaborate control patterns governing their relations to one another and to the environment. The most important and most complex agency of control is the body's central nervous system, analogous to the central processing unit in a computer that regulates its various activities. As psychoanalyst Emanuel Peterfreund explains, communication networks link molecules within cells, cells within tissues, tissues within organs, up to the highest level of cortical functioning:

> Biological order is achieved through a hierarchical arrangement of feedback-regulated, information-processing control systems ... All are integrated or "programmed" into the over-all normal activity of the living organism ... An understanding of the nature of the information processing in existing computers has provided, perhaps for the first time in history, a conceptual framework that allows us to begin to understand certain fundamental aspects of the activity of the central nervous system, and the psychological experiences that correspond to that activity.[4]

The hypothesis that people are information-processing beings implies optimism about the human condition, since human "software" can be revised:

> I believe that we can say that the "grand strategy" of successful advanced living forms is the ability to learn; they are programmed to be able to reprogram themselves. This is another way of saying that they are programmed to adapt to new information, whatever its source.[5]

The basic idea here is that people, like computers, process information, or – in computer terms – execute programs. Some of the steps in this processing occur within the span of conscious attention, as when a chess player deliberates about her or his next move. But most information-processing occurs below the threshold of awareness.[6] According to this account, depth psychology, correctly understood, is the investigation of this processing. Psychopathology, in brief, is information-processing gone awry.

CRITIQUE OF ARTIFICIAL INTELLIGENCE

Information-processing models have been constructed to explain the gamut of psychological phenomena: cognition, communication, emotional life, social relations, and psychopathology. In certain areas, cognitive science can contribute to our understanding of basic human capacities. For example, the minute movements that the eye makes in order to perceive an object appear to be directed by an information-processing strategy of a kind. But as a general theory of the mind, cognitivism has little explanatory value, some critics claim.[7] One of their criticisms of information-processing simulations of human mental functioning is that they are context-blind. Because the computer program's "knowledge" is of the explicit, propositional type – a "knowing that" rather than a tacit "knowing how" – it cannot supply the background knowledge that is required to perceive or understand anything in a human way. For example, a language comprehension program that holds the *Oxford English Dictionary* in memory, will not know whether the word "pen" in "The pig is in the pen" refers to an animal sty or to a writing implement, since it lacks the relevant contextual knowledge that would allow this distinction to be made. Of course, we can take this bit of information and load it into the machine's memory, but this only patches over the problem, since new situations will arise in which the absence of background knowledge defeats the program's language deciphering efforts. This knowledge, like the skills involved in playing a musical instrument or writing a poem, cannot be unpacked as a finite collection of representations about the world. Hence the simulating program will fail at problems of pattern recognition that even an infant – or a family pet, for that matter – can solve at once, without drawing upon any propositional knowledge.

This introductory summary does not do justice to the standard critique of artificial intelligence, nor have I said anything about the responses that believers in artificial intelligence modeling have given to their critics.[8] Rather than plunge into this long-standing controversy, let us concentrate on only one of the areas in which information-processing concepts have been applied: psychotherapy. Such clinical applications are really too simple to count as "cognitive science," yet they illustrate the ideological pitfalls of cognitivist explanation. One reason that information-processing approaches to psychotherapy fail is that they cannot solve the problem mentioned above; they are oblivious to contextual relationships that are critical to any clinical encounter.

INFORMATION-PROCESSING PSYCHOLOGY: A CLINICAL ILLUSTRATION

Peterfreund's analysis of the therapeutic usefulness of information-processing principles has inspired work along similar lines by subsequent theorists of clinical practice.[9] He argues that psychoanalytic treatment, in particular, can be recast within an information-processing framework. Here is one of his case illustrations:

> A patient of mine could not allow herself to recognize that her husband was a rather disturbed person. To have done so would have activated a "branching tree" of decisions to be made, with innumerable associated problems and conflicts. For example, if she were to recognize that her husband was ill then she would have to face the decision of separating or not separating from him. If she decided to separate then she would have to face a decision concerning

remarriage. If she decided not to remarry, then she would have to face innumerable problems and conflicts concerning sexuality, living alone, caring for her children, and so on. On the other hand, if she decided not to leave her husband, then she would have to deal with her husband's illness, how to cope with the rage that he provoked, and so on. If we analyze the situation carefully we find a host of contingently related processes, each of which "triggers" the next, and the branching tree of decisions to make with associated problems and conflicts expands enormously. It is comparatively simple to think about these clinical phenomena in information-processing terms.

Peterfreund diagrams this decision tree in the form of a flow chart (Figure 11.1).[10]

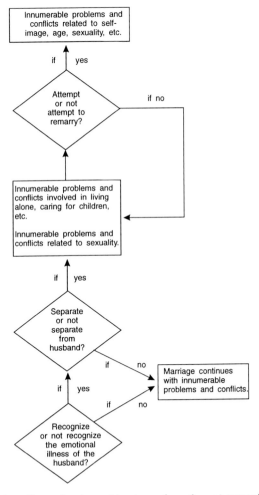

Figure 11.1 Flow chart illustrating branching tree of contingent emerging decisions, problems, and conflicts in a patient

This analysis faces a problem similar to the one, outlined above, that artificial intelligence designers find difficult to solve; formalization of a patient's situation so that it may be fitted into an information-processing scenario omits from consideration crucial contextual aspects of that situation. In the case of Peterfreund's woman patient, these aspects include her nearly total isolation and the social constraints on her available choices. Peterfreund's framing of her predicament as a kind of logic problem conceals its culturally and historically specific character. Within a different social world, where marriage did not strip people of their other relationships of companionship and support, the problem this patient faces could be addressed by a community of persons instead of being shouldered entirely by the spouse.

Peterfreund's flow chart diagram specifies that the decision to separate from the husband (second diamond from the bottom) implies "Innumerable problems and conflicts involved in living alone" (center rectangle). As Peterfreund has represented her situation, her connection to the world is solely marital. If that relationship is severed, she will be connection-less. Built into this either-or-logic is the exclusion of any third possibility. The woman is either with the husband or separate from him (and therefore totally on her own), as a binary bit is either one or zero. The flow chart does not completely mistake her predicament. The isolation of information-processing procedures from a larger matrix of relationships mirrors a culturally constructed reality; no social network is available which both husband and wife might turn to for help with the responsibilities and suffering that their relationship inflicts on both.

Immediately above the center rectangle of the chart, representing the problems that the woman will face if she separates from her husband, is the single alternative that this situation generates: "Attempt or not attempt to remarry?" Once again, it is simply taken for granted that she has no community of friends or family to fall back upon. Her only conceivable connection to the world is through a husband. Should she decide to attempt remarriage, then she will face "Innumerable problems and conflicts related to self-image, age, sexuality, etc." (top rectangle of the flow chart). Notice the objectification in these categories. Peterfreund's discussion of this case assumes that it is the patient's "age" itself which will make her life difficult, not the meanings that are given to a woman's age within a youth-obsessed culture. "Self-image," too, may interfere with her marrying again, Peterfreund suggests, as if the woman's image of herself, rather than the image and identity that the social world attributes to a middle-aged divorcée, is apt to get in her way.

Peterfreund might reply to this objection by amending his account: "What we need to add to the decision tree is a fuller list of relevant factors. In the rectangle at the top of the flow chart, for example, let us include *ageism* as well as *age*, *sexism* as well as *sexuality*, etc." This proposal for fixing Peterfreund's model fails because it eliminates the computational features of the model's decision tree structure. A computer program might conceivably take into account "age" and "sexuality," inasmuch as they are defined as purely biological, quantifiable variables. "Ageism" and "sexism," on the other hand, are qualitative, socially constituted notions. They assume meaning only within a network of cultural interpretation and power relations that cannot easily be represented in terms of sequential computational procedures.

Suppose that an information-processing device severs its communications link-up with one computer and attempts to re-establish them with another. Various problems may need to be addressed, including compatibility of protocols and rate of data transmission. But in this case, each problem is clearly defined, independent of every other, and involves relatively simple decision procedures. Where there are interdependencies, their structure is explicit in such a way that they can be systematically handled. This is not the situation that Peterfreund's woman patient faces. The possible obstacles to her remarriage – including ageism, sexism, and her self-image – are neither precisely defined, mutually independent, nor measurable parameters like those that a computational device handles. They are bound together within a matrix of relations, an experiential "lifeworld," that remains hidden within the psychoanalytic therapy that Peterfreund describes. His account, inasmuch as it occludes these relations, degrades clinical perceptions and intuition, and contributes to the illness that it pretends to alleviate.

THE COMPUTERIZATION OF PSYCHOTHERAPY

If a therapist perceives a client as an information-processor whose pathology consists in faulty programming, then the therapeutic function will be to enable the client to reprogram and recompute. For example, Peterfreund's patient needs, he believes, to carry out a certain decision procedure whose structure he specifies. But if this is the cure, then a machine might assist a patient as effectively as a human clinician. Computer-assisted instruction (CAI) is helpful for learning a variety of skills; why not include the skill of reprogramming oneself?

Just this conclusion has been reached by a number of theorists at the "cutting edge" of therapeutic innovation.[11] On the basis of his own research and several other studies attesting to the effectiveness of computer-administered therapy, psychiatrist Michael Zarr concludes that "computerized psychotherapy devices can produce changes and may be highly acceptable to certain patients. There is some evidence, as well, that such programs may be as effective or even more so than human therapists, in the delivery of certain modes of psychotherapy." An additional advantage of therapy of this kind is that a patient can keep a therapeutic adjunct close by, in the form of a personal computer: "Homework via computer provides a standard and interactive format that would keep patients involved with therapy and enable the therapist and patient to have immediate analysis of data, thereby increasing the power of therapeutic interventions."[12]

The logic here is simple: pathology is faulty thinking, therefore it can be alleviated by machines that help people think better. Zarr envisions therapists who will see patients long enough to diagnose their condition and set them up with a computer program that will "listen" to them in a technologically sophisticated way, monitor their progress, and modify their treatment plans if necessary.

Drawing on psychoanalytic concepts, Kenneth Colby, another of the pioneers in this area, refers to the positive and negative relationships that develop between patients and programs in computer-mediated psychotherapy. Having observed that most who are exposed to therapy of this kind became frustrated and irritated, he attributes their reactions to negative "transference." But Zarr asserts that this negativity provides no insurmountable obstacle to the therapeutic process. On the contrary:

> The patient-centered format enables the program to encourage exploration of these negative transference feelings, just as the human therapist would. Hence it is possible that such feelings could be manipulated in a therapeutic way in the context of computer psychotherapy to produce change, particularly in adult patients with good reality-testing.[13]

The negative reactions of patients to computer-administered therapy can become the subject of therapeutic exploration, to be worked through like any other issue! The author does not consider the possibility that the nature of the therapy, rather than the pathology of the patient, might be responsible for the patient's resistance.

Realizing that therapists as well as patients may be reluctant to prescribe or get involved in computer-administered treatment, Zarr argues that:

> The greatest obstacle currently slowing down progress of research in computer-mediated psychotherapy is the fact that unless the physicians using it truly believe in its effectiveness, even the most sophisticated computer technology will fail ... The introduction of computer technology into psychotherapy offers the significant advantages of flexibility, consistency, and economy that would make psychotherapy more effective and more readily available to a much broader patient population than the one presently benefiting from such treatment.[14]

It is not enough, Zarr claims, that psychotherapists should remain open to the feasibility of computer-mediated therapy of this kind. For it can succeed only if they "truly believe in its effectiveness." If patients are not helped by the machines that treat them, this apparently provides *prima facie* evidence for a failure of faith on the part of the therapist.

Zarr points out that there are economic reasons for placing computers in therapeutic roles. By his account, technology eliminates the need for therapists to devote personal attention to particular individuals, clearing the way instead for machine-administered treatment of the masses. As the prescription of anti-psychotic medication makes it possible to handle mental patients with minimal effort by human care givers, so interaction with a computer may now substitute for the dialogue that has traditionally defined psychotherapy. Carried to an extreme here is the separation of system requirements (such as the "flexibility, consistency, and economy" cited by Zarr above) from patients' needs for the kinds of exploration and understanding that are possible in the context of open-ended dialogue and mutual recognition.

Advanced industrial societies, in an era of chronic economic stagnation and recession, take as their top priority profit-generating economic activity. Those who serve this purpose are valued and rewarded. Society's so-called "non-productive" individuals, on the other hand – those homeless, addicted, elderly, physically impaired, or mentally disturbed, for instance – receive minimal resources. Psychotherapy is as vulnerable to this logic as any labor: a computer stands in for more expensive human service providers.

HISTORY VERSUS CLOCKED TIME

Peterfreund does not go as far in a technological direction as Zarr and other advocates of computerized psychotherapy. He is not ready to substitute a machine for the human therapist. Yet his invocation of technological metaphor to understand psychoanalysis transforms the discipline's meaning and mission. Filtration through the conceptual framework of information-processing psychology eliminates from social relationships and personal identity qualities that make them irreducibly human.

These qualities include categories as fundamental as space and time. How illuminating is cognitive science's simulations of these dimensions of our lived experience? Can an information-processing model explain, for example, the crucial role of personal history in psychotherapy? At first glance, information-processing simulation of the temporal aspect of human existence seems to pose no special difficulty. Typically, information-processing systems are acutely sensitive to the passage of time. Not a fraction of a microsecond goes by without a computer's central processing unit assessing the consequences of the previous fraction and preparing for the next. In a single second, a modest microcomputer can carry out millions of sequential operations.

But what is the quality of this time? The linear time that regulates a computational process is divisible into "slices" of precisely equal length, meted out by the computer's clock. This structure affords memory of a kind; a computer can take information generated at a particular moment and place it in electronic storage, where it may be accessed and subsequently used. Take the example of a chess-playing program that, first, modifies itself based on past successes and failures, and secondly, examines the future consequences of various moves in order to determine which move should now be made. Since in this sense a chess-playing system learns from its past "experience" and evaluates future alternative courses of action, we might say that its judgments are historical. History of this kind is not, however, human history. Unlike a human being, a computer system is "immortal" not only because it could possibly exist indefinitely into the future, but in the stronger sense that it is not really "embodied" in the world at all. Such a system, like an equation or mathematical theorem, is essentially a formal structure, existing beyond the categories of physical space and time and therefore invulnerable to the forces that generate or destroy material beings.

Past, present, and future *matter* for humans because it is within the compass of a particular life narrative that each unique personal identity is formed. Within our personal and interpersonal histories, we locate and identify others and ourselves.[15] As people get to know one another, their sharing of a history, consisting not only of their lives before they met but also of their own unfolding relationship, is essential to their recognition of one another. This is part of the reason that separation from a lover is a misery, for it is a separation from the path that two have traveled together and a loss of the identity made possible by their journey. If my lover dies, our history continues to exist as a heap of empirical facts. I can peer at the old photographs and recall our past. But this history no longer provides the ongoing vehicle of our reciprocal recognition, the mirror wherein we may see and acknowledge each other as the unique beings we are. The loss of our history together signifies an annihilation.

What is true of lovers applies also to wider relationships; the history of one is bound up with the history of all. If decades ago, my friends and I participated in the social movements of the time, these experiences are now interwoven with our lives in ways that continue to connect and identify us. Although some of us may regard this past as a naive and youthful folly, our common history nevertheless continues to define us, even at the moment of recantation. The only way of making sense of where we have been and of what we have become is through a recollection and re-examination of social as well as individual narratives.

Our history, then, is bound up with our personal identities not as a set of past and now irrelevant events, but as the enduring source of life's meaning and continuity. Unlike computers, people are constituted by their past as well as their current involvements. Unless we grasp the historical interweavings of our lives with cultural traditions and communities, we shall mistake the character of those lives. Because theorists such as Peterfreund construe human involvements in terms of information-processing programs operating on context-independent "data," they misunderstand the ways human beings create their history and in the process form themselves.

THE EXPERIENCE OF TIME IN PSYCHOTHERAPY

Cognition-based therapies tend to regard the past as significant only in so far as knowledge of what has happened in a person's life affords leverage for altering the future. The purpose of psychotherapy is to replace the patient's current pathological programming with programming that is more functional. On this account, "solving" a life problem is analogous to solving a chess problem; one doesn't care how the pieces got into their current positions – the challenge is to assess the existing situation and to devise a winning strategy.

In contrast to this information-processing approach, psychodynamic therapy views the uncovering of a person's unique history as important not only for the purpose of diminishing or altering its hold on the present, but also because it may contribute to a recognition that makes healing possible. Personal recognition means acknowledgement not only of who another person *is*, in the present, but also of who that person *has been*. Experiences from the past are brought into the therapeutic relationship in the form of "transference": the therapist is cast by the client in the roles of others who have figured significantly in his or her life. Within the transference, fears of intimacy and emotional vulnerability arise and are dealt with in ways that contradict earlier deprivations and disappointments, empowering the client to reappropriate a personal history that has never been understood or assimilated.

Psychodynamic psychotherapy does not always work this well, of course. In many ways and for many reasons, it may fail. But when it succeeds, it does so in large part because of an "I–thou" relationship of a kind established between human subjects. For all of their talk of "information-processing" and "reprogramming," I suspect that the effectiveness of cognitivist therapists like Peterfreund depends on the personal rapport they establish with those they seek to help. As Freud noted, intellectual understanding alone is impotent to affect change. Suppose that a machine could correctly diagnose a clinical problem: "Patient was unloved by parents;" "Patient's feelings of anger get in the way of intimate relations." How much good would this do? Of critical importance in effective psychotherapy is the presence of an other who listens, understands, and cares.

In New York, a special treatment program for addiction was devised that relied on microcomputer delivery of information and counseling to black adolescents. When asked which they preferred, computer or human service delivery, this group split 8 to 1 in favor of human service providers. The main objection the adolescents had to the computerized program was that it could not relate to human problems. As one of them said, "Computers can't take drugs." The complaint here was not that the machine was not a user, but that, being inhuman, it *could not* be.[16]

Such results remain unintelligible within an information-processing framework. If pathology is a matter of intellectual malfunction, then an astute machine that conveys factual information and encourages rationality could be expected to address and repair the situation. But if therapy works because of a human relationship, involving empathy and mutual vulnerability, then machine simulation is a hoax.

GAME THEORY AND PSYCHOTHERAPY

In Peterfreund's case illustration, the patient's predicament is represented as if it were a kind of puzzle, a game in which she has to learn the right moves. It is not accidental that advocates of information-processing psychology are attracted to game theory. For the codified rules of a game exhibit an independence of social and historical context that characterizes information-processing logic as well. In chess problems, for example, we are given a diagram of an initial arrangement of pieces on the board, and then asked to figure out what steps must be taken to obtain a winning position. It is immaterial how this initial configuration came into being. Peterfreund represents his patient's predicament as similarly rule-governed and solvable by logical means. But that predicament, as well as the information-processing procedures that promise to adapt her to her own life, are inextricable from an historical context that remains invisible within an information-processing perspective. Only through this history is the relationship between women and men created, including the divisions of labor between them, the forces that attract them to one another and that drive them apart, and their dependencies on one another.

Peterfreund's therapeutic method obliterates this context. To the extent that he communicates to his patient his information-processing model of what her life is about, his image of her may merge with her image of herself – an image that is likely to imply self-reproach, since it focuses on her inadequacies of internal programming and biology (the fact that she is growing older, for example). Were she to recognize her predicament as culturally shaped and as shared with many other women in similar circumstances, she might reject the representation of her situation that Peterfreund's model provides. This in itself would not amount to a "cure." But understanding the origins of one's anxieties and unhappiness does play an important part in shaping a different future.

One of the reasons that the information-processing model seems illuminating is that it is self-confirming, becoming true to the extent that we believe in it. This theoretical approach contributes to *forming* the very human nature that it claims to explain. When we treat ourselves or respond to one another in procedural, instrumental ways, aiming to "program" our lives, we validate a distorted image of ourselves. The complex realities of our social relationships, our personal histories, and our identifications are misconstrued by reading computational concepts into human experience as cognitivists like Peterfreund have done. We would do well to read them back out again.

Chapter 12

Technology and authority

In every society, people internalize cultural values and standards of behavior. Protestant self-discipline and Freud's superego, for instance, refer to aspects of internalization that are characteristic of industrializing nations. In post-industrial settings, however, the self's regulation of itself is differently organized and finds new metaphors for its own functioning in the technological apparatus of production. In this chapter, I'll suggest that information technologies serve to legitimate a "colonization of the lifeworld" characterized by bureaucratic structures of hierarchical authority. If this is so then the following question arises: is there any viable alternative to these structures, short of abandoning the technologies that support them?

In the economic realm, post-industrial authority is fundamentally contradictory. On the one hand, its ideology is laced with ideals of participation and self-determination. There is a vast literature on the importance of "involving" workers in the decisions that shape the workplace. Many administrators and managers today realize that self-motivated employees who feel that they have a say about how their own labor is structured are likely to turn out a higher quality product than workers for whom it is "just a job."

On the other hand, post-industrial production typically takes place under highly regimented conditions, organized by corporate enterprises, many of them multinational, that dictate terms not just to individual workers, but to unions, communities, local and even national governments. Today, capital is globally integrated, and its governing structures appear as scarcely comprehensible, let alone, controllable, by local agency of any kind. Toward the end of understanding the influence of technological innovation upon these structures, let us begin with microeconomic observations about the individual firm, and then extend our discussion to the broader prospects for democracy in post-industrial societies.

Technology's role in the distribution of power and authority is complex, and depends on the particular roles played by those who invent, fabricate, and make use of technological objects. For example, a programmer who writes software to operate a computer does not experience the device in the same way as a factory worker who assembles its circuit boards, or a typist who enters data. Similarly, an automated bank-teller has a certain significance for a customer, quite another for banking personnel responsible for monitoring or processing its transactions, and yet another for the technician called in to repair the system when it breaks down.

For some, technological interactions are empowering; the machine extends the reach of one's knowledge and facilitates the swift performance of previously laborious or even impossible tasks. For others, information technology *dis*enfranchises: automation takes away some jobs and de-skills others; computerized storage of information violates the privacy of those whom the machine "knows about." Information technology, then, like any other instrument, is incorporated within a social matrix that allocates power.

WHO'S IN CHARGE?

"Allocation," however, implies the existence of alternatives and the possibility of human choice. But within an information-based order, it is as if power allocates itself. Bureaucratic authority, which once was only one form of governance among others, has become institutionally standard and tends to efface the very possibility of an external perspective or critical stance.[1] Post-industrial settings differ in this regard from those that pit individuals directly against one another. In a traditional factory environment, for example, there exists a particular person or group of persons in charge, against whom workers can articulate their grievances and launch a strike. In a patriarchal family, where authority is located squarely in the person of the father, other family members may rebel against him. When the authority in question is a rationalizing system (e.g. corporate or state administration), on the other hand, it is less easily discerned or challenged. The size, complexity, and apparently seamless logic of the system appear to render it unalterable.

In keeping with the relatively personal structures of a small-scale manufacturing or commercial enterprise, Freud's model of individual self-formation turns upon the introjection of ideals exemplified by a particular person or persons with whom one identifies. This process begins in childhood but continues thereafter; human beings find in educational and work settings authority figures with whom or against whom they can identify and situate themselves. Today, these external, personalized models are for many people not in place; the query "Who's in charge?" admits of no satisfactory response. This is not to say that authority structures have been leveled or democratized; on the contrary, they continue to subordinate those who are submitted to them. Yet their negative consequences tend to remain hidden or ill-defined. In the workplace, for instance, individual problems may be labeled by health practitioners as anxiety disorders, psychosomatic complaints, or matters of "low self-esteem," thereby covering over rather than explaining the underlying issues.

Even research into the nature of post-industrial work conducted by social scientists tends to overlook or misconstrue the ways that work is hierarchically organized. One of the better-known recent studies of hi-tech workplaces is Shoshana Zuboff's *In the Age of the Smart Machine*.[2] In the various settings she examines, system rationality, incorporated in computerized machinery, is represented as the autonomous agent of the reorganization of work. Zuboff's book not only examines but evidently endorses this representation: "A noted Harvard social scientist," its back cover informs us, "provides the most complete and important book to date on how today's advanced computer technology fundamentally changes the nature of work and power." The presumed actor here is "technology," whose passive object is the social structure of the workplace. In each of the contexts that Zuboff examines, the legitimacy of the prevailing system rationality is taken for granted. Workers and managers alike understand their purpose as adaptation to system requirements. A manager at a pulp mill being computerized describes the new work environment:

> With the evolution of computer technology, you centralize controls and move away from the actual physical process. If you don't have an understanding of what is happening and how all the pieces interact, it is more difficult. You need a new learning capability, because when you operate with a computer, you can't see what is happening. There is a difference in the mental and conceptual capabilities you need – you have to do things in your mind.[3]

The reference here to "the evolution of computer technology" suggests that technology develops along a path of its own determination, independent of anyone's interest or will. Human agency is reduced to an anonymous "you" that performs the various system-defined roles: "You need a new learning capability," "you have to do things in your mind" – these functions and authority structures are what the system requires to operate, and also what workers need to operate within the system. Any distinction between the system's needs and those of the individuals it engages has been effaced.

If this were only management's perspective, it would not be surprising. But Zuboff's study indicates that participants at every level within automated work environments are prepared to adapt to their logic. At Piney Wood, a large pulp mill in the process of computerizing production at the time of Zuboff's study, she reports workers' attitudes about changing skill requirements:

> They anticipated that workers would need a great deal of education and training in order to "breed flexibility." "We find it all to be a great stress," they said, "but it won't be that way for the new flexible people."[4]

Flexibility, in this case, designates readiness to reshape oneself to function effectively within the new system. Ambivalences and emotional conflicts about the changing structure of the workplace barely surface in statements like "We find it all to be a great stress." When this remark is followed immediately by another that is more reassuring: "it won't be that way for the new flexible people," is this optimism heartfelt or rather an effort to save face in front of the interviewer or other workers? Might the interviewees be wondering whether the better-educated workers of the future will include themselves? As far as we can tell from reading her book, Zuboff's research did not ask such questions.

A mill "operator" (the company's term for non-managerial personnel) describes the way computerization has reshaped his responsibilities:

> If something is happening, if something is going wrong, you don't go down and fix it. Instead, you stay up here (in the control room) and think about the sequence, and you think about how you want to affect the sequence. You get it done through your thinking ... I am always wondering: Where am I at? What is happening? It all occurs in your mind now.[5]

To perform adequately, one must mentally reproduce the logical structure of the system whose functioning one monitors. Authority here is literally made internal: workers learn to monitor and respond to the system's display of its own condition – via meters, lights, and other indicators – as if that condition were their own: "It all occurs in your mind now."

THE "NEW MANAGEMENT"

Internalized in this way, patterns of reasoning become so much a part of one's identity that they cannot simply be put aside when one leaves work and returns to the lifeworld of family and friends. Mind workers tend to bring their work home with them, even if they walk in the door with their briefcases empty. Influence travels also in the opposite direction: institutions, without losing their rationalized character, import personal life into themselves. The workplace may even provide a "second home" of a sort, standing in for the family and affording a new intimacy fostered by the corporate culture.

In this corporate "home away from home," authority relationships assume new forms. "Working is like parenting – or being parented," Charles, a programmer and systems analyst, tells me. He explains:

> The manager of our team is a woman who looks after us with a lot of affection, while keeping her eye on what we are supposed to get done. In a way, we are her family. We, in turn, serve as teachers and surrogate parents of the user community that we build our systems for. Recently I carried a beeper, so that people at the test site [where a new information system was being installed] could call me any time, day or night, to ask questions and notify me when anything went wrong. My responsibility was "hand-holding," as it is called in the profession: you coddle users until they get familiar with the new system. I wanted – like my manager, in relation to those of us under her wing: to be a responsive, helpful parent.

The metaphor here invokes a mothering, not a fathering parent. Traditional patriarchal authority – which functions by laying down the law, punishing infractions, establishing superego controls – is not effective in getting programmers to program well, social workers to handle their cases effectively, or personnel to make intelligent use of newly introduced technology. "Maternally" structured authority works better, in this respect, but it also raises new issues about closeness and separation. Charles dreamt:

I have a bunch of files in my [computer] directory named akins1, akins2, akins3, *etc. "These are my files," I tell myself. But of course they belong to the company.*

Associations: These files are like someone else's kids I'm babysitting. My work's like that. I do it for others, I develop their software like a nursemaid who cares for someone else's children.

akins is Atkins minus the *t*. Ted Atkins is about to join me on this project. I eliminated the *t* from the file names. Maybe I don't want him coming on board!

akins has the word *kin* inside. The files in question are birds of a feather, look-alike siblings. But *akins* is also like *a*moral or *a*sexual, meaning "*without kinship.*" Files in a computer have no real relation to one another, they aren't literally brothers or sisters. They can't belong as kin to one another. There's no room for that sort of thing in the work I do. Colleagues belong maybe to the same "team," but not to the same family. Thank heaven it is so!

Babysitting is the initial role in which the dreamer sees himself. He manages the files in his directory as an adult supervises a child. These files are under his jurisdiction, however, only in his role as agent of the larger system, the company that owns everything he produces. He ends up comparing himself and his co-workers to the files themselves; although they are "birds of a feather," they "have no real relation to one another."

Charles works for a large corporation that organizes work around specific projects. If a customer puts in a request for an information system, a team is assembled to design and build it. On completion of the project, the team is dissolved. Such projects typically last one or two years. During that time, team members are apt to work extremely closely together. Charles describes this situation as follows:

You see the people you're working with day in, day out, and for that time you share everything – meals, breaks, the works – and talk over with them everything in your life, down to the raw details. But in fact these aren't your friends, and both of you know your companionship will end abruptly when the project terminates or for some other reason, you or they get shifted out of the project. So you let yourself go only so far and you remember that it will last only for this while, when you're working together. Once I'm out of here, or they're out of here, we won't keep up the relationship. You're intimate with someone one day, and on the next you're prepared to move on and never see them again. So you only get so close, knowing that before too long it will be all over.

Relationships among people parallel those among the "akins" files in the dream; they are situated together today, but tomorrow one or all of them may be moved elsewhere. For this reason, appearances notwithstanding, they are "without kinship" and do not belong "to the same family," as the dreamer puts it.

With a keystroke, a file can be deleted; Charles felt similarly dispensable. He mentioned the possibility that his current position might be eliminated, and that the man who was about to join him on his current project at work could conceivably take over his responsibilities. He could not bring himself to talk to his colleagues or manager about the uncertainty of this situation. As he pointed out, his work is such that feelings of any kind, but especially those that might bring people into conflict, tend to remain unacknowledged:

> We work in a pretty "sanitized" environment. Sisters and brothers [referring again to the dream] squabble and beat on one another. We don't. My manager treats me politely, and I return the favor. Likewise for the rest of us. Like files in a computer we might sit side-by-side, but no one publicly trashes anyone else. On the rare occasion that someone gets angry, it's like a dysfunction and everyone regards them as out of line.

Given this work ambience it was difficult for Charles to voice his fears and frustration about a situation that he felt powerless to control.

Where was power located? Higher up in the corporate system. But it seemed unattached to anyone in particular. Sometimes Charles felt anonymous himself, that he was not anyone in particular. Paradoxically, while he felt separate from his co-workers, he also experienced a lack of differentiation. He dreamt:

> *We were in a waiting room, filling out papers. Then the door opened and we were admitted into a chamber filled with glass objects, where everything was transparent and reflected everything else. We were all transparent and reflected one another. So there was the strange sensation that there was only one person, or no persons, in the room.*

Associations: This was like a world of video-terminals. Each is a window of kind through which you enter the system and do your work. At work everyone has their own screen, into which they stare hour upon hour. We all connect into the same system, as "nodes" it's technically called. Any node can see through to any other, but each is also invisible – an abstraction not in space-time, so there's nothing to see.

In this dream nothing opaque separates anything from anything else. Minds, substanceless and separate from bodies, are transparent to one another. Under these circumstances, the dreamer would be taking a risk to feel angry, since in a world without privacy or boundaries of any kind, one person's feelings instantly affect everyone else.

THE INVISIBILITY OF TECHNOCRATIC AUTHORITY

An invisible "abstraction not in space-time" – so Charles describes himself and his fellow employees. As in the case of Zuboff's millworkers, the logic of the system is joined to the functioning of those who interact with it. Reflecting on the character of post-industrial work, I am reminded of Karl Marx's comments, made over a century ago, about the consequences of automation for workplace relationships. Notwithstanding the qualitative differences between industrial and post-industrial social structures, there is also a continuity that Marx's account brings out. I am thinking here of his observations, made not when he was speaking out optimistically about the revolutionary "mission" of the proletariat, but in his private writings – in the preparatory texts for *Capital*, for instance, consisting of notes that he did not anticipate would ever be published. Marx describes what happens to the character of work when production is automated:

> [L]abor appears ... merely as a conscious organ, scattered among the individual living workers at numerous points ... subsumed under the total process of the machinery itself, as itself only a link of the system, whose unity exists not in the living workers, but rather in the living (active) machinery which confronts his individual, insignificant doings as a mighty organism.[6]

Laborers are disunited and dependent. Unity and mastery reside in the machine. Note that no mention is made here of capital or capitalists, as if the technical system itself takes charge and subordinates everything that is human to its own purposes.

Elsewhere, Marx pictured a proletarian whose manual strength and dexterity is harnessed to capitalist production, but whose mind is left free to comprehend and eventually, in solidarity with others, to resist and overturn his situation. Under conditions of automation, however, the worker's labor becomes reduced, in Marx's words, to "individual, insignificant doings." Marx continued to believe, of course, that the system of capitalist production is antithetical to the best interests of working people. Yet his analysis calls into question the prospect that they will recognize their own situation. On the contrary, the institutional rationality of advanced capitalism tends to automate out of existence possible opposition to itself.

We are referring here to a condition which Marx was able only to anticipate. In his day, industrial social relations could still be perceived in personal terms. The "capitalist system" operated according to a certain logic, to be sure, but this did not preclude identification of the enemy: the "ruling class," consisting of those persons who maintained their stranglehold over the economy and over the lives of workers. In post-industrial settings, on the other hand, it is more difficult to identify the particular individuals responsible for the structure or rationale of social organization. This returns us to an earlier theme; authority is experienced as located not in human individuals but in an anonymous structure to whose logic everyone is submitted. (Kafka's fiction provides an early literary representation of such depersonalization; Max Weber offers the classical theoretical formulation.) When, for example, a bank-teller reports that she cannot enter a transaction because "the computer has gone down," the client cannot very well get angry at her, since computer-maintenance falls entirely outside her jurisdiction. Who then is to blame? Where conflict involves impersonal agency, located in a corporation, bank, or government agency, as local as City Hall or as global as the International Monetary Fund, no obvious image of the adversarial "other" comes to mind. The best we can do is to imagine a banker with a top hat and money bags, or an Uncle Sam pointing his finger – we feel compelled to personalize. What has been so convenient about Iraq's Saddam Hussein is that he is a clear-cut "enemy," visible on TV, who can possibly be confronted and defeated.

COMPUTER LOGIC AND SOCIAL HIERARCHY

In an economically and culturally integrated world, the desire to return to smaller-scale, more personal and participatory communities appears anachronistic. Systems theorists argue that the organization of large-scale, complex social institutions inevitably assumes bureaucratic, hierarchical forms. To think otherwise, to envisage a decentralized, consensual social order, is on this view "hopelessly out of touch with social reality."[7] This belief in the necessity of top-down implementation of social control receives support in two ways from information-processing technologies. First, they serve as the "intelligence" of administrative systems: computers help to organize and manage the vast volumes of data that corporations and state agencies handle. Secondly, technological and social hierarchies mirror one other on a metaphorical level:

1 *Information system*: Software coordinates and integrates the various functions of a computer. Software accomplishes this task most efficiently, moreover, if it is hierarchically organized.
2 *Social system*: Economic and state administration coordinates and integrates the various functions of our social institutions. As in the case of the software–hardware relationship, administration accomplishes this task most efficiently when it is hierarchical.

The implication of this comparison between technological and social order is that hierarchical rationalization is indispensable for both. Its function is to coordinate the modules within a system by way of fulfilling the goals that the system serves. This logic seems as sensible and value-free as any in mathematics or science.

Ruled out here is the possibility that modern social institutions could be democratically run. On the contrary, efficient governance is bound to assume centralized, hierarchical forms since, as Nobel Prize winner Herbert Simon argues:

> Whenever highly complex programs have been written – whether for scientific computing, business data processing, or heuristic problem solving – they have always turned out to have a clear-cut hierarchical structure. The over-all program is always subdivided into subprograms. In programs of any great complexity, the subprograms are further subdivided, and so on. Moreover, in some general sense, the higher level programs control or govern the behavior of the lower level programs, so that we find among these programs relations of authority among routines that are not dissimilar to those we are familiar with in human organizations.[8]

Hierarchy has several meanings. *Analytic* hierarchy, referring to the division of a category into subcategories, as in the relation of genus to species, is not at issue here. A genus is hierarchically above, but does not exercise authority over, the species. A *command* hierarchy, on the other hand, consists in relations of authority and obedience. It is hierarchy of this kind, Simon argues, that is as essential to a well-ordered society as to a well-ordered computer program.

In comparing what has "always turned out" to be the case in programming to what "we are familiar with in human organizations," Simon stops short of explicit advocacy. His argument remains in the descriptive mode in this passage and in many others. For instance, "Hierarchic subdivision is not peculiar to human organizations. It is common to virtually all complex systems of which we have knowledge" and "The near universality of hierarchy in the composition of complex systems suggests that there is something fundamental in the structural principle that goes beyond the peculiarities of human organization."[9] There is an assumed stance here of value neutrality; no *oughts* or *shoulds* are to be found in these sentences. Nevertheless, Simon's professed scientific detachment and objectivity scarcely cover his enthusiasm for technocratic authority.

Plato, over two millenniums ago, was equally taken with the idea of hierarchical order. But he viewed that order as something absent from the real, corrupted world. Simon, on the other hand, argues from the fact of what exists – nearly ubiquitously, he believes – to what must be and should be the case. It is natural and inevitable, he says, that the structural logic of efficient information systems will be applied as well in the realm of social organization. Innovative here is not Simon's preference for hierarchical arrangements, but his reliance on the logic of computer technology to back up his social analysis. This reliance lends a certain credibility to his position, inasmuch as formal logic, realized in a computer process or mathematical proof, carries with it a unique quality of binding authority and even inexorability.

Herbert Simon was one of the first to compare computer logic to the logic of social institutions. By now this theme has become a favorite among some authors of programming primers. In their introductory text on structured programming, Hughes and Michtom argue that "It is necessary to have one module control the activities of the other modules in a program, in much the same way a president of a company supervises the firm's employees." They go on to elaborate the parallel between an optimally structured program and a well-run business. Vertical control characterizes both:

> A lower-level module should not make decisions that a higher-level module must follow. To illustrate this point, return to the analogy of the organization chart. We would not expect an employee to make decisions that his manager, his manager's manager, or other departments would have to follow. We would expect him to receive directions from his manager and report back as to whether or not he was able to carry them out successfully.[10]

As in Simon's account, the explicit meaning here is not a *prescription* about how social institutions should be organized, but only a *description* of their actual organizational logic. Hughes and Michtom compare what is "necessary" in a corporate decision-making environment to what is necessary in an information-processing system. The implication is that the prevailing authority structure of the social world is as logically compelling and inevitable as theorems in mathematics or computer science. We would, in Hughes and Michtom's words, "not expect an employee to make decisions that his manager, his manager's manager, or other departments would have to follow," any more than we would expect to add two and two and get five. By definition, company presidents and managers, like high-level modules in a computer program, issue instructions; employees, like low-level modules, carry them out and report back to their superiors. The only question is how this is to be accomplished most efficiently.

The comparison of corporate to programming architectures involves more than analogy. For those architectures directly implement management's control functions. As Ramoorthy points out, "The hierarchical arrangement of a structured program provides a natural organization for the assignment of jobs."[11] The logic of the program merges with the social division of labor, engaging the programmer in what appears to be a seamless system of technologically determined social control. In this way, structured programming serves to regulate, to some extent, to de-skill and disempower the programming workforce:

> Modules – which are simply discrete components of a larger program – can be parceled out to a low-level programmer who must follow rigid coding guidelines in writing the program fragment. He or she no longer needs to know anything about the overall system of which it is a part, or even how the module fits into other modules.[12]

Figures 12.1 and 12.2 illustrate the resemblance between software and corporate hierarchies. The first is a diagram of the main module for a job scheduler that a teams of consultants, including myself, helped to design for an industrial firm, and the second is a (simulated) diagram of the company's organizational structure. In planning the first of these systems, we were not, to my knowledge, consciously imitating the second. Yet the resemblance of the structure of the program to that of the company is striking.

What are the implications of this similarity? Simon begins with the premise that the hierarchical organization of programs is rational and desirable. Indeed, the software package mentioned above seems to be organized in a sensible way: hierarchically arranged relationships contribute to the clarity, efficiency, and easy modifiability of the code. Simon then infers that hierarchical arrangements are natural and appropriate also for social institutions. Is this conclusion justified?

SOCIAL DARWINISM

By way of approaching this question, let us examine the underlying form of Simon's argument. Reasoning of this kind proceeds as follows: social order is viewed as analogous to some other domain, and then principles thought to apply appropriately in the latter case are presumed to be rational in the former as well. For example, social institutions have often been compared to an individual human organism, with the implication that just as the mind (or brain) is assigned by nature to exercise authority over the body, so it falls to the state to govern the "body politic," and to management to run the corporation.

A similar lesson is drawn from the comparison of human to other biological species: a human "pecking order" is assumed to be as natural as the hierarchies that govern non-human animals. In the nineteenth century, Social Darwinism claimed the support of Darwin's theory of the evolution of species. According to this view, the fittest survive, both in the human and animal kingdoms. This is nature's way of weeding out the weaker members of a social order and of preserving the hardiest. Interference with this competition, through social welfare legislation or other measures that help those who cannot help themselves, supposedly debilitates humankind as a whole.

This Social Darwinist analogy resembles Simon's and Hughes and Michtom's comparison above of social to computational hierarchy. In each case, we are required to abandon our apparently Utopian illusions and resign ourselves to the status quo: "You can't change human nature," in the first instance; "You can't fight logic," in the second. There is one difference between the two arguments, though. Social Darwinism legitimates competitive *laissez-faire* capitalism, partly explaining the popularity of Darwinist metaphor among advocates of the "free marketplace" of material commodities and entrepreneurial skills. But in the twentieth century, the *laissez-faire* model is at odds with the logic of capital. The overall movement of industrial economies is toward integration and bureaucratic administration, as smaller units of production are consolidated horizontally and vertically into larger enterprises. These economies still include a competitive sector, consisting of numerous, typically small firms that vie with one another for market share and profits. But the monopoly sector, made up of such companies as those in the Fortune Five Hundred, has become predominant during the twentieth century. The logic of relations among and within these firms cannot be understood along the lines of a Social Darwinist no-holds-barred competition between biological individuals for survival.[13]

A more adequate model for post-industrial integration is the organization of a computer; this comparison finds a warrant for social hierarchy not in the evolutionary processes that have created us but in the computational processes that we create. Structured programming, with its emphasis on top-down design and the harmonious weaving together of disparate functions, provides an ideal for administrators of large institutions. Computer programs work well when they are hierarchically structured. Why not expect the same of social and political arrangements?

CORPORATISM AND COMPUTER TECHNOLOGY

The problem with the society–computer analogy is that the participation of humans in a social organization is quite unlike that of modules in a computer system. (A similar argument refutes Social Darwinism: its plausibility rests on fallacious inferences from the realm of animal behavior to that of human culture.)[14] Modules

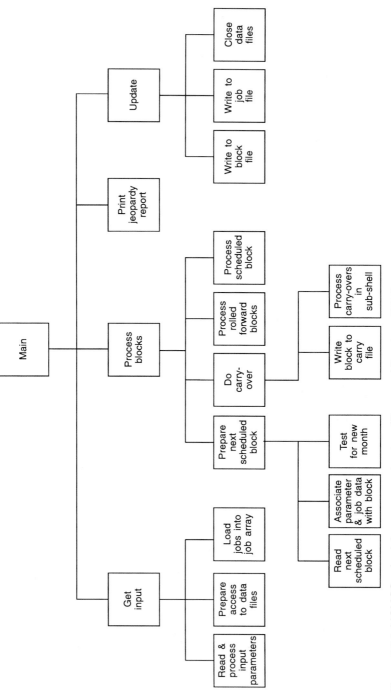

Figure 12.1 MCMCS scheduler program structure (Raymond Barglow, 1984)

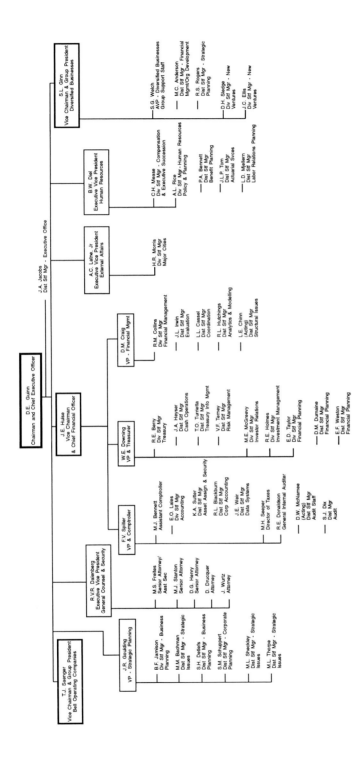

Figure 12.2 Pacific Bell organizational chart (1984)

are designed to contribute to the aims of the overall system to which they belong. These aims, in turn, are imposed on the system by its designers/users. Hence a computer system is appropriately viewed as serving external ends not of its own determination. The elements of a corporation such as a telephone company, on the other hand, include human beings, with needs and purposes not necessarily congruent with those of the corporate administration. A social institution typically mediates interests that clash.

This is obscured by the commonplace use of first person plural locutions to talk about the usefulness of information-processing technologies: *We* are entering the information age, which is bound to transform *our* lives by making computers available to *us*. Conveniently overlooked here is the differential influence of the new technologies on various social classes, ethnic groups, women and men, within a context of social inequality and domination. The job scheduling program discussed above, for instance, serves certain interests at the expense of others. The system does not have the same impact on supervisors whose planning it facilitates as it does on those whose labor it monitors. Those who service, repair, or key data into the system also are advantaged or disadvantaged in different ways. Viewing a human institution as if it were structurally parallel to the organization of a computer system effaces these differences, since logical relations among modules, unlike social relations among people, are non-adversarial. The internal structures of digital devices, in contrast to the social structures of their deployment, do not directly involve a dialectic of mutually defining but also mutually conflicting interests.

The clash of interests is what industrial and post-industrial engineering aim to preclude. Herbert Simon's views about how society should be organized, which have antecedents in nineteenth- and early twentieth-century pronouncements by industrial and financial magnates and their spokespersons (Carnegie, Edison, Taylor) about the virtues of large-scale technocratic organization, have long been attractive to corporate planners. In the 1980s, American businesses recommended top-down administration as an approach to governance that would break with the "divisive" and even "anarchic" politics of welfare state pluralism that were popular in the 1960s and early 1970s. Trilateral Commission researcher Samuel Huntington has written explicitly about an "excess of democracy" that, in his opinion, interferes with effective governance. He presents the classical case for technocratic control:

> In many situations the claims of expertise, seniority, experience, and special talents may override the claims of democracy as a way of constituting authority. During the surge of the 1960s, however, the democratic principle was extended to many institutions where it can, in the long run, only frustrate the purposes of those institutions.[15]

President Clinton evidently agrees with this perspective. His administration favors a reorganization of the economy, planned and implemented by specialists, that presumably will "make the United States competitive again." If the problems that the United States face as a nation are regarded as difficulties of coordination and efficiency, exacerbated by excessive claims brought against the social order by its diverse constituencies, then an appealing model for their solution is the design of a computer system. Effortlessly it seems, without provoking even the slightest discord or resistance, a computer organizes its environment and itself internally, allocating available resources and handling in an orderly fashion the competing demands made on the system by its component modules. This representation of social order as free of conflict and disruption is the "Utopian" ideal of technocratic planning.

THE NEW CARTESIAN DUALISM

Such planning may regard the entire globe as its appropriate domain. The "New World Order" will signify, then, not only the slogan of a past Republican presidency, but a reconfiguration of the planet's political economy along Cartesian lines: the "intelligence" of international corporate/financial institutions, no longer held back by nation-state borders, will organize and administer the "body," consisting of the totality of the world's material and human resources. Economic integration into this system will involve a sharp polarization of classes in each member country, placing design, planning, and administrative functions in the hands of a relatively small stratum of professionals, including high-level managers and technical specialists, while the rest of the population is unemployed or engaged mainly in low-paid sectors of the economy.

This division of labor, well underway in most parts of the world, is proving difficult for local communities, or even nation states, to influence.[16] Large corporations and financial institutions can often resist quite effectively attempts to influence their policies. If a government proposes legislation to insure minimum wage standards or protect the environment from pollution, for instance, a company can threaten to retaliate by laying off workers or even moving its operations abroad. In this respect, economic authority structures are extraordinarily mobile and disanalogous to traditional mind–body dualism. Within a single individual, mental and physical capacities are mutually dependent; the professional jogging on the track early in the morning before going off to work realizes that without the body's minimal cooperation, the mind will no longer function. But international capital resembles a mind that can skip from one embodiment to another more hospitable: "If employee or government demands interfere too much, we'll go abroad!" General Motors, for example, has been closing plant after plant in the United States, but has already become the largest private employer in Mexico.[17]

SPECIALIZATION, EFFICIENCY, AND DEMOCRATIC PARTICIPATION

If ordinary citizens "can't change city hall," what are their chances of successfully challenging the ways in which multinational institutions shape the world? To some extent, the perception that the basic social structures of our lives have been laid down once and for all – a perception shared by many members of the middle class as well as by urban rioters – accurately reflects the absence of democratic norms and popular participation in governing highly industrialized societies. Inasmuch as relationships among human beings are governed by institutional "reason" that pre-empts their own reflective and decision-making powers, they are apt to experience themselves, to one degree or another, as incompetent and helpless. The contemporary "crisis of the self" derives partly from such disempowering arrangements. On the one hand, freedom of thought and action ("taking the initiative," "thinking for yourself") remain highly valued ideals in post-industrial societies. On the other hand, submitted to structures of authority not of their own making and seemingly beyond the scope of their own control, people can scarcely sustain an image of themselves as self-initiating and self-determining agents.

This image of human action may be somewhat illusory, expressing an individualism built on false premises about what it is to be free. But this does not give us reason to give up our traditional ideals altogether. We do need to re-evaluate, however, what "individualism" and "freedom" can mean within an economically and technologically integrated world. We might begin by questioning the ideological underpinnings of post-industrial organization, including the identification of political authority with technical expertise. In many contexts, people rely on experts to specify the consequences of various policy alternatives; but *evaluation* of these consequences may in principle be arrived at through democratic discussions among all the participants. For example, someone who is regarded as an "authority" on nuclear power, because of technical expertise in that area, need not be regarded as an "authority" in the political sense and given responsibility for deciding whether nuclear power plants are to be built in the first place.

In the domain of computer programs, there is no place for the distinction between technical and political authority, since modules do what they are told without asking questions. We human beings, on the other hand, do not function automatically in this way, but are able to reflect on our social involvements. The *technical* division of labor, whereby various persons develop expertise in diverse areas of relevance to an enterprise, will certainly influence, but need not determine the *political* division of labor: the policy-making structure of that enterprise.

The dilemma "efficiency versus democracy" is, moreover, a false one. In many contexts *only* participatory structures can govern effectively.[18] Indeed, the traditional hierarchical division between management and labor makes for organizational inefficiency and failure, especially in occupational settings where information production, processing, and/or distribution are essential. Where the method for deploying new technologies is a "rationalization from above" that preserves or reinforces hierarchical structures and takes from people their sense of themselves as capable, self-determining agents, it is unlikely to increase productivity.[19] Robert Howard and Leslie Schneider argue that the use of information-processing technologies transforms the structure of labor:

> Work becomes more conceptual and abstract. Responsibilities are expanded and
> broadened ... successful work organizations are those that dismantle rigid

hierarchies and build flexible organizations based on a broad distribution of skill, decentralization of decision making, and increased worker initiative ... As the automation of discrete functions is increasingly replaced by the integration of entire computerized work systems, effective work will increasingly depend upon broad worker knowledge of both technology and the work organization itself.[20]

Beyond the link between productivity and participation, however, there is a more fundamental reason why democratic governance of institutions is desirable; it encourages creativity, solidarity, and self-determination. Efficient production is worse than useless if it does not serve humane ends. Because people identify and validate themselves in their relationships with others – through the kind of work they do, for example – more democratic participation will help to alleviate feelings of isolation, powerlessness, and loss of meaning.

Experimentation with workers' self-management structures has been carried out for decades in many settings. The Scandinavian examples have been the most impressive. Especially in Sweden and Norway, workers' participation in determining the conditions of their employment and the character of their work is extensive, and has even become a legal right. Some enterprises have successfully set up work-teams that are given near total responsibility for production. From such experiences, much has been learned about the advantages of collectively exercised authority.[21]

QUESTIONING "TECHNOLOGICAL NECESSITY"

This does not mean that if people were to participate actively in determining the structures and aims of their institutional involvements, then their fundamental anxieties and insecurities would simply vanish. Let us recall that in Scandinavian countries, where democratic forms of institutional life are relatively well developed, alienation and existential insecurity remain prevalent. One may argue, in fact, that not even the most thorough democratization of society will be sufficient to restore communities and personal identities which are based on face-to-face interactions within stable institutional settings; hence institutional democratization will not automatically dispel the insecurities about their own identities to which contemporary selves are subject. Yet there is much that can be done to further a reconciliation of the subjective and objective aspects of our lives. Much of the alien objectivity of contemporary social structures could dissolve if people were able to set their own agendas, to participate in shaping the frameworks that in turn shape them. Even granting that institutional complexity and specialization are essential to productive efficiency, there are countless ways in which these can be organized, some more conducive to freedom and social justice than others. Taking the ideal of democratic participation seriously entails at least the liberty to experiment with alternative social arrangements, the opportunity for society's members to discover for themselves where the constraints lie and how they are to be taken into account.[22]

The ends that information technologies are designed to serve are much more diverse than those served by previous technological forms. Whereas the primary function of an automobile, for example, is to provide transport from one physical location to another, a computer can serve any number of purposes. The range of its applications is limited only by the imagination of the programmer or user. We may view social reality too as subject endlessly to reconfiguration, as capable of serving any number of possible purposes. There is no single "right" way of organizing an institution, for example, any more than there is a single "right" way of configuring an information-processing system. The implication is that social arrangements are always somewhat arbitrary, and that structures radically different from our own might be equally valid.[23]

TECHNOLOGY'S CONTRADICTORY PROSPECTS

Technology, then, lends itself as readily to the legitimation of social change as to legitimation and preservation of the status quo. This is not the same as saying that technology is "value-free," a neutral instrument serving pre-existing aims. Rather, machines embody social meanings and implications that precede any particular user's interaction with them. The social character of a technological system does indeed play a part in structuring the beliefs and desires of those who form and use it, but it does so in contradictory ways. This point is easily overlooked, even by those highly critical of technology's social consequences. Viewing technology itself as responsible for technocratic authority, their opposition to that authority leads them to believe that technology itself is the enemy. Herbert Marcuse is driven to that conclusion:

> Not only the application of technology but technology itself is domination (of nature and men) – methodological, scientific, calculated, calculating control. Specific purposes and interests of domination are not foisted upon technology "subsequently" and from the outside; they enter the very construction of the technical apparatus ... Technological rationality thus protects rather than cancels the legitimacy of domination and the instrumentalist horizon of reason opens on a rationally totalitarian society.[24]

Marcuse and other critics rightly reject the positivist account of technology as merely instrumental, a means to the satisfaction of ends that technology serves but does not profoundly influence. Technology represents a *social* project, a logic not only of what may be done with machines but also with and to people. But this project is internally divided. Technology carries the authoritarian implications that Marcuse attributes to it, to be sure. These can be seen in the seventeenth-century European philosophical tradition that associates reason with social hierarchy, in the contemporary identification of human well-being with "technological progress," and in Herbert Simon's advocacy of social engineering. That technology has abetted coercion and domination is as evident in the aggression against nature that simple hand-tools serve (Figure 12.3) as in the machineries of human destruction

Figure 12.3 Print from *De Re Metallica* (*On Metals*, Agricola, 1556)

today. Nuclear-tipped ICBMs are computerized, as are government and corporate surveillance agencies. Networked computers make up the nervous system of the multinational corporations that dominate Third World economies and cultures. Domestically, workers lose their jobs when companies computerize their operations. The very concept of software control of hardware echoes the corporatist ideals that govern these enterprises.

Yet technology is not destined by its nature or by our own to be used in exploitative ways, nor to reflect back to human beings machine-like images of themselves as manipulators and masters. For instance, the fact that automation has resulted in unemployment and poverty for millions of workers in the United States is a consequence of social priorities that are not inherent in the machines themselves. We can imagine them serving quite different ends. Much of the factory and office labor that a post-industrial society requires is tedious. Automation of this labor could be the occasion not for laying off workers, but for shortening the work day, thereby freeing human beings to turn their attention to more enjoyable and fulfilling pursuits.

Technology does not necessitate any particular form of society or worldview. On the contrary, it simultaneously empowers and disempowers human beings, affords new opportunities for cooperation but also walls people off from one another, makes possible the construction of a materially prosperous civilization but also of weaponry capable of annihilating everything we have built, opens up ever more powerful channels of communication while restricting access to them. That is, technology is essentially contradictory; as a cultural "text" of a kind, it articulates and extends the fissures and inconsistencies that characterize our lives. We can let that text be written by the interests that currently organize the planet; or we can decide that we are going to write that text collaboratively and democratically, so that technological innovation enlarges the scope of human freedom and self-determination instead of contributing to new forms of irrationality and domination.

Chapter 13

Restoration of the self

"Self" has become a popular word in contemporary psychotherapy. The traditional aims of that enterprise – insight and ego-strength, diminished anxiety and defensiveness – are apparently no longer adequate. Serious therapy aims at transformation of the self. But does this project ever reach its goal? It seems that in our culture there always remains more work to be done on the self, if not by means of therapy, then through a special diet or by visiting a new hair stylist. Information technologies provide metaphors that describe this observing and reshaping of our own identities. It is quite unexceptional now to find self-improvement plans that are advertised as providing a "reprogramming" of the mind, or (in the case of weight reduction and physical fitness) of the body.

Acquiring this kind of leverage implies a certain separation of the one who does this work from the target worked upon: oneself. Ironically, the project to remake ourselves as subjects means that we view ourselves as manipulable objects. At the same time, though, we continue to attach value to the uniqueness, authenticity and spontaneity of each person. The dilemma is that planning and spontaneity, objectivity and subjectivity pull in opposite directions, and that the process of bringing the self within the scope of technical control seems as likely to efface as to enhance human freedom and self-determination.

These are familiar themes to new social movements critical of the ways in which freedom, objectivity, and individuality are currently defined in industrially advanced societies. The feminist, peace, and ecology movements that have emerged during the past several decades have addressed such specific issues as women's and workers' rights, militarism, and environmental pollution. But they offer also a more basic critique that looks at technology in relation to the larger social context of its invention and deployment; that context, not technology alone, is partly responsible for the meaning deficits and "crisis of the self" in modern societies. Only by transforming the social world, changing the ways we are involved in the reality that we reason about and manipulate, can this "crisis" be addressed. Lessening exploitation in all of its forms, and building relationships that respect and cherish not only all human beings but also our natural surroundings, would go a long way toward alleviating anxieties and insecurities about "the self."

But can these anxieties and insecurities be chalked up simply to a badly organized social order? They may also be responding to a threat to human subjectivity and individuality that no political party or platform can address. The threat arises, I have suggested, out of a set of cultural circumstances that both exalt the individual self and call its very existence into question. This dialectic of affirmation and denial is not necessarily historically stable or even viable. In the past, the contradictions inherent in the traditional notion of the individual self could be contained, because that notion, even if illusory, served as an organizing principle of industrial societies. But today this ideological underpinning is coming undone. The notion of the "self" is closely linked to two other traditional notions, "individuality" and "subjectivity," both of which are problematic. The ideal of the individual, epitomized in the sturdy and self-reliant bourgeois, is scarcely intelligible, let alone realizable, since it overlooks the essential social character of human identity. As for subjectivity, that too slips away from us as the world becomes increasingly objectified, due in part to the expansion of scientific discourses and technological innovation.

In this chapter, we will reexamine both of these challenges to the status of the individual self. The first, based on the observation that the presumed separateness and independence of individual persons is an illusion, is one that we can answer if we are willing to give up outdated ideas about what individuality is. Objectification, on the other hand, is more profoundly disturbing to our notions of who we are. Hence this book must come to an unsatisfactory conclusion. Instead of tying up loose ends in this final chapter, the fabric will further unravel. Our task is not merely to adjust or correct misguided technological applications so that we can get back on the right path again; at issue, rather, is the uncertain prospect of reconciling subjectivity with objectivity – reconciling the diverse traditions and myths that make our lives personally meaningful, with an objectified world scientifically explained and technologically organized.

THE SELF AS RELATIONAL

The social character of the self has been an axiom of twentieth-century sociology. Durkheim, Mead, and more recently Habermas present a strong case that the notion of the autonomous self is untenable. Especially in highly organized and integrated post-industrial settings, the idea of an imperial and typically male subject who single-handedly confronts and masters his surroundings makes little sense. Consequently, if the fate of the self is tied to the preservation of traditional individualist concepts and values, then its "crisis" will indeed remain chronic and irresolvable.

But the self need not be understood in this way. One of the insights of feminism, elaborated also by ecologists and social critics like Habermas, is that human beings are essentially relational creatures. Their identity consists not simply in their separateness from others, but in the myriad affiliations that link them within a shared lifeworld. "A subjective world of experiences to which the growing child has privileged access," Habermas writes, "takes shape complementary to the construction of a common social world."[1] Human reality is intersubjective; our life histories and language are bound up with those of others, in relation to whom we become the persons we are.

This perspective on human identity illuminates many of the case histories and dreams that have been presented in this book. In these lives, uncertainty about one's identity and hyperbolic self-objectification are of a piece with chronic isolation. The dreams we have discussed use many metaphors to express this condition:

> *I looked in the mirror, but all I could see was an outline, like a metal cookie-cutter with nothing inside. I was a gingerbread man with no ginger and no bread ... Suddenly, I'm looking down at my own body, it's like a scaffolding or erector set – all girders, frame, but no substance.*
>
> *I was seeing my mind as a vast empty space, subdivided by an interface or membrane ... I felt entrapped. I had to break through, or suffocate and die.*
>
> *An atomic particle occupies a closed box which is otherwise empty. The particle moves in a straight line and keeps bouncing off the walls of the box ... I am the bouncing particle.*
>
> *Image of a head – it might be of a cat, or human – and behind it is suspended a computer keyboard ... I'm this programmed head!*

The dreamer does not just happen momentarily to be alone in these dreams. They express, rather, a sense of solitude experienced as existential and inescapable, built into the structure of the world.

In the dreams that Freud analyzed, on the other hand, such extreme isolation is rarely a central theme. In Freud's dream of Irma's injection, discussed in Chapter 3, he is receiving guests on a social occasion. For a brief moment he goes off to the side to examine Irma's mouth, and he panics. But he is soon returned to the safe company of others, the doctors who assist him in arriving at a diagnosis. The social bond is momentarily called into question in the dream, but is restored in short order. In the contemporary dream experiences above, however, restoration of this bond, assuming it ever existed, is out of the question. Totally isolated, the self seems irretrievably lost to itself.

Shall we say, then, that these dreams reveal a more serious pathology, a profound insecurity about the self, that Freud and his patients did not suffer? I do not know the answer. Issues of aloneness, fragmentation, and loss of identity certainly existed for Freud and his patients, but perhaps they were better defended against recognition of these issues. It is also relevant to note that the ways in which human deficiency and failure are *described* change from one epoch to another. Metaphors of disintegration and loss of self that have become idiomatic in some Indo-European languages (in English: "falling apart," "cracking up," "going to pieces," etc.) are more commonplace today than they were during Freud's lifetime.[2] That we use such expressions to characterize our experiences does not entail, one might argue, a qualitative transformation in the experiences themselves.

But "experiences themselves" cannot be neatly separated from the cultural dimensions of our lives. The feelings of isolation expressed in the dreams described above reflect a social reality far removed from Freud's Vienna at the turn of the century. Freud and his contemporaries could be "individuals" only against a background of relationships such as the dense interpersonal network that linked Freud himself to his colleagues, friends, patients, and family. For many contemporary individuals, on the other hand, a background of that kind is perceived as not in place, and connection/belonging becomes the theme about which their lives seem to revolve. Failure or absence of relationship, of meaningful social ties, is almost always at issue in experiences of loss or fragility of the self.

The subject–object split, in which the self observes itself in a detached way, and the world too is viewed as other and alien, signifies a breakdown of communicative relationships linking self and other, a deficit of what Habermas calls "intersubjectivity." This deficit can be made good through the creation or restoration of a shared symbolic reality:

> Doubling of the relation to the self is only unavoidable so long as there is no alternative to this observer-perspective; only then does the subject have to view itself as the dominating counterpart to the world as a whole or as an entity appearing within it ... As soon as linguistically generated intersubjectivity gains primacy, this alternative no longer applies.[3]

While Habermas's solution to the problematic status of the divided subject seems too easy, his point about the reparative value of mutuality and communication is well taken. We make headway against isolation when we form a world together. Intersubjectivity, on this account, implies reciprocal dialogue and recognition that dismantle the rigid structures that privatize experience. Communicative action makes possible the initiation of new forms of collective and individual identity.

The "individual" does not disappear, under these circumstances, but is transformed. Carol Gilligan, in her studies of the psychology of ethical reasoning, observes a contrast between two conceptions of value, each associated with a different view of human individuality:

1   Values based on the "view of the individual as separate and of relationships as either hierarchical or contractual";
2   "[T]he values of care and connection, salient in women's thinking, [which] imply a view of self and other as interdependent and of relationships as networks created and sustained by attention and response."[4]

Contemporary object relations psychoanalysis and self-psychology[5] break with the classical Freudian assumption that the aim of early development is separation and autonomy – becoming an individual as defined by the first set of values cited above. Formation of identity begins not with Oedipal repression, around the age of 3 years, but with a prior dialectic of connection and sharing with another, who for most children is the mother. This new psychoanalytic thinking, attentive to Gilligan's second set of values, rejects the traditional dilemmas of development: autonomy versus dependence, separation versus attachment. As Jessica Benjamin points out, attachment to others contributes to the security of the child's sense of self. Mutuality of recognition and respect, not the cutting of close emotive ties, enables a child to form a personal identity.[6]

OBJECTIFICATION AND REIFICATION

If human identity is relational in nature, it does not need to live up to the traditional ideals of individualism in order to survive or flourish. But there is another, more fundamental challenge to the identity that children and adults face: objectification. Modernizing processes in the West have distinguished subjectivity from objectivity, culture from nature. These distinctions are neither self-evident nor universal. In pre-industrial societies, tribal societies in particular, all of nature retains human attributes; aspects of nature that modern science regards as inanimate are typically personalized: within trees, mountains, and rivers spirits dwell. In industrially and technologically developed societies, on the other hand, subjectivity is no longer ubiquitous. Nature is "disenchanted" and objectified; people are treated impersonally as, say, labor power, sex-objects, targets of advertising, potential votes for politicians, or records in a computer database. Modernization culminates in an information-based social order, where virtually any aspect of our lives and surroundings, private or public, can be submitted to analysis, redesign, and rational administration.

A crucial distinction needs to be made, though, between objectification and reification.[7] Objectification is essential to any thoughtful experiencing of the world. One's surroundings are necessarily objectified inasmuch as differentiations are made and boundaries drawn in every act of perception or cognition, whether as concrete as the experience of a table or chair, or as abstract as the laws of physics. Reification, on the other hand, is objectification in the service of domination. In Ralph Waldo Emerson's words, "Things are in the saddle and ride mankind." Reification is our attribution of "hard," thing-like qualities to reality, so that any dialectic between them and ourselves is attenuated: we seem compelled to adapt our lives to "requirements" not subject to negotiation or alteration. Such requirements – imposed for example when institutional rationalization occurs "from above" and is planned and administered by experts – are apt to be experienced as coercive and disenfranchising. "At work *they're* putting in a new computer system" is quite different from "At work *we're* putting in a new computer system." What "we" are doing for ourselves brings us together as a community of self-determining social actors, in at least partial control of our lives; what "they" are doing for us, on the other hand, divides "us" from "them" and from the environments that are the product of their social engineering. Under these circumstances, objectification signifies disempowerment and alienation.

MASTERY AND OBJECTIFICATION: THE CRITIQUE MADE BY NEW SOCIAL MOVEMENTS

It is objectification in this sense that the ecology, feminist, and peace movements question. One of the aims of these new social movements has been to address the myriad ways that human beings become detached from their surroundings and even from themselves. The ecology movement has examined the impact of contemporary patterns of production and consumption on the environment. In an industrial, technologically "mature" social order, our natural surroundings – forests, oceans, mountains – are perceived as "resources," to be mapped and exploited. The word "exploited," referring to the use of physical nature as well as the abuse of human beings, is appropriate here, for it points to the fateful intersection of our attitudes toward inanimate objects and our attitudes toward persons. The "forward march of history," whereby nature is to be mastered and humankind liberated, has proven far more problematic than past promoters of industrial "progress" – including not only captains and managers of industry but also such social critics as Marx and Engels – would have anticipated. Sociologists in the Critical Theory tradition[8] formulate the contradiction in these terms: mastery of *external* nature, exemplified by scientific inquiry and engineering that have helped to shape the modern world, is bound up with mastery of *internal* nature, with a colonization of consciousness that detaches human subjects from one another and from themselves.

In keeping with this dynamics of domination, "rationality" has been regarded as masculine and active, and the world upon which it operates as feminine and passive. Reason imposes not merely order but also regimentation; irrational nature must be tamed and bridled. Feminist theory has examined the import of the culture/nature and subject/object polarizations for male–female relationships. Seen and rated by men, women simultaneously identify with and distance themselves from the mirror-images that reflect back to them the way they appear to others. Men too are submitted to standards that they or others have imposed. Objectification and domination are joined, governing the relationships not only among but also within individuals. As a surveyor measures and subdivides a terrain, converting it into an abstract topography, so we apply analytic techniques for assessing and organizing ourselves.

There is aggressivity in these techniques, whether directed toward ourselves or toward our natural and social surroundings. The most striking conjunction of objectification and aggression is the one that peace movements worldwide address: the development and use of instruments of war. This convergence of coercive attitudes toward nature and violence against human beings is not a recent development. Woodcuts in a popular sixteenth-century compendium of mining methods, Agricola's *De Re Metallica*, illustrate the forcible extraction of minerals from the earth (Figure 12.3, p. 181). Although much less damage is being done by this miner than by our modern practices of strip-mining and clear-cutting of forests, there is an unmistakable belligerence visible in his action.

This anger can be turned against people, in the form of violence organized by the state. In one of Peter Bruegel's prints, *Justice* (Figure 13.1), issued a few years prior to the publication of Agricola's work, the nature that is subjected to domination is human, not inanimate. Justice, blindfolded at the center of this representation, does not see what is being done in her name. At the lower left, a man is being tortured upon the rack. Elsewhere a man's hand is being cut off, while another is about to be beheaded. Just beyond the elevated platform, a flogging proceeds. A crowd of common people observes, powerless to prevent what is happening. Those nearest the foot of the stairs have turned their heads toward the platform, where they witness the cruel punishments being administered. Were they to attempt to mount the stairs to intervene, they would encounter first the militia man who immediately blocks their way, and then the might of the other armed figures stationed at various locations on the platform. This administration of "justice" is "rational" in a sense: torture, mutilation, and execution are legally sanctioned and carried out in an orderly way. In the trial scene at the lower right, three servants of the court are busily at work, recording the relevant information about each case. Notice the symmetry between the pair of men at the lower left who administer the water, and the pair of scribes at the right, sheltered behind a triangular desk. Their information-processing labor contributes to the system no less than the activities of those who carry out the physical punishment.

NEW SOCIAL MOVEMENTS: PROSPECTS AND LIMITATIONS

Western rationalization has historically involved domination and violence directed against nature, women, and those regarded as "criminal" or "the enemy." The subject–object dualism characteristic of our civilization creates an "other," distant, alien, and threatening, that the subject feels compelled to subdue or annihilate. Insight into this dynamic, as well as alternative structures of decision-making and participation, are among the significant contributions made by new social movements. Green parties in Europe, for example, have built into their own organizations egalitarian structures and procedures that contrast with and counteract the technocratic and militarist political regimes they oppose. Similarly, the peace movement in this country and Europe regards non-violence not only as a means but as an end itself, as a way of life consonant with fundamental human values of caring and cooperation.

But can the ideals of such movements govern large-scale social institutions, or, thinking even more ambitiously, the economy or body politic as a whole? What happens when feminist or ecological principles come up against "real world" economic, technological, and political constraints? In Europe, when representatives of ecology movements have been voted into public office, they have often dis-covered that it is difficult to live up to their values within the social system they criticized previously from the outside. Should they be willing, for example, to compromise their principles by joining alliances to increase their political clout? How is respect for consensual decision-making to be upheld in situations of conflicting social interests? How is technical expertise to be incorporated into democratic political processes?

I agree with radical activists who believe that such contradictions can be overcome. We are capable of building institutions that are much more participatory and humane than our current ones. Yet, although exploitation and isolation might

Figure 13.1 Justice (Peter Bruegel, 1560)

be greatly diminished in a differently organized social world, human insecurities and longings would not go away. On this point, Freud's psychoanalytic perspective concurs with the insights of existentialism and of Critical Theorists like Theodor Adorno: human beings are inevitably divided, unsatisfied creatures. Hence the project that some socialists, feminists, and other critics of modernity have proposed – a reconciliation of subject and object, of human beings with each other and with nature – can at best be imperfectly realized.

Reason itself stands in the way of any total reconciliation. Human understanding depends upon the use of categories that, at least to some extent, distance and depersonalize the world to which they apply. For example, when ecologists warn about depletion of the atmosphere's ozone layer or global warming, and when peace activists point out that vast resources are wasted on armaments, they rely on statistical evidence and argumentation that, like any analytic technique, abstracts from the experiences and viewpoints of particular individuals. Similarly, the very categories of radical feminist analysis – for example, *male* and *female*, *public* and *private* – objectify and "package" human reality, in the interest of representing gender relationships.

This logic of objectivity produces a certain irony in the writings of those whose criticism of Western culture and colonialism has been most trenchant. Léopold Senghor, poet and statesmen of Senegal, eloquently articulated a distinction between Western and African ways of perceiving:

> Let us consider first the European as he faces an object ... [as] an *objective* intelligence, a man of will, a warrior, a bird of prey, a steady gaze. He first distinguishes the object from himself. He keeps it at a distance. He freezes it out of time and, in a way, out of space. He fixes it, he kills it. With his precision instruments he dissects it in a pitiless factual analysis ...
>
> The African is as it were shut up inside his black skin. He lives in primordial night. He does not begin by distinguishing himself from the object, the tree or stone, the man or animal or social event. He does not keep it at a distance. He does not analyze it. Once he has come under its influence, he takes it like a blind man, still living, into his hands. He does not fix it or kill it. He turns it over and over in his supple hands, he fingers it, he *feels* it.[9]

The estrangement of the European from his or her surroundings that Senghor describes here is something that he understood all too well and to which he himself was vulnerable. His own categories for distinguishing Africa from the West exemplify a classifying, analytical attitude that represents his own assimilation into the very culture whose values and interpretation of the world he wanted to call into question. This is a contradiction that Senghor constantly wrestled with, as an artist and as a politician. He tried to synthesize African intuitions and culture with the European humanist tradition, thereby creating a "Civilization de l'Universel." Yet he could not help but observe, in the process of constructing his own account, the problematic character of this unification.

TOWARD A GLOBAL CULTURE

Senghor's dilemma is also our own. In Western societies, we have learned to observe from a distance, to think critically, to deliberate on our relationships and ourselves. Rational scrutiny dissolves the "glue" of tradition that held the world together for our ancestors, but does not furnish an adequate substitute. Freud argues that reason cannot provide human beings with a *Weltanschauung*, or worldview.[10] The science of psychoanalysis, he notes, is incapable of bestowing upon us belief in the Biblical sense: that of Moses in a living God and a chosen people; belief of the pious Christian, Muhammadan, or Hindu that there exists a divine plan that renders the universe and our place within it ultimately intelligible and meaningful.

Conviction of this quality harks back to childhood, when we wanted to believe that our parents knew everything and would take care of every need. A longing for such security is one of the deepest and most enduring human emotions. There is an immense and incomparable satisfaction in the conviction that one is taken care of in an ultimate, transcendental way. Religion may be an illusion, as Freud argued,[11] but if so it is one that has proved remarkably long lasting. On the one hand, its hold upon the human psyche has gradually been loosened, in the West at least, by the steady advance of secular and scientific systems of explanation and technical control. On the other hand, a backlash against the assault by objectivity on religious faith has been one of the defining features of our age: Christian, Islamic, and other forms of fundamentalist revival flourish in many parts of the world.

In the long run, though, these doctrines are unlikely to withstand the corrosive influences of modernity. Even in Iran, some of the more conservative ayatollahs have been displaced by pragmatic politicians whose religion is tempered by their recognition of the need for Western technology and for a well-informed and professional work-force. In order for orthodox Islam to remain hegemonic, it would have not only to eschew Western technologies of production, but also to close off access to Western television, movies, radio, and printed materials that reach audiences worldwide. In the cities of the Islamic republics, ruling officials are finding that their power to control the influx of Western commodities, material or cultural, is limited.[12] Anti-modern religious ideologies remain popular, but the worldwide integration of economies and means of communication makes it virtually impossible to isolate a society from modernizing cultural and technological influences.

However different non-Western cultures may be from our own, a television receiver or computer manufactured or used in Singapore, San Salvador, or Cairo works just about the same, using identical procedures and an identical logic, as the corresponding technological devices produced or deployed in Japan or the United States. On a technical level, very little having to do with understanding or using these machines is culturally relative.[13] And although technological devices can be used for widely divergent purposes, to some degree the medium is the message. The dissemination of contemporary technologies – including television, cinema, video-games, and computers – integrates local communities within a global system that is at once economic, technological, and ideological.

Paradoxically, though, this integration is also fragmenting, since persons whose lives have been formed within these communities are confronted with evidence of the partiality or one-sidedness of the traditions and rituals that their identities depend on. "Internal colonization of the lifeworld" signifies that process wherein scientific and technical objectivity renders local traditions and belief systems *merely* subjective, and therefore marginal. The unifying cosmologies of the past, such as tribal creationist myths or medieval Christianity, could be hegemonic only in the absence of competition. But today, thanks in part to communications linking cultures worldwide, more and more people on this planet are learning that their local customs and way of life represent only one among countless alternatives. The totems or gods one worships, like the rituals one practices, are provincial.

To some extent we can attribute this disenfranchisement of local beliefs and practices to "cultural imperialism." But then we face the challenge of building a world in which scientific and technological development could coexist comfortably with alternative cultural perspectives. Is a pluralism of fundamentally different beliefs and practices viable within a globally integrated world? I ask the question not to encourage skepticism about multiculturalism, but to call our attention to the problems. Scientific knowledge can be interpreted in various ways, some of which I discuss later. But as traditionally understood in the West, science leads toward skepticism about any alternative worldview. Consider for instance accounts of the origins of life: Darwin's theory of the evolution of animal species, as elaborated and amended by contemporary biological sciences, does not count as just one more story about how the world came to be populated by living beings. On the contrary, it seems to undermine all of its competitors, relegating them to the fictional status of creationist *myths*.

Whether or not the rationality and credibility of the natural sciences is in some sense "objectively" superior to that of such rivals as creationism, tribal magic, shamanism, alchemy, astrology, and "Christian science" is too large a question to take up here. Some historians and philosophers of science have called into question the allegedly timeless and universal validity of scientific/technological reason.[14] While such objections may help to curtail the facile extension of that reason to encompass social and psychological domains, it is questionable whether they will undermine the consensus that stands behind scientific/technological belief systems and methodologies. These have the advantage of a manifest and reproducible precision and functionality, in comparison with which alternative traditions and practices appear arbitrary and merely subjective. One can hardly dispute that a watch or television set or computer works, whereas the efficacy of a tribe's magical or shamanistic practices, for example, will not necessarily be evident to anyone who is not already sympathetic to that tribe's traditions and lore. Western medical technology, too, tends to marginalize or eradicate cultural alternatives to its concepts of objectivity and truth. In some instances, Western medicine has made a real contribution to human health in Third World countries, as was the case with the introduction of smallpox vaccination in India. Yet this advance did away with the cult of Sittala Devi, the goddess whom one relied upon previously to deal with this illness.[15]

Scientific reason tends to take no interest in presumed knowledge that cannot be fitted within its own parameters. Hence such traditional practices as acupuncture, herbal treatments, and techniques of meditation are driven to legitimate themselves in terms of the predominant Western paradigm, and we are told of scientific studies attesting to the value of these alternatives. As a result, the hegemony of the ideal of objectivity is consolidated: "We are willing to accept as valid your traditional beliefs and practices, provided that they can be integrated within the framework of Western rationality and science."

This does not mean that all local customs and beliefs which remain unassimilated into the mainstream are fated to dwindle and die. On the contrary, we may cling to them all the more fervently, for they seem to define the very substance of our being. The worldwide outburst of divisive ethnic and religious loyalties is the flip-side of the rationalizing processes that have been reorganizing the planet. This dynamic is influential not only in Third World countries, but in the post-industrial heartland as well. In the United States, the ideal of the "melting pot," of the assimilation of diverse ethnicities and religions, is challenged today as never before in American history. None of the unifying myths of the past, whether associated with the American Frontier, Manifest Destiny, or the Red Scare, are ideologically compelling. Political leaders stand discredited, a large fraction of the population does not bother to vote, millions of workers lose their jobs and are rendered economically superfluous, while organizations of the ultra-right long nostalgically and sometimes fanatically to restore outdated value systems.

This cultural fragmentation creates an intolerable vacuum. The more that public, institutional life becomes rationalized, the greater the effort to compensate by invigorating private, non-institutional life with emotional excitement and intensity. War has been and remains one of the favored ways of renewing a sense of vitality, but more habitual cultural representation is also harnessed to this end. Television and movie thrillers have to be maximally violent, Gothic novels hyper-romantic, the human senses enlivened with Ecstasy or designer drugs, to make up for the meaninglessness and monotony of everyday post-industrial existence. As factories, offices, and bureaucratic agencies become increasingly planned and automated, life away from the machines and procedures hungers all the more for sensation, feeling, passion – experiences providing evidence that subjectivity has not been extinguished. This may partly explain why post-industrial cultures, notwithstanding the advances that have been made in prolonging average life expectancies, remain obsessed with images of dying and death. We recognize that the world we inhabit, comprising not only the natural environment but also shared traditions that connect our lives in meaningful ways, is endangered. Civilization's "progress" may be perceived as an impoverishment of subjectivity, divesting human experience of its spontaneity and vigor, as if more machines meant less life.

TRANSCENDING THE SELF?

To some extent, this impoverishment can be remedied by a "politics of meaning" that contradicts post-industrial forms of repression and alienation. But can we hope ever to fulfill the human desire for a world that is profoundly personal in a spiritual or metaphysical sense, in which our status as subjects is not vulnerable to objectifying frameworks? Our best chance may lie in Eastern teachings that call into question the rifts between subject and object that Western conceptions cannot close. In the above discussion, certain polarities have been assumed: religion versus science, culture versus nature, subjective versus objective. Perhaps these oppositions can be dissolved by transcending the Western metaphysics of the self on which they rest. True the individual self loses its bearings in a post-industrial world. But doesn't the East teach us that it is our attachment to the self that gets in the way of our emancipation? If so, then we need not mourn its loss. From a spiritually inclined perspective, the disintegrative influence of post-industrial institutions and technologies on the foundations of Western civilization, including its notions of "individual," "ego," and "self," might even be a good thing.

These very technologies, moreover, can link East and West in mutually beneficial ways. In some instances, information-processing devices might even help us to rescue endangered ethnic and religious traditions, as an advertisement for Apple Computer (Figure 13.2) suggests. Tibetan Buddhism is kept alive not only as an oral tradition of the smiling monks in this representation, but also with the assistance of the notebook computer that the man at the center, presumably himself a student of Buddhism, displays for us to admire. On its screen we see the title of a document, *The Tradition of Drepung Loseling*, and immediately beneath, a description of the enforced relocation of this monastery from Tibet to India following the occupation of Tibet by Chinese Communist forces in the 1950s. The juxtaposition here of a recent and highly sophisticated Western technology with an ancient Eastern tradition implies that the former is not only compatible with, but may even lend support to, the latter. At the lower right of the advertisement, we see the Apple trademark, a multi-colored apple with a bite taken out of it; contrary to what we read in Genesis, there is no reason to fear the quest for knowledge.

The text visible on the video-screen speaks also of the monastery's history and recent worldwide tours, "performing 'Sacred Music, Sacred Dance for World Peace' in over 100 cities in North America and Europe." The current tour "applies traditional Tibetan practices for the purification and healing of our troubled planet." The manifest thesis here is that the colonization of traditional beliefs and practices by Western technological rationalization can be turned around, so that our most sophisticated technical instruments are placed in the service of helping, for example, Tibetan communities to preserve and share their culture with the world.

But let us look for a moment at the semiotic subtext of the advertisement, at the way it is visually organized. The monks are represented as circling the Westerner, who links the two cultures and holds in his hands the computer, whose operations he, not they, has mastered. Meaning is drawn down from the peripheral figures and

PowerBook.

It's from Apple.
It's not just a new computer.
It's a new idea.

It makes numbers scream.
It makes words sing.
It makes people smile.

It can talk to computers.
It can talk to fax machines.
It can talk.

It does more than you imagine.
It costs less than you think.

The power to be your best.

Figure 13.2 PowerBook™ and Tibetan monks
Source: Utne Reader (July/August 1992)

lodged in the information-processing object, around which this entire scene is centered. The text to the right of the image drops the reference to Tibetan religion entirely and speaks only of the machine:

PowerBook.^{TM}

It's from Apple.
It's not just a new computer.
It's a new idea.

It makes numbers scream.
It makes words sing.
It makes people smile.

It can talk to computers.
It can talk to fax machines.
It can talk.

Offered to us in haiku-like form, this advertising copy renders respect for the technical instrument verbally explicit and nearly reverential. The computer assumes the qualities of a secular icon. The formal design of the advertisement's visual imagery is comparable to that of traditional Christian representations of Madonna and Child (Figures 2.5, p. 32, and 2.6, p. 33); male figures replace Mary and her admirers, and a laptop computer displaces the Christ Child as the center of wonder and authority. The computer has become the Incarnation!

What appears, then, from one perspective to be a humane international relationship – between a Tibetan tradition and Western technological rationality – seems from another to count as yet one more instance, however subtle and disguised, of cultural imperialism: a hi-tech iconography incorporates a non-Western religious way of life within a Western, technology-centered and market-centered concept of how the world is put together. Hence the advertisement functions like a Gestalt image that can be read in at least two ways: as an enheartening model of intercultural communication, or as commercial exploitation.

Viewing the advertisement from this second perspective, both its visual and verbal texts invoke a colonial code that articulates a relationship of social as well as technical power between male representatives of the two cultures on display. This code collapses the distance between East and West, and assimilates a discourse that originally was foreign and "other." A religious tradition that at one time could not be easily fitted into a Western frame now becomes readily accessible: Tibetan monasticism is "interesting," perhaps even "fascinating"; how friendly its representatives seem, decked out in their colorful robes and ceremonial caps.[16]

The beliefs and practices of these Tibetan monks on tour are unlikely to remain unaffected by their experiences in a world remote in every respect from that of the monastery in their original homeland. Relevant here are not only the obvious Western influences – the emphasis on consumption and "getting ahead," for instance – but also "materialism" in the metaphysical sense of the word. Tibetan religion has so far outlasted political and military assault, but can it withstand as well a different danger: incorporation within a scientific, secular worldview that dismisses any alternative to itself?

In the past, human beings in every culture have attributed intentionality, purpose, and design to the world they inhabit. In this way, life has been made meaningful and coherent, and members of tribes, communities, and nations have found their own identities within mythic or narrative frameworks that explain and legitimate their forms of life. In post-industrial societies, however, the various "stories" that human beings have relied on in the past tend to be supplanted by a narrative of scientific explanation and technical achievement that denies the existence of occult, religious, or mystical entities, forces, or states of mind.

Let us recall the ways in which religious traditions have interacted with scientific and technical innovations in the past. In the late Middle Ages, the most advanced technologies, including machines for milling grain and clocks for measuring time, played prominent symbolic roles within a Christian social order. Mechanical timepieces exemplified a celestial and divine harmony that linked all aspects of the Creation, "like the wheels in clock works, which turn, so that the first to the beholder seems still, and the last, to fly," Dante tells us in his *Paradiso*. Notice the attention that Dante gives to the detail of the wheel train belonging to the clock mechanism. Clocks were, says David Landes, "the technological sensation of their time."[17] Mounted on church spires and towers of the towns and cities, their bells reminded urban citizens of their duties and coordinated their disparate activities. In 1335 in Amiens, France, to cite a typical instance, the king acceded to the request made by the city's officials:

> that they might be permitted to issue an ordinance concerning the time when the workers of said city and its suburbs should go each morning to work, when they should eat, and when return to work after eating; and also, in the evening when they should quit work for the day, and that by the issue of said ordinance, they might ring a bell which has been installed in the Belfry of the said city, which differs from the other bells.[18]

Time for the medieval peasant was natural and concrete, marked by the rhythms of the seasons, the rising and falling of the sun, the phases of the moon. Time in the burgeoning cities, measured first by clocks and eventually by watches, became an abstract and precisely reckoned quantity, capable like money of being saved or misspent, introducing a new order into all of the activities of daily life, including labor, prayer, and recreation.[19]

Medieval Christian institutions embraced the new clock-work technology and drew also upon its symbolic associations. Clergy taught their parishioners that internal discipline and moral balance are analogous to the methodical ticking of a timepiece. In Benedictine monasteries, clocks served not only as metaphors for the orderly, temperate life, but were central also to the daily regimen of religious practices. They measured the canonical hours and called the brothers to their prayers, meals, ceremonies, and work activities. One might have believed at the time that technology was only religion's "neutral" instrument, placed in the service of established religious practices. But we can see in retrospect that technical devices, and the mentality associated with their construction and use, contributed also to a transformation of the medieval world, culminating in the forms of rationalization of private and public life instituted by the Protestant Reformation several centuries later.

THE DALAI LAMA'S VIEW OF BUDDHISM AND SCIENCE

The early inventors and users of time-keeping technologies could scarcely have imagined these changes. Do we today have any better idea how our world will be influenced by our involvements with the newest machines? The current Dalai Lama of Tibet anticipates no contradiction here. He is convinced that Western and Eastern forms of reason are compatible. In fact, the ease with which he bridges cultural traditions has in the past confounded those who do not know him well. In 1955, the Dalai Lama was invited to China and met with Chairman Mao Tse Tung on several occasions, the last of which he describes in his autobiography. Mao congratulated him for having seen through the illusions of religion, for recognizing that religion is a poison of a kind that "neglects material progress." The Dalai Lama was astonished by the Chairman's misunderstanding:

> How could he have misjudged me so? How could he have thought that I was not religious to the core of my being? What had caused him to think otherwise?... He surely could not have failed to notice that every day I spent at least four hours in prayer and meditation and that furthermore, all the time I was in China, I was receiving religious instruction from my tutors. He must have known too that I was working hard towards my final monastic examinations ...
>
> The only possible explanation was that he had misinterpreted my great interest in scientific matters and material progress. It was true that I wanted to modernize Tibet in line with the People's Republic and true also that my cast of mind is basically scientific ... I have always been open to the discoveries and truths of modern science. Perhaps this is what tricked Mao into thinking that my religious practices were nothing more to me than a prop or convention.[20]

I do not doubt the accuracy of this account of Mao Tse Tung's total misreading of the Dalai Lama's outlook on life. Yet, while the "Great Helmsman" may have mistakenly assumed that the Tibetan monk's respect for science was incompatible with his religious beliefs, might Mao have been right about the long-run relationship between the secular and the sacred? The "scientific worldview" (a phrase that aptly captures the comprehensive aim of scientific inquiry) may disallow and eventually dispel perspectives and practices that are rooted in prescientific religious beliefs and ethnic traditions.

The Dalai Lama concludes his autobiography optimistically, affirming his conviction that on the very deepest levels, the Eastern and Western concepts of reason and methods of inquiry are the same. He reminds us that, after all, "Both science and the teachings of the Buddha tell us of the fundamental unity of all things."[21] But the "unity" in which the devout Buddhist believes is not identical to that postulated by science. Religion's unity is *spiritual*; there is design and purpose in the universe – God's master plan, Allah's *shari'a*, Buddhist karma and the reincarnation of souls. Science's unity, on the other hand, characterizes a universe – whether we regard it as consisting ultimately of particles, energies, and/or waves – that is populated only by physical processes and forces, and governed by natural laws rather than spiritual or ethical principles. Materialism in this sense is fundamentally at odds with every one of the world's major religions.

To be sure, there are differing opinions about the appropriate metaphysical assumptions for the natural sciences. Much has been made of the idea, for example, that so-called "objective" reality has no properties that are prior to or entirely unconnected to the subject who observes and measures them. In this sense, the known world cannot exist independently of the one who knows it. This seems to make natural science less impersonal and more human, more intrinsically related to ourselves. Indeed many scientists, probing the fundamental structures of nature, express a sense of mystery and awe that seems akin to the religious variety. Interpreters of science like Bateson, Bohm, and Capra argue that its fundamental assumptions and methodologies coincide with those of religion.[22] Yet the structures of these two enterprises remain radically different. Superficial analogies (for example, mystical experience stands to mystical knowledge as the evidence of the senses stands to scientific theory) afford a reconciliation of spirituality with materialism that obscures a possibly fundamental divergence.[23]

Given the nearly universal respect attributed today to Western science and technology, the synthesis of Eastern and Western traditions, as projected in the Apple advertisement and endorsed in a more sophisticated way by spiritual leaders like the Dalai Lama, may add up to a false unity that all but surrenders to the West. The Dalai Lama and other Tibetan monks have willingly participated in scientific research conducted at American universities regarding the physiological correlates of their meditative practices, including their abilities to raise and lower their body temperatures, withstand pain, and induce alpha-state brain waves. Tibetan Buddhism, the Dalai Lama assures us, is fully consistent with empirical science.[24] If he and his fellow monks continue in this direction, however, they may discover that little remains of what they originally believed. After all, if a monk's experience is closely associated with and causally dependent on a brain state, then its claim to reveal any kind of transpersonal or spiritual truth is at once called into question. A brain state is something happening inside the skull of a particular individual; the skeptic will be quick to scoff at any claim that this state, however unusual the amplitudes or frequencies of its registrations upon an EEG monitor, is in an epistemologically privileged position to ascertain the fundamental nature of the universe.

FALSE RECONCILIATIONS

On an economic and political level, the West has been scarcely more supportive of

Tibetan culture than on a metaphysical level, appearances notwithstanding. True, India and the Western world have provided the Tibetan refugee community with asylum. But by shoring up the brutally oppressive ruling classes of Tibet in the decades prior to the Chinese takeover in the 1950s, Western governments helped to prevent progressive social change in that country. Asylum cannot compensate for this deplorable history. On the contrary, many Tibetan immigrants discover, upon reaching the United States, that Western "freedom" does not permit them to find jobs or put food on the table. Nor are their interactions with technology always as felicitous as those represented in the Apple advertisement. Lhapka Dolma, formerly a schoolteacher in Tibet, describes her experience as follows: "In America you are always talking to machines. You go to the bank and you talk to a machine. You go to the BART [Bay Area Rapid Transit] and you talk to a machine. You call your friend on the phone and you talk to a machine."[25] Many of those who arrive on the shores of the "promised land" find themselves confronting a machine-like social world.

The segmentation of that world, which privatizes inhabitants of the same city, neighborhood, or even the same household, is itself a technological product. Today, one can bank, shop, and work from home, using computer telecommunications (illustrated in Figure 8.6, p. 114), thereby dispensing with unplanned or unintended contact with other human beings. Our encounters with social strata other than our own are increasingly mediated by mass communications. These make it possible for us to learn about what is going on in remote parts of the world – about the predicament of the Tibetan community, for example. But sophisticated technology is also quite compatible with superficial and manipulative coverage of issues by television and printed media, as well as computerized relationships that narrow rather than expand the horizons of our awareness. Michael Dertouzos, Director of MIT's Laboratory for Computer Science, has written extensively about the use of new technologies to facilitate communications. He proposes that the United States make a major investment in a "National Information Infrastructure" (NII) that will enable us to reconstruct our social relationships:

> Philosophically, the NII should be viewed as a new means of controlling our personal locality – choosing our working associates, vendors, entertainers, and perhaps even friends – without being limited to those that happen to be physically near. With the importance of physical proximity diminished, every person on the national information infrastructure could assemble his or her own electronic "neighborhood."[26]

This prospect is appealing, inasmuch as it promises to extend the range of human choices and communications. Yet it is also frightening, because "choosing," in this case, also means excluding. In a computerized world, will each of us populate our respective "electronic neighborhoods" only with people who are more or less like ourselves, and in whose company we can feel socially and intellectually comfortable? We might welcome into our "neighborhood" the smiling Tibetan monks in the Apple advertisement, but we need not have anything at all to do with less advantaged immigrants to the country, or with the homeless or disenfranchised who are not sending us electronic mail.

Computer communications technologies are advertised as providing a basis for a more connected and integrated world, seemingly in keeping with the Dalai Lama's dream of a worldwide community of peoples. But implementation of this concept may amount to little more than the construction of a network of tunnel visions: a world totally compartmentalized along lines of social class and professional specialization. When automobiles first were mass produced, they too were advertised as a technology that would bring us together by making everyone accessible to everyone else. But automotive travel turned out to have quite different implications, including the formation of suburbs insulated from the ghettos of the inner city. Similarly, the "information superhighway" is as likely to atomize as to integrate. Confronted with the fragmentation of contemporary social life, the self will find its purpose and identity within an electronically contrived virtual reality inhabited only by like-minded others.

Granted, this is not the only possible outcome of our involvements with the new technologies. Preparing to enter a new millennium, we are challenged to come to terms somehow with a world that can no longer be made meaningful or coherent in the traditional ways. Whether we can do so, whether we can form communities and personal identities that do not rely upon old or new illusions, remains to be seen.

Conclusion

I arrive at the doctor's, a pleasant setting in a clean-cut suburb, streets lined up orderly in rows and columns. But there is nowhere to park. About 3 or 4 prescribed spaces are all filled. Someone else manages to fit their car in, but I can't do that. I just have to wait outside.

Associations: I see myself from outside, I am just one more car that has to find parking, just one more case for the doctor to diagnose. This reminds me of when I'm using a program and I myself am one of the data records to be processed – a mailing list program for an organization of which I'm a member, or writing a payroll module for a company that has hired me on.

A beautiful April day. From the hilltop my friend and I unloose our kites into the sky. Our spools of string unwind, forming two parallel arcs. Like two curving rainbows, each begins from our hands and reaches to ... infinity. They are like endless programs, or our lives, that we write.

Associations: We noticed that our kite strings had wound about one another. I could release mine, or my friend hers, and neither would escape. Our lives are bound up in one another now – this happened when we weren't even thinking about it or trying ... I see our kites lift and dive and shimmer in the sun.

Sandy, with whose dream of a dolphin I began this book, reported the two dreams above which occurred about two weeks apart. The themes expressed in the one on the left side of the page include isolation, anxiety about finding one's place, being outside and wanting in, taking an objective attitude toward oneself: "I see myself from outside, I am just one more car ... just one more case ... I myself am one of the data records to be processed ... " The dreamer is divided into someone observing and someone observed. This cleavage into subject and object, "I" and "me," takes place in waking life as well as in the dreams of many of the people whose experiences we have discussed in previous chapters.

In the dream on the right side of the page, however, this division is no longer evident. In the company of her kite-flying friend, self-objectification and isolation have been, for the moment at least, overcome. Being with another involves constraint of a kind: "Our lives are bound up in one another now." Yet fear of closeness and loss of control – feelings by no means foreign to this dreamer – do not predominate here.

Both dreams make covert reference to the one they were recounted to: in my role as interviewer and author, I could stand in for the "doctor" in the first dream, and for the "friend" in the second. In the first dream, Sandy was reproaching me for my presumed objectivity: "I am just one more case for the doctor to diagnose" – she wanted to be healed, not just to serve as an object of research, "one of the data records to be processed." In a way, Sandy was right. Her dreams, like those of others with whom I talked in preparing to write this book, served as "data." I was friendly and listened carefully to those who were willing to share their experiences with me. But there was something unsatisfying about these encounters. Our intimacy would be so short-lived. With most of the interviewees, I would share a few moments, or a few hours if we were involved in a therapeutic relationship, and then, we would part ways. Our lives were not destined to be "bound up in one another" like the kites in Sandy's dream.

There is nothing unusual about this. In most interviewing/therapy contexts, one person talks and reveals herself or himself to another. The other person, cast in the role of helper or researcher, listens and perhaps takes notes, but remains relatively invisible. During my meetings with Sandy, for example, she told me of her experiences, while I said very little. The dolphin in Sandy's earlier dream, "pure thought cutting through the water like a knife, silent and invisible," is a metaphor for her view of herself, but also of me. "When someone is using a program I've written," Sandy remarked about that dream, "all they see of me are some symbols splashed on their screen." These splashings might also represent to her my behavior, beneath which I, in my role as interviewer, remained unseen. (Might Sandy also have been suggesting in her kite dream that I "Go fly a kite"?)

As Sandy represented me, so I suppose I am. I am therapist, consultant, author, etc. These are among the surfaces I present to others, and they present themselves similarly to me. Most of the people whom I encounter during any given day enter my life in partial, specialized ways, and a short while later they are gone. In the morning a plumber visits my house to repair my kitchen sink; an hour later I am in an office, playing my "professional" role. At lunch, I interact briefly with a waitress in a restaurant, and then with the cashier on my way out. As the day progresses, I am sequentially engaged with a host of people whom I know only or mainly in relation to the roles we perform, and they are acquainted with me in the same way. My relationship with you, dear reader, is similarly partial and transient. You will spend a few hours with this book (if I am lucky enough to hold your attention for that long), and then our paths will diverge. Our respective roles as writer and reader bring us together, but also keep us safely apart.

As performers of multiple roles, we may scarcely identify with any of them. On the contrary, we may feel anonymous and invisible behind the public faces we present to the world. Technological involvements, especially those that are incorporated into most institutional structures, reinforce these experiences. More than fifty million Americans interact directly with computers on a daily basis. In such interactions, people not only work with abstractions, but also view themselves and others abstractly. A computer program, whether as simple as a mailing-list application or as complex as an ICBM delivery system, typically works in a context-independent and person-independent way: it is indifferent to the identity of those who operate, benefit or suffer from its operations.

Machines neither supply nor demand the respect or special consideration that human beings ask for. We use them for our own purposes, and they do not object to being treated in that way. But these appropriate attitudes toward things may slide over into our attitudes toward persons. In a world in which human connections are often fragmentary and mediated by impersonal structures, objectifying and manipulative relationships among persons are common. These relationships tend to be contradictory, since no one wants to be handled merely instrumentally, as a means to an end. People objectify one another and themselves, yet each wants to be recognized as a subject, as a unique being whose particular experiences and interests are to be respected.

The inconsistency of our lives, then, is as follows. On the one hand, the contemporary social world is technologically highly complex and organized in terms of formal procedures and protocols. The daily work we do, in the course of planning and managing our lives, implies an impersonal detachment and objectification of our surroundings and ourselves. On the other hand, ours is also a culture that claims to value subjectivity, emotional rapport, and intimacy.

AN ETHICS OF TECHNOLOGY

This predicament is typically worked out in practice through the partitioning of our lives into public and private domains: in the private domain we get "personally involved"; we regard ourselves as treating others in a personal way and expect to be treated similarly by them. We care for those who are close to us, sharing our lives with them and giving to them much that we have and are. In public, on the other hand, we behave less intimately and more impersonally, more "rationally"; others are kept at a safe distance. The situation of the homeless exemplifies this division: those of us who have homes are not about to invite those without a roof over their heads to share ours with us.

We like to think of ourselves as treating others well: persons are not to be manipulated as objects, but are to be regarded as ends-in-themselves whose value exceeds that of even the most sophisticated machines. This ideal is a basic premise of Western humanism, belied however by the splitting of the social world that disengages us from one another; what goes on in the lives of others, in the ghettos of the inner city, for instance, has seemingly little to do with me, and it requires a riot before I will pay any attention at all. The separation here is intellectual as well as geographical. Formally "well educated," many of us have learned to filter reality through a network of abstractions that avoids experiences of homelessness, illness, abuse, poverty, and neglect we would rather not acknowledge. Managing our own perceptions in this way, perhaps we can remain "information-processors," safely uninvolved.

But this "safety" is apt to turn against itself, to detach and unsettle the human subject. Our enclaves of privacy lose their anchoring in a shared social existence. The intention is to find one's own path and pursue one's own aims, without being held back or dragged down by complicating entanglements. The price paid may be isolation, loss of meaning, and loss of purpose. Personal identity and integration become problematic in post-industrial settings that claim to value the freedom and flourishing of the individual, but are in fact organized around the impersonal administration of people and things. Life's fragmentation is partly the consequence of a culture that divorces intellectual performance from emotional expression and from the senses; that parcels knowledge out into the countless professions; that celebrates the limitless opportunities afforded by the Information Age while making meaningful, creative employment available only to a few.

These are among the contradictions of the contemporary social order. In each, technological innovation is involved, providing metaphors as well as machines that reorganize our experiences of one another and even our perceptions of ourselves. Those of us who are accustomed to this order, so much so that we may have resigned ourselves to its priorities and given up on the possibility of changing it in any fundamental way, can perhaps scarcely imagine any other. Our views of the "self" and "personal identity" remain equally static, frozen in place by our inability to envision a qualitatively different reality. In the mental health professions, my colleagues regard "ego strength" and a "unified self" as criteria of psychological health partly because of our experiences with clients isolated and disempowered by their surroundings, whose only alternative seems to be to "get it together," to think about and organize their lives strategically in order to survive. Nor are we, the presumed "healers" and "caretakers," exempt from this same logic. On the contrary, we are apt to experience coping strategies and self-management as necessary not only for our clients, but also for ourselves, since the reality they confront is not so different from our own. Consequently, restoration of the self becomes defined in terms of repairing and bolstering a faltering and vulnerable psychic structure. Whatever fortifies or reassures or promises to unify that structure we regard as good, everything else as foreign and potentially dangerous.

Psychological maneuver is, however, not our only possible response to a world that in so many ways objectifies and disintegrates human beings (not to mention its assault also upon the environment). To the extent that the forces that tear at the self have been socially and historically constituted, its restoration calls for a transformation that is collective as well as personal. If the world could be made more subjective, in part through greater participation by people in determining institutional structures so often experienced as alien, and if technical "rationality" and "efficiency" were no longer fetishized at the expense of other values, then our underlying assumptions about human nature and human identity might be called into question. Under these circumstances, the self might no longer need to be "unified" to adapt to environments enforcing certain standards of intelligence and performance.

Life subject to those standards tends to eliminate incongruity and cultural difference – anything that doesn't fit with what is already familiar and "known." We have learned to associate disagreement and conflict with lots of negatives, including strife between social classes, war between nations, and the psychic splitting between "good" and "evil" that engenders psychological and social pathologies. Hence the Dalai Lama's preoccupation, discussed in the preceding chapter, with finding common ground, bringing diverse communities together, and discovering the unity in all things. But in a freer, less exploitative and less violent world, this convergence might not have to remain the highest priority. People could become more open to difference and division in their lives, and the dimensions of the self might unfold in directions that currently we cannot begin to fathom or anticipate.

Notes

INTRODUCTION, pp. 1–8

1 That special bonds link dolphins and humans is a theme with a long history. Aristotle told stories about dolphins' friendships with children. Dolphin images occurred on Ancient Greek coins, mosaics, and paintings. In some of these instances, dolphins are phallic symbols designating male power, but connotations of helpfulness, intelligence, and playfulness are also common. In France, dolphins were associated with royalty; for centuries, the oldest son of the king carried the title of "dauphin," the French word for dolphin. See Dudley Herschbach, "The Dolphin Oracle," *Harvard Magazine* (January–February 1993), pp. 57–59.
2 Jürgen Habermas, *The Theory of Communicative Action*, Vol. 2, *Lifeworld and System: A Critique of Functionalist Reason*, translated by Thomas McCarthy (Boston, MA: Beacon Press, 1981), p. 356. Colonization of the lifeworld (*Lebenswelt*, in German) is not a uniquely modern phenomenon, however. One might argue, for example, that in the Middle Ages, the lifeworld was "colonized" by Church and state authority.
3 For Jürgen Habermas, colonization of the world of lived experience may be contested by communicative action on the part of those whose lives are being rationalized. One of the problems with the theories of rationalization proposed by Max Weber and Michel Foucault is that they cannot take such resistance into account.

1 THE TECHNOLOGICAL MIRROR, pp. 11–18

1 Michel Foucault discusses Plato's dialogue in *Technologies of the Self: A Seminar with Michel Foucault*, edited by Luther Martin, Huck Gutman, and Patrick Hutton (Amherst, MA: University of Massachusetts Press, 1988), pp. 23–30.
2 Christopher Lasch, *The Minimal Self* (New York: W.W. Norton, 1984); Christopher Lasch, *The Culture of Narcissism* (New York: W.W. Norton, 1979).
3 George Miller (Professor of Psychology, Harvard University), quoted in B. Rensberger, "Man and Computer: Uneasy Allies of 25 Years," *New York Times*, June 27, 1972, p. 43.
4 Creativity, for instance, is often experienced as a kind of "drive" that impels creative persons, seemingly independently of their consciousness or consent. Creativity flourishes best, it has even been suggested, when we abandon the "illusion of the self."
5 The difference between these two types of internal object is indicated also by our dissimilar responses to their loss. When an automobile breaks down, it is as if the use of a bodily appendage is now unavailable. If, on the other hand, a computer ceases to function, it is as if the mind has been dismantled. Someone who has been interacting intensely with the machine may experience this as strangely disturbing.
6 "Technology," as I am using the word here, includes any material instrument or

implement. Every society has its own technologies in this sense, however "advanced" or "primitive." In a narrower sense, something counts as "technology" only if its development involves the application of theoretical science, physics for example.

7 Paul Feyerabend, *Against Method* (New York: Verso, 1988); Paul Feyerabend, *Farewell to Reason* (New York: Verso, 1987); Thomas Kuhn, *The Structure of Scientific Revolutions* (Chicago, IL: University of Chicago Press, 1970).

8 For an overview of the early history of Critical Theory, see Martin Jay, *The Dialectical Imagination: A History of the Frankfurt School and the Institute of Social Research, 1923–1950* (Boston, MA: Little Brown, 1973). Also good is David Held, *Introduction to Critical Theory: Horkheimer to Habermas* (Berkeley, CA: University of California Press, 1980). Herbert Marcuse analyzes the social structure of technology in many of his essays and in *One Dimensional Man* (Boston, MA: Beacon Press, 1964). This subject is taken up also by Habermas in *Towards a Rational Society*, translated by Jeremy J. Shapiro (London: Heinemann, 1970).

9 Jürgen Habermas, *The Theory of Communicative Action*, Vol. 2, *Lifeworld and System: A Critique of Functionalist Reason*, translated by Thomas McCarthy (Boston, MA: Beacon Press, 1981). In subsequent interviews and essays, Habermas has continued to explain and elaborate his "internal colonization" thesis.

10 A presentation of the views of major figures in the object relations tradition is given in J. R. Greenberg and S. A. Mitchell, *Object Relations and Psychoanalytic Theory* (Cambridge and London: Harvard University Press, 1983). Heinz Kohut sets out his theory of the self most clearly in *The Restoration of the Self* (New York: International Universities Press, 1977). Jessica Benjamin integrates feminism, psychoanalysis, and Critical Theory in "The Decline of the Oedipus Complex," in *Critical Theories of Psychological Development*, edited by John Broughton (New York: Plenum, 1987). See also Jessica Benjamin, *Bonds of Love* (New York: Pantheon, 1988).

11 A collection of Jacques Lacan's essays is presented in *Ecrits: A Selection*, edited by Jacques-Alain Miller, translated by Alan Sheridan (New York: W.W. Norton, 1977). An excellent introduction to Lacan is Richard Boothby's *Death and Desire: Psychoanalytic Theory in Lacan's Return to Freud* (New York: Routledge, 1991).

2 NARCISSISM, MASTERY, AND IDENTITY, pp. 19–42

1 Quoted in Sergio Pacifici, *A Guide to Contemporary Italian Theatre* (New York: World Publishing, 1962), p. 215.

2 Max Weber, *From Max Weber: Essays in Sociology*, edited and translated by H.H. Gerth and C. Wright Mills (New York: Oxford University Press, 1946; orig. 1919), p. 155.

3 Various theoretical perspectives, including object relations psychoanalysis and self-psychology, affirm that the "self" is a valid psychological construct. See Stephen E. Toulmin, "Self-Knowledge and Knowledge of the 'Self'," in *The Self: Psychological and Philosophical Issues*, edited by Theodore Mischel (Oxford: Basil Blackwell, 1977). For the French psychoanalyst Jacques Lacan and his followers, on the other hand, the "self" of American psychoanalysis signifies an illusion, evading the recognition of a fundamental lack of being and absence of definition that human beings cannot bear. We will return to the issue of the reality of the self in subsequent chapters, especially Chapter 6.

4 Joseph Weizenbaum, *Computer Power and Human Reason: From Judgment to Calculation* (San Francisco, CA: W.H. Freeman, 1976); Terry Winograd and Fernando Flores, *Computers and Cognition: A New Foundation for Design* (Reading, MA: Addison-Wesley, 1987); Hubert Dreyfus, *What Computers Still Can't Do: A Critique of Artificial Reason* (Cambridge, MA: MIT Press, 1992).

5 Robert Coles, *Privileged Ones: The Well-off and the Rich in America*, Vol. 5, *Children of Crisis* (Boston, MA: Atlantic Monthly, 1977), p. 380.

6 Ibid., p. 381.

7 Michel Foucault, *The History of Sexuality*, Vol. 1, *An Introduction*, translated by Robert Hurley (New York: Random House, 1978), pp. 58–60. See also Volume 3 of this work, and Michel Foucault, *Technologies of the Self: A Seminar with Michel Foucault*, edited by Luther Martin, Huck Gutman, and Patrick Hutton (Amherst, MA: University of Massachusetts Press, 1988). Foucault would not agree with psychoanalytic object relations theory or self-psychology that the self can be an ahistorical, substantialized entity.

8 Coles, op. cit., p. 406.

9 Douglas D. Noble, "Mental Materiel: The Militarization of Learning and Intelligence in US Education," in *Cyborg Worlds: The Military Information Society*, edited by Les Levidow and Kevin Robins (London: Free Association Books, 1989), p. 30. See also Douglas D. Noble, *The Human Arsenal* (Bristol, NJ: Taylor & Francis, 1991).

10 Christopher Lasch, *The Minimal Self* (New York: W.W. Norton, 1984), p. 57.

11 John Broughton (forthcoming) speaks of "hi-gender" and "low-gender," in parallel with the distinction between "hi-tech" and "low-tech." New gender definitions reflect a shift away from corporeal identification (body as anchor of gender) to mental fantasy (mind as phallus).

12 In *Technology and War* (New York: Macmillan, 1989), Martin Van Creveld points out that as military operations became more technologically intensive during the sixteenth and seventeenth centuries, artillery and engineering became specialized military occupations. In the nineteenth century, he adds, professionalization and bureaucratization were accelerated – a trend which continues today (p. 146).

13 Ibid., p. 248. See also David Segal, *Recruiting for Uncle Sam: Citizenship and Military Manpower Policy* (Lawrence, KA: University Press of Kansas, 1989); Chris H. Gray, "The Cyborg Soldier: The US Military and the Post-Modern Warrior," in *Cyborg Worlds: The Military Information Society*, edited by Les Levidow and Kevin Robins (London: Free Association Books, 1989), p. 59.

14 Such expressions are especially prevalent in English. The concepts of wholeness and fragmentation, basic to self-psychology as developed by the psychoanalyst Heinz Kohut and his followers, are not as easily formulated in other languages. It is as if Kohut had to migrate from Germany to an English-speaking country in order to find a congenial idiom, since expressions like "falling to pieces" have no equivalent in his native language.

   In German, anxieties about the ontological status of the self are typically not articulated in terms of the wholeness/fragmentation metaphor, but draw instead upon a related polarity: organization/disorganization.

15 Peter Berger, "'Sincerity' and 'Authenticity' in Modern Society," *Public Interest* 31 (Spring 1973), pp. 81, 86.

16 Heinz Kohut, *The Search for the Self: Selected Writings of Heinz Kohut: 1950–1978*, edited by Paul H. Ornstein, Vol. 2 (New York: International Universities Press, 1978), pp. 780–781. Incoherence and disintegration of the self have indeed been central themes in twentieth-century literature. Kohut might equally well have cited these illustrations:

> Sometimes it seems to me that the forms of life are suddenly emptied of their contents, reality is unreal, words are nothing but sounds bereft of sense, these houses and this sky are no longer anything but façades concealing nothing, people appear to be moving about automatically and without reason; everything seems to melt into thin air, everything is threatened – myself included – by a silent and imminent collapse

into I know not what abyss, where there is no more night or day ... it is clear I can never know who I am, or why I am.

Ionesco, quoted in Ralph Harper, *The Existential Experience* (Baltimore, MD: The Johns Hopkins University Press, 1972), pp. 28–29.

Life was a hollow shell all round him, roaring and clattering like the sound of the sea, a noise in which he participated externally, and inside this hollow shell was all the darkness and fearful space of death, he knew he would have to find reinforcements, otherwise he would collapse inwards upon the great dark void which circled at the center of his soul.

D. H. Lawrence, *Women in Love* (New York: Modern Library, 1950), p. 368.

As I've mentioned earlier, women writers have also dealt with these issues, from perspectives different from those of most male authors. In Virginia Woolf's *The Waves*, for instance, the identity of each character sooner or later disintegrates.

17 What object relations theorist, Margaret Mahler, refers to as "separation–individuation," presumably a universal stage of child development, is to some extent an historical artifact, a function of our particular modes of representation (for example, Giotto versus Cimabue).

18 Christine de Pizan's writings in defense of women are discussed in Joan Kelly, "Early Feminist Theory and the *Querelle des Femmes*," *Women, History, and Theory* (Chicago & London: University of Chicago Press, 1984), pp. 65–109; see also her essay in the same book: "Did Women Have a Renaissance?," pp. 19–50. For an examination of women's public and private roles during the Early Modern period in Europe, see Merry Wiesner, "Women's Defense of Their Public Role," in *Women in the Middle Ages and the Renaissance: Literary and Historical Perspectives*, edited by Mary Beth Rose (Syracuse, NY: Syracuse University Press, 1986), pp. 1–27.

19 Ludwig Binswanger, "The Case of Ellen West," in *Existence: A New Dimension in Psychiatry and Psychology*, edited by Rollo May, Ernest Angel and Henri Ellenberger (New York: Basic Books, 1958), p. 247.

20 *The Nation*, December 31, 1990, p. 825.

21 Christopher Lasch, *The Culture of Narcissism* (New York: W. W. Norton, 1979), pp. 87–88.

22 Michael Beldoch, "The Therapeutic as Narcissist," *Salmagundi* 20 (1972), p. 138.

23 Jessica Benjamin discusses the relationships between individuation, identity, and mastery in "The Decline of the Oedipus Complex," in *Critical Theories of Psychological Development*, edited by John Broughton (New York: Plenum, 1987). See also Jessica Benjamin, *Bonds of Love* (New York: Pantheon, 1988).

24 Lucien Lévy-Bruhl, *Primitive Mentality*, translated by Lilian Clare (New York: Macmillan, 1978), p. 113.

25 H. Callaway, "The Religious Systems of the Amazulu," in *Relations des Jesuites dans la Nouvelle-France (1655–1656)* Vol. XLII (Quebec: Canadian Government, 1868), pp. 150–152.

26 Robert Bly, *Iron John* (New York: Random House, 1990); Alexander Mitscherlich, *Society Without the Father: A Contribution to Social Psychology*, translated by Eric Mosbacher (London: Tavistock Publications, 1969). Recognition that an "absent father" is a problem in many men's lives does not entail, however, that we accept the reinstitution of masculine rituals or the other remedies that the poet prescribes.

27 Psychoanalytic object relations theory and self-psychology have rightly emphasized the crucial role that a "mothering" parent plays in a child's earliest interpersonal experiences.

But by allocating this role exclusively to women, while locating only men as performers of "paternal" functions, these accounts reproduce oppressive gender ideologies. Among the first to point this out was Nancy Chodorow in *The Reproduction of Mothering: Psychoanalysis and the Sociology of Gender* (Berkeley, CA: University of California Press, 1978). See also the excellent discussion in Benjamin, op. cit., "The Decline of the Oedipus Complex."

28 Bly, op. cit., pp. 22–23, 92–102.

3 THREE DREAMS, pp. 43–59

1 Space limitations, along with considerations of confidentiality, prevented me from including more of the background information relevant to interpretation of the dreams presented in this book. I have thoroughly disguised the identities and circumstances of the dreamers.

2 See for example Fredric Jameson, *Postmodernism, or The Cultural Logic of Late Capitalism* (Durham, NC: Duke University Press, 1991); Ian Reid, *Narrative Exchanges* (London: Routledge, 1992). Of course the dichotomy I am proposing is highly simplified. Neither Henry James' nor Conrad's writing, to mention only two exceptions, fits neatly into the mastery-versus-identity polarity I outline here.

3 Sigmund Freud, "Creative Writers and Day-Dreaming," in *The Standard Edition of the Complete Psychological Works of Sigmund Freud*, edited and translated by James Strachey, Vol. 9 (London: Hogarth Press, 1959), p. 150.

4 Sigmund Freud, *The Interpretation of Dreams*, edited and translated by James Strachey (New York: Basic Books, 1961; orig. 1900), p. 382.

5 Ibid., p. 357.

6 J. R. Vrooman, *René Descartes, A Biography* (New York: G.P Putnam's Sons, 1970), pp. 56–58; I have modified Vrooman's translation from the French text which is given in *Oeuvres de Descartes*, edited by S. S. Sacy (Paris: Club français du livre, 1966), pp. 75–77.

7 René Descartes, *Discourse on Method*, Part I in *Discourse on Method and the Meditations*, translated by F. E. Sutcliffe (New York: Penguin, 1968; orig. 1637), p. 33.

8 Vrooman, op. cit., p. 59.

9 Descartes, op. cit., Part VI, p. 78.

10 René Descartes, *Rules for the Direction of the Mind*, Rule 5 in *The Philosophical Writings of Descartes*, translated by John Cottingham, Robert Stoothoff, and Dugald Murdoch (Cambridge: Cambridge University Press, 1985), p. 20.

11 Genevieve Rodis-Lewis, *Descartes: Textes et Debats* (Paris: Le Livre de Poche, 1984), p. 32.

12 René Descartes, *Meditations on First Philosophy*, edited and translated by John Cottingham (Cambridge: Cambridge University Press, 1986), pp. 15, 54.

13 Rodis-Lewis, op. cit., p. 32; Descartes, op. cit., *Meditations*, p. 56.

14 Freud, op. cit., *Interpretation of Dreams*, p. 107.

15 Among the dream's analysts are D. Anzieu, *Freud's Self-Analysis*, translated by P. Graham (New York: International Universities Press, 1986); Erik H. Erikson, "The Dream Specimen of Psychoanalysis," *Journal of the American Psychoanalytic Association* II(1), pp. 5–56; Alexander Grinstein, *Sigmund Freud's Dreams* (New York: International Universities Press, 1980). Anzieu offers this summary of previous interpretations:

> The 'hall' with its guests and Irma's 'throat' ... 'receiving' ... [present] an image of coitus ... The 'extensive whitish grey scabs' on 'some curly structures' are traces of sperm and represent impregnation ... According to Fliess, 'trimethylamin' was a key

ingredient of sexual chemistry; similarly, the examination of Irma's 'turbinal bones' was a kind of tribute paid by the dreamer to another of Fliess's theories, which postulated a connection between the nose and sex ... the 'injections' made 'so thoughtlessly' with a 'syringe' that 'had not been clean' – they refer to the need to resort to contraceptive techniques.

(Anzieu, op. cit., p. 136)

16 Freud, op. cit., *Interpretation of Dreams*, pp. 108–109, 118.
17 Jeffrey Masson, *The Assault on Truth: Freud's Suppression of the Seduction Theory* (New York: Farrar, Straus & Giroux, 1983); Peter Gay, *Freud, a Life for our Time* (New York: W.W. Norton, 1988), pp. 82–86.
18 Freud, op. cit., *Interpretation of Dreams*, pp. 192–193.
19 Ibid., p. 216.
20 Ibid., pp. 117, 119, 114.
21 Ibid., pp. 110–111.
22 Ibid., p. 119.
23 Ibid., p. 116. Lacan and Anzieu, in their analyses of Freud's Irma dream, also point out various triplets to which it may allude. Their way of locating the people in Freud's life into groups of three differs from the one that I present. See *The Seminar of Jacques Lacan*, Book II, edited by Jacques-Alain Miller, translated by Sylvana Tomaselli (New York: W.W. Norton, 1988; orig. 1955), pp. 156–159; Anzieu, op. cit., pp. 147–149.
24 To bring out more clearly the similarity between chemical and social structures, I have diagrammed only two of the compound's three methyl groups.
25 Freud, op. cit., *Interpretation of Dreams*, p. 116.
26 Descartes, op. cit., *Meditations*, p. 33.
27 Freud, op. cit., *Interpretation of Dreams*, p. 111.
28 Ibid., p. 113.
29 Gay, op. cit., p. 138.
30 Stefan Zweig, *The World of Yesterday* (New York: Viking Press, 1943), p. 77. Zweig refers to unmarried women in particular, but characterizes in similar terms the lot of middle-class women in general (pp. 67–91). The repressive consequences of Austrian culture for Viennese women at the turn of the century were made into theater by Arthur Schnitzler; see the comparison of the dramatist to Freud in Sidney Bolkosky, "Arthur Schnitzler and the Fate of Mothers in Vienna," *Psychoanalytic Review* 73 (Spring 1986), pp. 1–15.
31 Freud's famous query, "Was will das Weib?" is quoted in Ernest Jones, *The Life and Work of Sigmund Freud*, Vol. 2 (New York: Basic Books, 1955), p. 421. See also Freud's "New Introductory Lectures on Psychoanalysis," *Standard Edition*, op. cit., Vol. 22, p. 116, where he acknowledges that psychological explanation "is unable to solve the riddle of femininity."
32 Sigmund Freud, *The Origins of Psychoanalysis* (New York: Basic Books, 1954), pp. 318, 319, 183, 290.

4 INDIVIDUALISM: THE PERPLEXING PROJECT, pp. 60–65

1 See, for example, John O. Lyons, *The Invention of the Self* (Carbondale, IL: Southern Illinois University Press, 1978).
2 Clifford Geertz, *The Interpretation of Cultures* (New York: Basic Books, 1973).
3 The "decline of the individual" has been a favorite theme of the Frankfurt School. David Riesman and other American sociologists have also elaborated this idea.
4 Skepticism about the self is a recurrent theme in Nietzsche's writings; see, for instance, Part I, Section 13 of *On the Genealogy of Morals*, edited and translated by Walter

Kaufmann and R.J. Hollingdale (New York: Random, 1967). Belief in God and belief in the individual are internally linked. In the Western philosophical tradition, the individual was invented partly to answer a certain argument against God's existence. If the Creator exists, the atheist suggests, then by definition He is omniscient, omnipotent, and totally benevolent. Therefore, He would create a perfect world. But our world is notoriously flawed, as the widespread existence of human suffering attests. How are we to square the existence of God with a world that is defective in so many ways? One of the traditional rejoinders to this "problem of evil" given by defenders of the faith is that human beings themselves, being relatively free and autonomous individuals whose existence is in this respect patterned after their Creator, are responsible for the world's apparent "imperfections." In this way the existence of free human individuals would make that of God more credible. Conversely, calling the existence of God into question threatens the status of the human individual, too.

5 Iris Murdoch, *The Sovereignty of the Good* (London: Routledge, 1970), p. 80.

6 Herbert Marcuse, *One Dimensional Man* (Boston, MA: Beacon Press), pp. 158–159.

5 BOUNDARY, pp. 69–80

1 Small children are of course not quite saying this, since the linguistic boundary between "me" and "not-me" is not yet securely in place. It is because we are linguistic beings – capable of "carving" the world with language, we might say – that it is possible to become a self at all. Daniel Stern argues, however, that infants are capable of making primitive boundary discriminations. See Daniel Stern, *The Interpersonal World of the Infant: A View from Psychoanalysis and Developmental Psychology* (New York: Basic Books, 1985).

2 Margaret S. Mahler, F. Pine, and A. Bergman, *The Psychological Birth of the Infant: Symbiosis and Individuation* (New York: Basic Books, 1975). Stern, op. cit., is critical of Mahler for underestimating behaviors of independence and separateness that even infants exhibit.

3 This dynamic does not begin with information technologies. Because technical instruments of any kind extend human powers, they dissolve and relocate power's boundaries. Consider, for example, the power of physical movement. So long as the human capacity for locomotion is foot-driven, there is a certain area that a human being is capable of traversing in a day. With the advent of rotary engine and eventually rocket transportation, that boundary expanded enormously. There is scarcely any conceivable limit on how far an astronaut may go in exploring space. The only insuperable constraint here is the finite lifetime of the space traveler. Perhaps one of the reasons that modern societies become obsessed with death – we are addicted to it on television, in the movies, and take vitamins and do our daily exercise to postpone it as long as possible – is that mortality remains to date the most stubborn, unsurpassable boundary in our lives.

4 Douglas D. Noble, "Mental Materiel: The Militarization of Learning and Intelligence in US Education," in *Cyborg Worlds: The Military Information Society*, edited by Les Levidow and Kevin Robins (London: Free Association Books, 1989), p. 26.

5 In Eisenhower's time, the complex of which he spoke existed mainly within the United States. Today, however, capital is internationally integrated, and pays less and less attention to nation-state boundaries. Enlargement of corporate boundaries is accompanied by their redefinition inside the firm itself. Because the requirements placed on contemporary capital change so quickly and so unpredictably, boundaries within as well as between enterprises lose their fixed character. As specific projects or product lines come into and pass out of existence, so do the associations of workers organized to carry them through to completion. Corporate and financial organizations have become more mobile than ever before, ready to expand or contract, to enter new markets or retrench,

in order to meet shifting requirements for survival or growth. Under these circumstances, boundaries are constantly being displaced and reconfigured.

6 Jürgen Habermas, *The Theory of Communicative Action*, Vol. 2, *Lifeworld and System: A Critique of Functionalist Reason*, translated by Thomas McCarthy (Boston, MA: Beacon Press, 1987), VIII, Part 2.

7 A. Adu Boahen, *African Perspectives on Colonialism* (Baltimore, MD: Johns Hopkins University Press, 1987), p. 96.

8 Alvin and Heidi Toffler, among others, have noted that corporate environments have become structures of instability. He points out that the production aims and organization of work, including a company's internal subdivisions as well as its relationships to other firms and to a client-base, are typically subject to constant revision in the light of changing circumstances; see Toffler's *Future Shock* (New York: Bantam Doubleday Dell, 1970), pp. 108–119, 128–151. Toffler fails to examine, however, the ways in which corporate change advantages certain social interests at the expense of others.

9 Paradoxically, William's perceptions of transience and absent boundaries coexist with his sense of the fixed and immutable character of institutional life. That the structures of his work environment could be differently organized is scarcely a possibility within his universe.

6 SUBJECTIVITY, pp. 81–93

1 David Hume, *A Treatise on Human Nature* (Oxford: Oxford University Press, 1978; orig. 1739), pp. 252–253.

2 Steven Toulmin, "Self-Knowledge and Knowledge of the 'Self'," in *The Self: Psychological and Philosophical Issues*, edited by Theodore Mischel (Oxford: Basil Blackwell, 1977). For an excellent conceptual overview and etymology of "self" see Charles Webel, "Self: An Overview," in *International Encyclopedia of Psychiatry, Psychology, and Neurology*, Vol. 1, *Progress,* edited by Benjamin Wolman (New York: Aesculapius, 1983), pp. 398–403.

3 Erich Auerbach, *Mimesis: The Reproduction of Reality in Western Literature*, translated by Willard Trask (Princeton, NJ: Princeton University Press, 1953), pp. 40–49.

4 Heinz Kohut, *The Restoration of the Self* (New York: International Universities Press, 1977), pp. 278–279.

5 Margaret Mahler, Fred Pine, and Anni Bergman, *The Psychological Birth of the Human Infant: Symbiosis and Individuation* (New York: Basic Books, 1975). In consideration of Daniel Stern's critique of Mahler, however, I regard the normal outcome of pre-Oedipal relationships as individuation, not separation. See Daniel Stern, *The Interpersonal World of the Infant* (New York: Basic Books, 1985).

6 Kohut, op. cit., p. 227.

7 Kohut, op. cit., p. 177.

8 Heinz Kohut, *The Search for the Self: Selected Writings of Heinz Kohut: 1950–1978*, edited by Paul H. Ornstein, Vol. 2 (New York: International Universities Press, 1978), pp. 781–782; Kohut, op. cit., *Restoration*, p. 269.

9 In *The Search for the Self*, Kohut suggests that the historical shift which has resulted in a contemporary prevalence of self pathologies may be explained in terms of the history of the family:

In former times the involvement between the parents and their children was overly intense. The children were emotionally overtaxed by their proximity to adults – be they the parents or nursemaids or others ... But now we seem to be dealing with the opposite problem. There is not enough touching, not enough genuine parental responsiveness; there exists an atmosphere of emotional flatness and sterility.

Kohut speaks quite generally in this passage about "parents" and "children" as if there were not crucial differences between the ways in which children from various social class and ethnic backgrounds are raised. Moreover, if there exists any overall tendency in the history of the family, it has been *away* from just the conditions that Kohut cites as conducive to self pathology. See Edward Shorter, *The Making of the Modern Family* (New York: Basic Books, 1975), pp. 168–204.

10 Anna Freud, *The Ego and the Mechanisms of Defense*, translated by Cecil Barnes (London: Hogarth Press, 1942), pp. 85–86. In other writings, Anna Freud does mention intellectualization on occasion, but it never plays a prominent role in her account of defensive functions.

11 Max Horkheimer elaborates this thesis in many places, including *Eclipse of Reason* (New York: Oxford University Press, 1947), especially Chapter 4, "Rise and Decline of the Individual"; and "Authority and the Family," *Critical Theory* (New York: The Seabury Press, 1972), pp. 47–128.

7 ETHICS, pp. 94–103

1 Charles Taylor, *Sources of the Self* (Cambridge, MA: Harvard University Press, 1989).

2 Emanuel Peterfreund, *Information, Systems, and Psychoanalysis* (New York: International Universities Press, 1971), p. 128.

3 Immanuel Kant, *Foundations for the Metaphysics of Morals*, translated by Lewis White Beck (Indianapolis, IN: Bobbs-Merrill, 1959; orig. 1785), Section 434, p. 53; also Sections 434–440.

4 Kant's ethics associates moral community with abstract reasoning and religious belief in ways that we may find unacceptable. Moreover, he regards ethical principles as timeless and transcendental, whereas we may view them as culturally relative and subject to historical development. Finally, as environmentalists point out, the Kantian distinction between merely functional, "dead" objects and alive, intrinsically valuable human subjects has been associated historically with exploitative attitudes toward our natural surroundings ("domination of nature"). Yet, for all of his faults, Kant does begin to get at an ethical basis for human relationships. Many post-structural critics would argue that no such basis can be found, but see Martha Nussbaum's reply in "Human Functioning and Social Justice: In Defense of Aristotelian Essentialism," *Political Theory*, 20(2) (May 1992), pp. 202–246. There are continuities as well between Critical Theory's communicative ethics and Kantian views. See Karl-Otto Apel, "Is the Ethics of the Ideal Communication Community a Utopia? On the Relationship between Ethics, Utopia, and the Critique of Utopia," *The Communicative Ethics Controversy*, edited by Seyla Benhabib and Fred Dallmayr (Cambridge MA: MIT Press, 1990), pp. 23–59; also Otfried Höffe, "Kantian Skepticism toward Transcendental Ethics" in the same volume, pp. 193–219.

5 "Deep ecology" would extend the domain of the intrinsically valuable to encompass non-human species and inanimate nature: the natural world in all its forms is to be respected and cherished.

6 Taylor, op. cit., p. 28, argues for an internal link between human identity and ethics: "To know who you are is to be oriented in moral space, a space in which questions arise about what is good or bad, what is worth doing and what not, what has meaning and importance for you and what is trivial and secondary." I worry, though, that his argument is transcendentally, and ultimately religiously, based. Taylor dichotomizes value, reserving a special ontological status for what he calls "hyper-goods." Although I find his discussion provocative, I am not quite convinced. Notwithstanding his criticism of

Kantian ethics, his elevation of certain goods to super-natural status (literally beyond naturalism) appears to accept a Kantian premise that I hope we can do without.

7 Lynn White, "The Iconography of *Temperentia* and the Virtuousness of Technology," *Medieval Religion and Technology: Collected Essays* (Berkeley, CA: University of California Press, 1978), 193–194.

8 John F. Kasson, *Civilizing the Machine: Technology and Republican Values in America, 1776–1900* (New York: Viking Penguin, 1977), p. 80.

9 Robert N. Bellah, Richard Madsen, Ann Swindler, and William Sullivan, *Habits of the Heart* (Berkeley, CA: University of California Press, 1985), p. 75.

10 Ibid.

11 Ulrich Beck, "The Anthropological Shock: Chernobyl and the Contours of the Risk Society," *Berkeley Journal of Sociology* 32 (1987), p. 159.

12 Jürgen Habermas, *The Theory of Communicative Action*, Vol. 2, *Lifeworld and System: A Critique of Functionalist Reason*, translated by Thomas McCarthy (Boston, MA: Beacon Press, 1987), p. 323.

13 Alasdair MacIntyre, *After Virtue: A Study in Moral Theory* (Notre Dame, IN: University of Notre Dame Press, 1984), especially pp. 27–31.

8 RECOGNITION, pp. 104–118

1 Colin Morris, *The Discovery of the Individual: 1050–1200* (London: SPCK for the Church Historical Society, 1972), p. 144.

2 Simon Schama, *The Embarrassment of Riches* (Berkeley, CA: University of California Press, 1988), p. 575. My interpretation differs slightly from Schama's.

3 None of these European settings was conflict-free, to be sure. Even where that conflict erupted in war, though, this did not necessarily drive a wedge between institutional and personal identities. To the contrary, when one city-state or religious sect or royal house was pitted against another, the respective identities of the contending parties tended to be reaffirmed.

4 Arthur Lovejoy, *The Great Chain of Being*, especially Chapter 9, "The Temporalizing of the Chain of Being" (Cambridge, MA: MIT Press, 1936).

5 Erwin Panofsky, *Early Netherlandish Painting*, Vol. 1 (Cambridge, MA: Harvard University Press, 1953), p. 203.

6 Ibid., p. 142.

7 *Dartmouth Bible*, Exodus 3:5, p. 82. These and other details of the painting are discussed in Panofsky, op. cit., pp. 140–144, and Herwig Guratzsch, *Dutch and Flemish Painting* (New York: Vilo, 1981), pp. 22–26.

8 Gerard Thomas Straub, *Salvation for Sale* (Buffalo, NY: Prometheus Books, 1988), pp. 36, 38. The attention given to viewers of evangelical TV programs does not cease when their hosts go off the air, because televangelists offer additional services to supplement viewers' born-again experiences. Robertson and Falwell make extensive use of the telephone for this purpose. On Robertson's program, viewers are encouraged to call a toll-free number to talk with a counselor who will hear and pray for their sins. His telephone counseling network has handled about 4.4 million calls annually. In addition there are "700 Club" counseling centers established by the Robertson organization in forty-four cities.

9 Direct-mail advertising adopts the same strategy. A computer-generated, personalized letter (no oxymoron, this) from American Express addresses its customers:

Dear [name of card holder]
Because you are a highly valued American Express© Card member, I am inviting you to apply for the Gold Card at this time ... Only a select group will ever carry the

Gold Card. So it instantly identifies you as someone special – one who expects an added measure of courtesy and personal attention ... The Gold Card says more about you than anything you could buy with it. We think it's time you joined the select group who carry it.

Another example of the "personalizing" of commercial services; upon dialing information on my telephone recently, I was surprised to hear the operator began by telling me who she was, "Hello, this is Shirley, how may I help you?" I was receiving attention from a named (therefore real!) person. Arlie Hochschild, in *The Managed Heart: Commercialization of Human Feeling* (Berkeley, CA: University of California Press, 1983), speaks of "emotional work," consisting of services that involve the production of personal rapport with clients.

9 IDENTIFICATION, pp. 119–133

1 Thomas Aquinas, *The Summa Theologica*, in *Great Books of the Western World*, edited by Robert Hutchins (Chicago, IL: Encyclopedia Britannica, 1952) Vol. 2, Supplement to Third Part, Q. 75, Art. 2, Reply Obj. 3, p. 936.
2 M. Merleau-Ponty, *Phenomenology of Perception*, translated by Colin Smith (London: Routledge & Kegan Paul, 1962), p. 98.
3 Ibid., p. 102.
4 Robert Bly, *Iron John* (New York: Random House, 1990), p. 93.
5 Alexander Mitscherlich, *Society Without the Father: A Contribution to Social Psychology*, translated by Eric Mosbacher (London: Tavistock Publications, 1969).
6 In educational institutions, for example, relationships between students and teachers become more abstract when personal contact gives way to impersonal administration. Standardized tests (for the efficient scoring of which we can thank computers), enable teachers to chart their students' progress "objectively." Even the act of teaching itself no longer requires a teacher's personal intervention: computer-assisted instruction substitutes for direct student–teacher contact. The legitimate concern about the possible abuse of children by their teachers provides an additional distancing influence. For example, a first-grade teacher may decide to discontinue the practice of holding hands with the students in his class; a child could report this touching to a parent or administrator, and the teacher might be accused of perversion.
7 W. Ronald D. Fairbairn, *Psychoanalytic Studies of the Personality* (London: Routledge & Kegan Paul, 1952), p. 138.
8 At the time that Andy told me about his dream of the computer "motherboard," I did not think of the association "mother bored." Andy's mother had apparently been quite neglected by his father, and at a loss about what to do with herself in the absence of his companionship.
9 On a traditional psychoanalytic reading, the syllable "pop" which occurs at several points in the dream and dream associations might be interpreted to allude to the dreamer's father, from whom Roger felt distant. Being French, though, Roger might not have been aware of this meaning of the word.
  The imagery of fullness and emptiness in Roger's dream tells us not just about his unique history, but about contemporary culture at large, as indicated by the evolution of English, Roger's second language. "Self-fulfillment," a word of relatively recent vintage is roughly synonymous with the more traditional expression, "self-realization." However, "self-realization" belongs to an Aristotelian ethics: one "realizes" oneself through the gradual and disciplined development of one's essential human powers, whereas "self-fulfillment" is a more recent metaphor: the self as a container that "fills" itself to be made mentally and physically substantial, self-sufficient, and whole.

10 Typically, the information presented in these various formats is not used by people actually to prepare their meals. Recipes are of interest, regardless of whether the reader or viewer ever implements them in the kitchen. Food literature is a new pornography of a kind – the fantasy is as attractive and absorbing as the reality.

11 Liz Atwood, "Buyers Expect All the Extras in New Homes," *Oakland Tribune*, August 20, 1989, Section F.

12 Michael Goldhaber, "The Human Meaning of the Information Revolution," in *New Ways of Knowing*, edited by M.G. Raskin and H.J. Bernstein (Totowa, NJ: Rowman & Littlefield, 1987), p. 168.

13 Francis Bacon, *The New Organon* (New York: Liberal Arts, 1960; orig. 1620), p. 25.

14 René Descartes, *Discourse on Method*, Part I in *Discourse on Method and the Meditations*, translated by F. E. Sutcliffe (New York: Penguin, 1968; orig. 1637), p. 33.

15 Francis Bacon, "The Masculine Birth of Time," in *The Philosophy of Francis Bacon*, edited and translated by Benjamin Farrington (Liverpool: Liverpool University Press, 1964), p. 62.

16 This story exists in several versions. Hewlett-Packard is not always the culprit company.

17 The manager of a systems analyst and programmer I worked with gave him a sheet of paper, to be entered into his dossier, on which he was to list his accomplishments. For the past two years he had been constructing the core of a complex system – those of us familiar with his work knew that it was excellent – he had carefully thought through and assembled an elaborate infrastructure. But he could not think of non-technical terms to describe it. Hence his work remained invisible not only to those who would use the system he was building, but also to managerial personnel responsible for his evaluation.

10 THE LOGIC OF COLONIAL ORGANIZATION, pp. 137–150

1 Gordon Pask and Susan Curran, *Micro Man: Computers and the Evolution of Consciousness* (New York: Macmillan, 1982), pp. 216–217.

2 Jürgen Habermas, *The Theory of Communicative Action*, Vol. 2, *Lifeworld and System: A Critique of Functionalist Reason*, translated by Thomas McCarthy (Boston, MA: Beacon Press, 1987), p. 356.

3 Peter Drucker, "The Coming of the New Organization," *Harvard Business Review* (January–February 1988), p. 48.

4 Franz Fanon, *Black Skin, White Masks* (New York: Grove Press, 1967), p. 219.

5 Victor T. Levine, "Political-Cultural Schizophrenia in Francophone Africa," in *Africa and the West: Legacies of Empire*, edited by Isaac Mowoe and Richard Bjornson (New York: Greenwood Press, 1986), p. 161.

6 Cheikh Hamidou Kane, *Ambiguous Adventure*, translated by Katherine Woods (New York: Walker and Co., 1963), pp. 150–151.

7 Ibid., pp. 149–150.

8 Albert Memmi, *The Colonizer and the Colonized* (Boston, MA: Beacon Press, 1969), especially pp. 20–51.

9 George Orwell, "Shooting an Elephant," in *Shooting an Elephant and Other Essays* (New York: Harcourt, Brace, Jovanovich, 1945), p. 8.

10 Ernesto Laclau and Chantal Mouffe, *Hegemony and Socialist Strategy: Towards a Radical Democratic Politics* (London: Verso, 1985).

11 Habermas, op. cit., pp. 154–155.

12 Betsy Collard, *The High-Tech Career Book* (Los Altos, CA: William Kaufmann Inc., 1986), p. 72.

13 Ibid., p. 69.

14 It is experience transformed in this way that cognitive psychologists believe they can

account for in terms of information-processing models of the mind. Inasmuch as life becomes calculative and procedural, it confirms cognitivism's view of it. See Chapter 11.

15 There is an extensive literature on this subject. See for example David Noble, *Forces of Production: A Social History of Industrial Automation* (New York: Oxford University Press, 1986).

16 Georgy Lukács, *History and Class Consciousness* (Cambridge, MA: MIT Press, 1971) quoted in *About Looking* edited by John Berger (New York: Random House, 1980), p. 17. My comments on the colonial character of contemporary relationships with animals draw on Berger's perceptive analysis.

17 Berger, op. cit., p. 12.

18 Berger, op. cit., p. 23.

19 Berger, op. cit., p. 28.

20 Amanda Cochrane and Karen Callen, *Dolphins and Their Power to Heal* (Rochester, VT: Healing Arts Press, 1992), p. 73. My discussion here results from conversations with Susan Hales from the Saybrook Institute and Terry Samansky from Marine World, USA. Richard Connor, who has studied dolphins in Shark Bay, pointed out to me that when males sequester a female, they may be "intending" not to copulate with her, but to keep her away from other males. So perhaps they are offering "protection"!

11 INFORMATION-PROCESSING PSYCHOLOGY, pp. 151–162

1 George A. Miller (Professor of Psychology, Harvard University), quoted in B. Rensberger, "Man and Computer: Uneasy Allies of 25 Years," *New York Times*, June 27, 1972, p. 43.

2 René Descartes, *Discours de la Methode* (Paris: Bader-Dufour, 1948; orig. 1637), pp. 21–22.

3 Sherry Turkle, *The Second Self: Computers and the Human Spirit* (New York: Simon and Schuster, 1984), especially pp. 58–60.

4 Emanuel Peterfreund, *Information, Systems, and Psychoanalysis* (New York: International Universities Press, 1971), pp. 105, 127–128.

5 Ibid., p. 189.

6 Ibid., p. 127.

7 Joseph Weizenbaum, *Computer Power and Human Reason: From Judgment to Calculation* (San Francisco, CA: W.H. Freeman, 1976); Terry Winograd and Fernando Flores, *Computers and Cognition: A New Foundation for Design* (Reading, MA: Addison-Wesley, 1987); Hubert Dreyfus, *What Computers Still Can't Do: A Critique of Artificial Reason* (Cambridge, MA: MIT Press, 1992).

8 See, for instance, Daniel Dennett, *Consciousness Explained* (Boston, MA: Little, Brown & Co., 1991), especially pp. 278–280, 435–440; David Chapman, *Vision, Instruction, and Action* (Cambridge, MA: MIT Press, 1991). In the past decade, cognitive scientists have shifted their model of mental functioning from single-tasking to parallel-processing computers, which answers some of the philosophical objections to their basic assumptions.

9 Not every cognitive scientist would extend the information-processing model to clinical contexts. Indeed, the explanatory value of information-processing concepts cannot necessarily be measured in terms of their adequacy in accounting for therapeutic interactions.

10 Peterfreund, op. cit., pp. 172–174.

11 See for example G.H. Lawrence, "Using Computers for the Treatment of Psychological Problems," *Computers in Human Behavior* 2 (1986), pp. 43–62; Christopher Mruk, "The Interface Between Computers and Psychology," *Computers in Human Behavior* 3 (1987), pp. 167–179; James Sampson, Jr, "The Use of Computer-Assisted Instruction in

Support of Psychotherapeutic Processes," *Computers in Human Behavior* 2 (1986), pp. 1–19; Michael Zarr, "Computer-Mediated Psychotherapy: Toward Patient-Selection Guidelines," *American Journal of Psychotherapy* 38(1) (January 1984), pp. 47–61. Kenneth Colby's contributions in this area are too numerous to cite here, but see "Computer Psychotherapists," in *Technology in Mental Health Care Delivery Systems*, edited by J.B. Sidowski, J.H. Johnson, and T.A. Williams (Norwood, NJ: Ablex, 1980), pp. 109–117.

12 Zarr, op. cit., p. 50.
13 Zarr, op. cit., pp. 50, 53, 55.
14 Zarr, op. cit., p. 60.
15 An information-processing system does not have an identity, in this sense, at all. Its hardware and software resemble other mass-reproducible commodities – typically, we are not interested in the manner or history of their production. Vegetarians are fond of pointing out that this attitude characterizes the perspectives of most people when they do their grocery shopping; they don't want to know too much about the origins of the neatly plastic-wrapped packages in the meat department.
16 Michael Moncher *et al.*, "Microcomputer-Based Approaches for Preventing Drug and Alcohol Abuse Among Adolescents from Ethnic-Racial Minority Backgrounds," *Computers in Human Behavior* 5 (1989), pp. 88–89.

12 TECHNOLOGY AND AUTHORITY, pp. 163–182

1 To be sure, this "harmony" is durable only on the condition that the system "delivers the goods." The point here is that contemporary institutions assimilate participants' intelligence and energy in a way that diffuses and disarms their discontent and makes the mobilization of organized resistance more problematic, as union representatives have discovered in post-industrial workplaces.

A striking illustration of the way in which institutional authority neutralizes criticism is provided by the history of Native American negotiations with federal agencies. Native Americans who oppose federal policies are compelled to conceptualize and articulate their situation in legal/bureaucratic terms – to speak in a language that Washington understands. But this language obscures the very experiences and concerns that are the basis for their case against the government.

2 Shoshana Zuboff, *In the Age of the Smart Machine: The Future of Work and Power* (New York: Basic Books, 1984).
3 Ibid., p. 71.
4 Ibid., p. 4.
5 Ibid., p. 75.
6 *The Grundrisse*, in *The Marx-Engels Reader*, edited by Robert C. Tucker (New York: W. W. Norton, 1978), p. 279.
7 Niklas Luhmann, "Interaction, Organization, and Society," in *The Differentiation of Society*, translated by Stephen Holmes and Charles Larmore (New York: Columbia University Press, 1982), p. 78.
8 Herbert Simon, *The New Science of Management Decision*, revised edition (Englewood Cliffs, NJ: Prentice-Hall, 1977), p. 113.
9 Ibid., pp. 110–111.
10 J.K. Hughes and J.I. Michtom, *A Structured Approach to Programming* (Englewood Cliffs, NJ: Prentice Hall, 1977), pp. 27–28, 31.
11 M. Ramoorthy, *Structured Programming* (Information Technology State of the Art Report, 1976), unpaged.
12 Philip Kraft, "The Routinization of Computer Programming," *Sociology of Work Occupations* 6 (1979), p. 148. A recent development in software design, "object-oriented

programming," continues to adhere to the principles of hierarchical organization and modularization that have characterized structured methodologies since their inception. Data encapsulation, a central feature of this new approach, favors the construction of modules that are "black boxes," meaning that what goes on in them is invisible from outside. Interpreted metaphorically, this contradicts the ideal of democratic governance understood as a kind of transparency that minimizes decision-making "behind closed doors." For a different but well-argued view, see Sherry Turkle, "Artificial Intelligence and Psychoanalysis: A New Alliance," *Daedalus* (Winter 1988), pp. 241–268.

13 Even in a post-industrial order, Social Darwinism remains ideologically useful, however. First, it provides a foundation for the legitimation of the competitive sector of the economy. Secondly, in the name of "survival of the fittest" it has been used to justify cutbacks of welfare payments and other state-funded social services.

14 M. Sahlins, *The Use and Abuse of Biology* (Ann Arbor, MI: University of Michigan Press, 1976); R.C. Leowontin, S. Rose, and L.J. Kamin, *Not in Our Genes* (New York: Pantheon, 1984).

15 M. Crozier, S.P. Huntington, and J. Watanuki, *The Crisis of Democracy* (New York: New York University Press, 1975), pp. 113–114. Edward Herman examines the contradictions between democracy and international capital in "The End of Democracy?" *Z Magazine* 6(9), September 1993, pp. 57–62.

16 Noam Chomsky, "Notes on NAFTA," *The Nation*, March 29, 1993.

17 The express aim of the North American Free Trade Agreement (NAFTA), according to Harry Gray, CEO of United Technologies, is "a worldwide business environment that's unfettered by government interference." Ibid.

18 For an overview of the arguments in favor of greater workers' participation in workplace organization and administration, see Michael Albert and Robin Hahnel, *The Political Economy of Participatory Economics* (Princeton, NJ: Princeton University Press, 1991); Michael Albert and Robin Hahnel, *Looking Forward: Participatory Economics for the Twenty First Century* (Boston, MA: South End, 1991).

19 Paul Strassman, *Information Payoff: The Transformation of Work in the Electronic Age* (New York: Macmillan, 1985), p. 163.

20 Robert Howard and Leslie Schneider, "Worker Participation in Technological Change: Interests, Influence, and Scope," in *Worker Participation and the Politics of Reform*, edited by Carmen Sirianni (Philadelphia: Temple University Press, 1987), pp. 71, 89. See also the books by Michael Albert and Robin Hahnel cited above.

21 David Schweickart, "Economic Democracy: A Worthy Socialism that Would Really Work," *Science and Society* 56 (Spring 1992), pp. 9–38; Andrew Martin, "Unions, the Quality of Work, and Technological Change in Sweden," in Carmen Sirianni, op. cit., pp. 95–139; *Technology and Work: Labour Studies in England, Germany and the Netherlands*, edited by Wout Buitelaar (Brookfield, VT: Gower, 1988); Fred Block, *Post-industrial Possibilities: A Critique of Economic Discourse* (Berkeley, CA: University of California Press, 1990); Diane Flaherty, "Self-Management and the Future of Socialism: Lessons from Yugoslavia," *Science and Society* 56 (Spring 1992), pp. 92–108.

22 Of course, many questions remain. Full workers' participation in policy decisions is an ideal that has attracted radical theoreticians of labor, including Karl Marx. But can we count on it to attract the long-term commitment of workers themselves? Can a society make the most efficient use of technology and expertise without according to certain individuals more decision-making powers than others enjoy? Will plain old individual selfishness and narrow-mindedness, though historically and contextually shaped, always throw a monkey wrench into plans for building egalitarian institutions? We cannot answer these questions definitively, although there is no reason why we should not explore further the realm of the possible. The bearing of technology on democratic values

in the workplace and elsewhere is examined by Michael Goldhaber in *Reinventing Technology* (New York: Routledge & Kegan Paul, 1986), and in Goldhaber's newsletter "Post-Industrial Issues," published in San Francisco, CA.

23 This is a favorite theme of contemporary popular culture evident, for example in fictional representations of technology's roles. In *Star Trek*, the starship Enterprise models a hierarchical, male-governed social order. Yet, one of the crew members, Mr Spock, who is partly human and partly "Vulcan," represents quite different values. The Vulcan world is fundamentally non-violent, egalitarian and participatory; its fundamental ethical principle is the belief that "the greatest joy in all creation is in the infinite ways that infinitely diverse things can join together to create meaning and beauty." See Stephen E. Whitfield, *The Making of Star Trek* (New York: Ballantine, 1968), p. 226; and Diane Duane, *Spock's World* (New York: Simon & Schuster, 1986).

24 Herbert Marcuse, *One Dimensional Man* (Boston, MA: Beacon Press, 1964), pp. 158–159.

13 RESTORATION OF THE SELF, pp. 183–202

1 Jürgen Habermas, *The Theory of Communicative Action*, Vol. 2, *Lifeworld and System: A Critique of Functionalist Reason*, translated by Thomas McCarthy (Boston, MA: Beacon Press, 1987), p. 139.

2 In English, these metaphors typically draw upon an imagery of fragmentation; in German, organization/disorganization provides a conceptual template for framing self-insecurities and pathologies. See Chapter 2, note 14.

3 Jürgen Habermas, *The Philosophical Discourse of Modernity*, translated by Frederick Lawrence (Cambridge, MA: MIT Press, 1987), p. 297.

4 Carol Gilligan, "Remapping the Moral Domain: New Images of Self in Relationship," *Mapping the Moral Domain*, edited by Carol Gilligan, Janie V. Ward and Jill M. Taylor (Cambridge, MA: Harvard University Press, 1988), p. 8.

5 The accounts that I have in mind include attachment theory (Ainsworth, Bowlby), object relations (Mahler, Fairbairn, Winnicott), and self-psychology (Kohut).

6 Jessica Benjamin, "The Decline of the Oedipus Complex," *Critical Theories of Psychological Development*, edited by John Broughton (New York: Plenum Press, 1987), pp. 222–227. This perspective on the self does not deny that Oedipal dynamics play an important role in the formation of its identity. But Freud's model – the toddler would like to kill the parent of the same sex and take possession of the parent of the opposite sex – is oversimplified, at best. It is inapplicable in situations (single-parent families, for instance) where the primary caretakers are not the mother and father of the traditional nuclear family. More importantly, the model tends to read adult attitudes back into children's experiences. The dynamic of the Oedipal triangle may be driven not by a child's wish to *destroy* the relationship enjoyed by the parents but rather by the wish to become *involved* in it. A theme that weaves through many of the dreams gathered for this study is a desire not for conquest but for connection, to both mothers and fathers, on the part of dreamers of either gender.

7 "Reification" is central to Lukács' analysis in *History and Class Consciousness* (Cambridge, MA: MIT Press, 1971). As many commentators have pointed out, though, Lukács does not distinguish adequately between reification and objectification.

8 A good summary of Critical Theory perspectives on the link between mastery of natural environments and self-mastery is given by William Leiss in *Domination of Nature* (Boston, MA: Beacon Press, 1974).

9 Léopold Sédar Senghor, *Prose and Poetry* (London: Heineman/Oxford University Press, 1965), pp. 30–31.

10 Sigmund Freud, "New Introductory Lectures on Psychoanalysis," in *The Standard*

Edition of the Complete Psychological Works of Sigmund Freud, edited and translated by James Strachey, Vol. 22 (London: Hogarth Press, 1959), pp. 181–182.

11 Sigmund Freud, *The Future of an Illusion* (New York: Norton, 1961).

12 These thoughts about Islamic fundamentalism are based on conversations with Minoo Moallem.

13 Of course there are cultural variations in the applications and user-interfaces that personal computers provide. A keyboard, for example, may employ Western, Japanese, or Chinese characters. More significantly, software may be written with a certain end-user community in mind. But these variations do not determine the underlying logic of the technology or of our interactions with it.

14 Paul Feyerabend, *Against Method* (New York: Verso, 1988); Paul Feyerabend, *Farewell to Reason* (New York: Verso, 1987); Thomas Kuhn, *The Structure of Scientific Revolutions* (Chicago, IL: University of Chicago Press, 1970).

15 Martha Nussbaum, "Human Functioning and Social Justice: In Defense of Aristotelian Essentialism," *Political Theory* 20(2) (May 1992), p. 203.

16 The people in the advertisement, I was told by a spokeswoman from Apple, are authentic monks not models.

17 David Landes, *Revolution in Time* (Cambridge, MA: Harvard University Press, 1983), p. 57.

18 Ibid., p. 73.

19 See Otto Mayr, *Authority, Liberty and Automatic Machinery in Early Modern Europe* (Baltimore, MD: The Johns Hopkins University Press, 1986), especially Chapter 2, "The Rise of the Clock Metaphor"; see also Lynn White, "The Iconography of *Temperentia* and the Virtuousness of Technology," *Medieval Religion and Technology: Collected Essays* (Berkeley, CA: University of California Press, 1978), pp. 181–204. An early analysis of the importance of clocks to medieval monastic life is that of Lewis Mumford at the beginning of *Technics and Civilization* (New York: Harcourt Brace & World, 1934).

20 The Dalai Lama, *Freedom in Exile: The Autobiography of the Dalai Lama* (New York: HarperCollins, 1990), pp. 99–100.

21 Ibid., p. 270.

22 Classics in this genre include: Fritjof Capra, *The Tao of Physics: An Exploration of the Parallels Between Modern Physics and Eastern Mysticism*, 3rd rev. (Boston, MA: Shambhala, 1991); David Bohm, *Wholeness and the Implicate Order* (London: Routledge, 1980). A more recent contribution is David Griffin's *The Reenchantment of Science: Postmodern Proposals* (New York: State University of New York Press, 1991).

23 Differences between empirical and transcendental experiences are discussed in Chapter 2, "The Problem of Proof," in Ken Wilber's *Eye to Eye: The Quest for the New Paradigm* (Garden City, NY: Anchor, 1983).

24 The Dalai Lama, Herbert Benson, and Robert Thurman, *Mind Science: An East-Dialogue* (Boston, MA: Wisdom Books, 1991).

25 John Flinn, "Tibetan Refugees' New Life in Bay Area," *San Francisco Examiner*, July 5, 1992, pp. A-11.

26 Michael Dertouzos, "Building the Information Marketplace," *Technology Review*, January 1991, p. 40.

Index